COLUMBIA COLLEGE CHICAGO

3 2711 00142 5531

W9-DHU-690

The Globe's
Emigrating Children

DEC 1 9 2008

Rethinking Childhood

Joe L. Kincheloe and Gaile Cannella
General Editors

Vol. 40

PETER LANG
New York • Washington, D.C./Baltimore • Bern
Frankfurt am Main • Berlin • Brussels • Vienna • Oxford

COLUMBIA COLLEGE LIBRARY
600 S. MICHIGAN AVENUE
CHICAGO, IL 60605

Kathleen A. Stark

The Globe's Emigrating Children

Teaching in a Second Language

PETER LANG
New York • Washington, D.C./Baltimore • Bern
Frankfurt am Main • Berlin • Brussels • Vienna • Oxford

Library of Congress Cataloging-in-Publication Data

Stark, Kathleen A.
The globe's emigrating children: teaching in a second language /
Kathleen A. Stark.
p. cm.— (Rethinking childhood; v. 40)
Includes bibliographical references.
1. English language—Study and teaching (Elementary)—Foreign speakers.
2. English language—Study and teaching (Elementary)—Foreign speakers—
Social aspects—United States. I. Title.
PE1128.A2S7256   428.2'4—dc22   2008010856
ISBN 978-1-4331-0262-2
ISSN 1086-7155

Bibliographic information published by **Die Deutsche Bibliothek**.
Die Deutsche Bibliothek lists this publication in the "Deutsche
Nationalbibliografie"; detailed bibliographic data is available
on the Internet at http://dnb.ddb.de/.

Cover art by Tom Stark after a child's drawing
Cover design by Joshua Hanson

The paper in this book meets the guidelines for permanence and durability
of the Committee on Production Guidelines for Book Longevity
of the Council of Library Resources.

© 2008 Peter Lang Publishing, Inc., New York
29 Broadway, 18th floor, New York, NY 10006
www.peterlang.com

All rights reserved.
Reprint or reproduction, even partially, in all forms such as microfilm,
xerography, microfiche, microcard, and offset strictly prohibited.

Printed in the United States of America

Dedicated to
Tom, Jamillah, Phillip and Joe-Joe
and
teachers and students everywhere

Contents

List of Figures

Acknowledgements

First and above all I want to recognize the help of Taylor Stoehr, friend and professor of literary and cultural history at the University of Massachusetts, Boston. He is a busy man with remarkable and important social projects and challenging work responsibilities, yet he carefully read every chapter, asked probing questions and after that, re-read my many new versions until they were clear. His insights and suggestions were gifts for a lifetime. I know that he grew fond of the children we were considering because when he finally saw photos of them, he hugged them. Words fail. Perhaps to say that Taylor is a gift to his time approaches what I mean.

I am grateful to my sister, Elaine O'Brien, for opening my mental door to the possibility that I could and should write a book. Not only did she inspire me, but she read many chapters and sent encouragement and suggestions with each reading. Cliff Nieuwenhuis at Foresite Software was amazing about getting the book into the computer language of publishing while remaining patient and unflappable. Friends and other family members, especially Jim O'Brien, Laura Hart, and Veronica Moore, asked important questions after reading selected chapters and led me to critical insights. Chris Myers and Sophie Appel at Peter Lang were extraordinarily graceful and patient guides throughout publishing operations.

The cover shows a self-portrait drawn by Mufdi at the end of his first year in school. The strings, books and globe were added later by my husband, Tom. It was his idea drawn from his understanding of of the text, which he knew well since he had carefully read and commented on every chapter. Only he could have come up with the perfect illustration for this book. I know how lucky I am that he is my friend and love.

I made every possible effort to contact Mufdi for permission to use his work, but was unable to trace him. I have not used his last name, or those of any of the children in this book, because I did not want to risk compromising their political security. The beautiful photographs of them were created by Whitney Curtis, who has given me permission to use them.

My thanks to Rhina Espaillat for permission to use *Bilingual/Bilingüe*, which I found in her book *Where Horizons Go*, published in 1998 by Truman State University Press. Charlotte Zolotow was also gracious in allowing me to use her poem, "People." Every reasonable effort was made to secure permission to use all other copyrighted material. If a rights holder wishes to question any usage, they should contact the publisher.

Chapter 1

Saying It for the First Time

"I have loved the word 'susurrus' for a long time, and I had never found another use for it."

- Reverend John Ames, in Gilead *by Marilynne Robinson*

Fifteen children sit on a classroom carpet, their faces and hair shining, their eyes alert. No one speaks and no one moves except for one or two cautious looks. This is their first day of school, and for most of them, their first day in any school. While I fill out first-day forms, they watch me. I count the girls and boys, see who takes a bus and note which one they take, who walks and who's coming for them, figure out their racial categories (futile to resist).... I hurry through the paperwork as fast as I can.

These children, native Arabic, Spanish, Vietnamese, Haitian and Somali speakers, are here to learn English in a first-grade sheltered English class. I'm their teacher, trained and experienced in language teaching. I will teach them how to learn in an English-speaking school system.

I won't teach them much and my education and experience will be useless if I can't make them happy to come to school. Accomplishing this goal is more important than anything else I will do today. I want the children's feelings of being alone to disappear, and I want the classroom to become a familiar, welcoming place for them.

I move to the carpet, find a space and sit down. I look around and smile at them while they solemnly watch me. I point to myself and say the first words I'll help them learn: I'm, name, your, and what's. "I'm Mrs. Stark. What's your name?" I look at a child who looks back at me without a word or change in expression. I smile at her, and because she looks a little frightened, turn to the class again.

I point to myself again, repeat my name, and now turn to the child on my left, a tall, solid boy with thick black hair precisely parted and painted down with water or gel. A few pieces stick up at the back of his head. I repeat the words, point to myself again, and then to him. "I'm Mrs. Stark. What's your name?" "Jayson," he says firmly, but without a smile.

"Jayson! Ah." I touch his hand. Around the circle the children begin to sit up straighter and watch with more interest. Jayson relaxes a little. " 'I'm Jayson'?" I repeat "I'm Mrs. Stark," pointing to myself, then point to him and ask, "What's your name?"

He says, "I'm Jayson."

"Nice to meet you, Jayson," I say. Now a little smile begins, and ends. The children in the circle focus their attention on us, expressions of curiosity all around replacing apprehension.

Soon I'll know how lucky it was that Jayson was the first child to respond. Although my students in past years have enjoyed this name-learning process, Jayson is excited to participate and I'm sure that he'll describe his victory at home tonight, repeating, "I'm Jayson" for his parents. His eagerness is infectious and his quick grasp of what we are doing is a piece of good fortune. His enthusiasm will be a blessing for the entire year, but will pose a challenge as well.

His parents are from El Salvador, and both of them brought Jayson to school this morning. They had kind, open faces and were dressed formally. Mrs. R., tall, solid and somewhat anxious-looking, was serious and reminded Jayson to behave. Mr. R., a bit shorter than his wife, seemed more at ease than she was and smiled good-naturedly at her concern that Jayson might misbehave. I later learned that in El Salvador Mr. R. had been a journalist, but in the United States his first job was in a restaurant. Mrs. R., working in a motel, was a homemaker in El Salvador.

They have emigrated from El Salvador to provide a safer environment for Jayson and his baby brother. Over the course of several months, informally at the classroom door and during parent conferences, I will learn why most of the children's families immigrated. The majority will say they've come to the United States to provide "more opportunities" for their families. A few, like Jayson's parents, will describe political reasons. No matter what the precipitating cause, at the core of the decision to immigrate is concern for the well-being of their children. Many say they hope to return to their home countries as soon as the economic status of the family is secure, or when dangerous political situations are resolved.

The possibility that my students will return to their countries of origin is one reason why I want to encourage not only the maintenance of their home languages but their development as well; they will need them. However, the primary reason is that I know how much a child's cognitive and psychological sustenance can be lost if the heritage language is lost; the language that carries the history and culture of the family and the child's early sense of identity.

Most of the rich resources a child first brings to school are embedded in the language of the home, the language with which children and parents can have the deepest understandings and discussions, and with which they tell stories of their past and present lives. Such experiences allow children to master the shape of oral narratives and to be confident that listeners will want to hear what they say—valuable assets that transfer to print literacy.

Without care, most of these resources can be lost. Even a heritage language can drift away and, with the heritage language, the psychological and cognitive benefits it holds for its speakers. Especially in an immersion situation this is a risk. Without opportunities to learn new vocabulary and practice speaking, facility with this first language can be greatly diminished, or the language can be entirely forgotten. In my experience, this process is especially marked in young children.

Most of my students' parents understandably think learning English is important for their children's survival or success. English has acquired hegemony for global communication in business, science, art, music, Internet use and other areas, and parents know this. But to acquire the benefits of English speaking for their children, many parents expact I will say they should speak only English at home and tell me, "I only speak English to them at home," and, "I make them speak English to their brothers and sisters," or, concerned, "I can't speak English with them at home...." Knowledge of English will be useful, but in their eagerness to help their children, they risk overseeing the loss of something irreplaceable. My advice to them is the opposite of what they expect, and they look both surprised and relieved when I say it.

I say that speaking their first language at home is probably the most helpful step they can take to support their children's learning at school. They can read and tell them stories in this language, teach them new words in it, have conversations and listen to songs in it. Their children will have ideational and artistic resources in several bodies of literature and an entre into two or more cultures. They will be in demand and valued anywhere they go. We, the parents and I, are in an ideal position to secure this advantage for their children when we work together. No parent has ever been sad to hear me say this!

On the carpet, helped by Jayson's model, I go through all the students' names and teach each one, "I'm...." To memorize their names I have to go back to review after learning six of them; then I can add two or three more. They smile at hearing their names learned, and watch each classmate I address. Will she remember the name? This focus helps; it draws their attention away from themselves. I make it a game.

I enjoy hearing them respond with the new words, and for them it seems like a game to say something foreign. If I forget a name, I ask again, "What's your name," and they repeat "I'm...." None of them makes an error in responding, although some of them haven't heard the /m/ of "I'm," and don't pronounce it clearly, adding instead a generic nasal sound, which they do hear. I see no rush to help them with this. They look proud of their victories, and that's what will make them enthusiastic about coming to school tomorrow. They watch to see how the others will do.

By the end of this process, they will have heard the new words over and over. It is repetition combined with comprehension that leads words and expressions into long-term memory, and through the year I'll use every strategy I know that will promote them in an engaging and natural way. With this naming process the repetition seems natural, and I'll have all their names memorized; a big help during the day. For them too it seems, because when they hear their names they look happy and their comfort creates a nascent feeling of ease in the room. If I'm careful, it will stay and grow.

Even foreign language speaking may seem less mysterious when they realize that they can name themselves in one, English, and I hope this realization will start the strangeness of the language and the place on their first steps out of the room. My work has begun. They've learned their first words.

I think of English teaching as a way to teach about languages in general. I'll have to ask my students how to say the expressions they learn in English in their languages. I'll remind them how lucky they are to speak two languages, and ask them to tell stories their parents and grandparents have told them. I'll model multilingualism with them, and illustrate its value when I talk to their parents. Even if I learn only a few words or a greeting in languages I don't know, like Somali and Arabic, they and their parents will be appreciative.

A language classroom needs to emphasize words and the vigorous work they do in communication. Vocabulary is the key I want to give my students. A vocabulary with depth and breadth is much of what leads to comprehension in reading and effective communication in important conversations. Vocabulary can take communication beyond enabling basic living to the realm of complex ideas and art. I want my students to own such a vocabulary, and to own the vocabulary in at least two languages.

As I look at my charges now though, as I gesture to accomplish even the simplest task, it's hard to imagine a time when they'll understand anything by words alone, let alone have important conversations in English. They will need so many words, and now they don't even know the most basic ones.

I get ready for them to move; they've been sitting long enough for six-year-olds. Since in this school everyone has to walk in silent lines, I prepare to show them how to line up and to teach them the words for it. There's a small girl with a lively, happy face and a mass of brown curly hair somewhat caught up in a pony tail.

"It's time to line up Rosalinda," I say. She looks at me without a trace of understanding, but with sparkling attention. I take her round, moist hand, and repeat "It's time to line up," indicating by my expression that it's something significant. She carefully studies my face for a second or two. Then she brightens, jumps up and comes with me. I lead her to the door, indicate with my hands that she needs to stay there, and say, "Stay here." She understands. Then I move to Ivan, bend over to take his hand, and say, "It's time to line up, Ivan." He looks down with a shy smile as he stands to come with me. I leave him standing behind Rosalinda. Now I look around and see a muscular boy watching me as if I were a mouse and he a hungry cat and I say, "Etienne, it's time to line up."

This time, rather than showing my meaning, I wait to see if he'll understand the words alone—he has paid such rapt attention. I fold my arms and smile a challenge at him. He immediately jumps up with a swift athletic move, a boy who loves action and is sure of his body. He walks to line up with the cocky flair we'll soon identify with him. After that display, I'm pretty sure the others will know what to do and will want to show it.

I stand apart now and call each child individually and randomly to get in line, repeating the words "in line" each time. The children watch me eagerly, waiting for their turns. When they hear their names, they stand up quickly, looking proud to know what to do. We're ready, and the children look excited and happy. Those happy faces—they're gold.

I'm taking them on a tour of the school, pointing out where the bathrooms are, the office, the nurse, the playground and the cafeteria. I use the words I think they'll need over and over again: cafeteria, line, outside, food, eat and choose, and then I introduce the cafeteria staff to them. All the students in the school will have free lunches, including my students, so there'll be no concern about collecting lunch money every morning. As we walk I take photos of the places we visit and the staff the children meet. In a few days, we will place these photos on the classroom bulletin board, enlarged to poster size and labeled.

From the cafeteria I lead the students to the playground on the route they'll take everyday. I hope familiarity will relieve some of their anxiety over being in a new situation without loved ones to help. Outside where we're alone I tell them that they can play "Play! Run!" and I gesture broadly with my arms and feet. There are shouts of joy and most of them run off, quickly assessing classmates to see who will be a friend. A few hesitate until I repeat: "Play! Run!" And off they go. Salam, an Iraqi boy, stays back. "Salam, you can go! Play!" I repeat, gesturing. He shakes his head. His demeanor speaks of reserve, maturity and self-knowledge and I trust his sense that waiting is right for him.

Tamathor, one of the five girls in the class and, like Salam, from Iraq, immediately runs off with the others, but quickly returns, unable to find someone who will play with her until Etienne runs up and tags her just as she nears me. The two of them, Haitian and Iraqi, communicate without a word.

She races to catch him, and to his surprise, does. Abubakar from Somalia now speeds after them and easily becomes part of the play. Jayson drifts by for a moment, on the run, to wave with a big smile, and Rosalinda takes my hand. Seeing this, Sara takes my other hand, and Brenda takes Rosalinda's as we walk around the schoolyard. I say a few words to them in Spanish, hoping to make them comfortable.

Usually I speak only English in class because research and my experience support keeping languages separate. Besides, it doesn't seem fair if I speak Spanish to Spanish speakers, but not Arabic, Vietnamese, Somali, Creole or Arabic to those speakers. Perhaps if I'm with Spanish speakers, I'll speak Spanish, and when I'm with the others, I'll try to learn a few words in their languages. We can share expressions for the same situation and compare the languages.

Laura has come and is holding Sara's hand. With the exception of Tamathor, all the girls are with me. Laura is quiet, even with the girls, and doesn't speak to me, her eyes averted and her face almost frozen. I'll never see Laura laugh, but she'll occasionally smile and will have secret, animated conversations in Spanish with her class friends. In a few months she'll move to another area of town as her mother tries to escape from an abusive boyfriend, and I will never see or hear from her again.

Soon I call the students back with large arm motions and ask them to make a *line*. I'm happy to see that now they know the word and what I mean. They form a noisy, approximate line. Once they know how to line up I won't need to have lines all the time, only in the halls and on some field trips.

While the class noisily assembles, Ali, Jayson and Elmer come up to me, flushed faces dripping with sweat.

"Ms. Stark," begins Ali. He was in an English immersion kindergarten class during most of last year, but oral language assessments show that he remained at a beginner's level. He stops trying to talk and makes a sign by pointing one finger to his opened mouth.

"You want to drink water?" I ask. I mime drinking out of a cup. The three boys nod gratefully with their telling, dripping heads. "Okay. Line up. Then we'll drink water," and I make the sign again with an exaggerated nod so they know their urgent need is understood. I hold up one finger to indicate, "Wait a minute." They look satisfied and return to the line.

Once we're back in the classroom I say: "Let's sit down," sitting down myself while motioning them to sit on the carpet. Jayson, Etienne and Sara figure out what to do first and the others follow.

"Come up closer to the chair," I say, gesturing. "Chair," I repeat, touching the chair. All of them have sweaty faces with beads of sweat on their upper lips, and wet hair clinging to their heads. One by one I send them to the class fountain for a drink while I pull out the big book we'll read. In a day or two I'll teach them to take turns going to the fountain without my supervision.

There are only fifteen children in the class this morning, but not for long. Ms. Olivas, the secretary, will come all day with new students and their parents. How lucky the school is to have this warm person in the office. She's equally fluent in Spanish and English and treats everyone with respect. By the end of the week we'll have twenty students, and by the end of the month, twenty-four. With each new student, the new words must be repeated and explained whenever an opportunity appears.

It's disruptive when students come late, but that's how the first days of school are for this classroom and surely for many others. Immigrant parents have numerous forms to fill out to enroll their children in school. They need to provide more documentation than U.S. citizens, and usually need to find a translator to help them. They often are unaware of the starting days and times.

The big book I've chosen is *Mrs. Wishy Washy*. It will be an early favorite until their English skills have grown and they prefer more complex stories. As I read, I need to explain several words—*wash*, and *mud*—but the illustrations help when I point to them. I have dirt in a bowl and add some water to make mud since in past years I've found it impossible to communicate orally what mud is.

"Euew!" say Abubakar, Sara and a few others, delighted with the muck.

Right away they catch the repetitive "wishy washy, wishy washy" phrase in the story and begin to repeat it, at first timidly, except for Etienne and Jayson. These two watch intently, figure out what to do, and begin, looking at one another in joined pleasure. I encourage them, moving my finger along the words, exaggerating the relationship between the spoken word and its written form. Then the others join, first one, then another until everyone is chanting "wishy washy, wishy washy," and watching my finger. It will be awhile before they separately hear these words in a stream of English speech, or recognize them in a written text, but I think I'm giving them a background for understanding with my pointing.

For awhile the children seem like friends, and they seem relaxed. Their willingness to jump in and participate is encouraging; they're already taking steps to English and literacy and I'm sure it's going to be a good year. Already they can say one expression, *I'm* and can recognize *name*, *in line*, and maybe *chair*. Tomorrow I'll show them a poem and teach them the jazz chant, "Where's Ernie?" from Carolyn Graham's *Jazz Chants for Children*, an enjoyable way to learn "good morning" vocabulary and conventions.

Exposing them to the poems and songs they learn all year is among my favorite strategies to cultivate students' reading, vocabularies and appreciation for language. The songs and poems serve as resources for the children all year in their writing and conversations. The frequent re-reading helps their fluency and automatic recognition of some of the words in print (sight words), produces memorized words and phrases for oral speech, and generally increases their familiarity with the language. Since they're useful in so many ways, I start to teach songs and poems immediately.

Once they're memorized, words and how they're combined are available for speech and writing. Otherwise, the verb/preposition, noun/verb combinations (collocations) commonly used together such as *wait for*, *take care of*, *forgive someone for something*, *keep a promise*, *pay a price* and *stroke of luck* are challenging to remember because they don't always make sense and are different among languages. Learning songs and poems is an enjoyable way to memorize them because the context is interesting.

Each week the children will receive an individual copy of a new poem and a new song after we've read them together from a large chart. They will glue their copies into poetry notebooks. These notebooks are not elaborate: colored construction paper covers that are stapled together with blank white pages inside. On the outside I write each child's name in my best script: *Jayson's Poetry Notebook*. When I hand them these notebooks they invariably smile with pleasure.

Sitting with their friends, they chat, read, draw, color and glue their poems into their notebooks, illustrating them as I've seen children do in French schools. Illustrators must think about the meaning of a text, so studying and understanding it is required. I think of illustrating texts as a valuable comprehension activity, in addition to being something children enjoy doing.

These are the children's notebooks and they can re-read their poems or not, as they like. I require that they keep them in their reading boxes so they'll know where they are, and often I see these notebooks pulled out and poems and songs re-read with friends during reading period. At the end of the year, they will take the notebooks home—all the songs and poems they learned in first grade.

I copy and illustrate all the same poems and songs by hand in a large format for the group to see, and we keep them hanging in the room. During reading period or early in the morning, before they become proficient book readers, the children will enjoy going around the room with or without pointers to read the charts with friends. Brenda and Rosalinda especially will like this, and so will Etienne and Abdulrahman. Their friends will join them.

At the beginning of the year when the children want to show their parents how they're learning to read, they will read these nearly memorized poems. Parents love this sign of learning, are proud that their children know what the words mean and can pronounce them, and believe that they can read each word.

I have to be honest with them. Because I believe parents should know exactly how their children are doing, I explain that although the children wouldn't recognize most of the same words in other texts, they do know some of the words by sight, and know how to use beginning letters to nudge their memories. There is much literacy growth to see in these shows for parents, whose faces sometimes barely can contain the pride they feel.

As the children enter on the second day of school, I'm pleased to see that they already remember to put their backpacks and other personal effects in the coatroom and to come to the carpet. The jazz chant "Where's Ernie?" is on a large piece of chart paper. The accompanying cassette is playing as they enter, with its jazz-style tune and simple lyrics. It has a call and response format that repeats several times.

At first they look surprised and don't know what to make of the lively music. It wasn't playing yesterday. When they come to the carpet they sit down and look up at me with searching expressions, and I begin to sing. Etienne quickly tries to sing along with the tape and me. Then a few others join. When everyone is seated, I start going over the song line by line as I point to the words on the chart as I sing them, not belaboring it; it's too soon.

Teacher: Good morning!

Children: "Hello!"

These two lines repeat.

Teacher: "Where's Ernie?"

I look left and right. "Ernie?" I ask, something that's not in the song.

The children on the tape say, "I don't know!" and I mime it, looking puzzled and extending my hands.

After that, the words are: "It's Ernie! Hello Ernie, It's Ernie, Hello Ernie, hello." One by one the children join me. We sing it once more, this time substituting Elmer's name for Ernie. He grins and looks proud to be chosen. Every morning I'll greet them with "Good morning," and it won't be long before they say "Good morning" to me and to other staff members. Over the course of a week we'll substitute all of the children's names for Ernie several times.

The expressions: *hello*, *Good morning*, *where* and *I don't know* will be useful for these early days of school. We'll sing the song every day for at least two weeks, and after that, whenever we feel like it.

Now we move to the calendar. Once they know what it is they'll look forward to it and remind me that "We didn't do the calendar," when occasionally I consider skipping it for some reason, like getting ready for a field trip. Since the children insist on doing the calendar, on those days I will manage to get by with a truncated and hurried version. It's hard to make them understand why. First graders' sense of schedule and time is nothing like an adult's.

They like to update the calendar because the work is active and they'll have a chance to perform; to say the date, to put it on the calendar, to say the month, to choose the correct month from all twelve months using first letter sounds or other clues, and then lead the class in reciting, "Today is Tuesday, September 4th, 20...." They'll grow to view it as a game of sorts, and their hands will wave eagerly to say the date and show all that they know—the date, the season, the year etc. They know the routine, and see their skills grow daily. When someone says "Today is..., and all the rest correctly, I write that person's name on the board with stars all around it. They like this, and they like leading the whole class, like a teacher.

Jayson will often call out the answer, which he will know right away. But this will be before the others have a chance to think. Everyone, including me, will be disappointed. His calling out the answer is the challenging part of his eagerness.

"Ai, Jayson! It's great that you know, but we want everyone to get a chance! You spoil the fun because people like to give their own answers." I mix my reminder with a compliment so that I don't discourage his cheerful enthusiasm. His waving hand, his efforts to achieve that elusive self-control and his eagerness to participate are unforgettable images of working with this group of children, and of Jayson. I need his cooperation so the others won't be discouraged from thinking.

At this early point of the school year, some children, rather than trying to participate, simply look around the classroom. I believe that to learn they need to pay attention: to look, listen and connect what they see with the words they hear. Calendar activities are important in this immersion class because they promote language development in a comfortable, comprehensible framework. Knowing how much they'll eventually like it and profit from it makes me confident that encouraging their participation is worthwhile. So I make sure that every child is paying attention. I will even say it more directly later in the year, "Your eyes are looking, but I don't see that your brain is working. Is it?" I'm careful to communicate that this is a genuine question, because I've been wrong on occasion. I've had children respond, "I'm listening," or "I'm thinking," and was persuaded that they were.

I consider insisting on their attention a way to convince them that they're important in the class, and that I'm sure they will learn if they pay attention. I show them that this is how they learn almost everything they want or need to know.

I call Abubakar's name. He looks up suddenly, startled, and I point to my eyes: "Abubakar, Look." I point to my ears: "Listen." He does, but will need another reminder in a few minutes. I look around. "Ali, Look. Listen." "Sara...." As the year progresses I will rarely need to do this.

Since it's September 4th, the /th/ sound surfaces as a language difference. It requires explicit instruction in most cases. I decide to work on it a little because no one can say it.

"Stick your tongues out like this," I say. Now that they're all looking and listening, they all stick out their tongues, with the exception of Salam, who hesitates at first with this undignified gesture, but eventually joins since no one is watching him.

"Thhhhhhhh." I ask each child to try individually and, for most of them, it's not apparent how to make the sound.

"You need air," I say, exaggerating a slight intake and slow release of air over my extended tongue. "Hold your hands (I show my hand) in front of your mouths. Do you feel the air? Air?" I add, blowing. Despite these unknown words, they understand. I know that some languages like Spanish don't require the release of much air when pronouncing certain letters, and this particular difference in our languages means that we'll have to have occasional practice for pronunciation. Later I'll explain, when their understanding of English improves, that languages are different from each other. The need to expel air will come up again as they learn to differentiate between letters for spelling. /P/ and /B/ in English require particular attention.

"Fourthhhhhh," I say. I ask each one to have a turn with this, and it's much harder for them. "Stick out your tongue." I stick out mine. This is funny enough to make them willing to try. Many say "fourt" because they're not used to the /th/ sound. Later when they line up for lunch I'll develop ordinal numbers further with "Brenda's first in line, Rosalinda's second, Laura's third, Sara's fourth...." I wasn't teaching it. Not yet. I was preparing them for future instruction with this background.

"It's hard, isn't it?" I make a face to communicate "hard," but there's a playful feeling because it's funny to stick out tongues, and the children are laughing and giggling. Eventually they'll all master the /th/ sound, but it will take weeks for some of them.

Quickly I move to the next task—shared reading of a poem. I don't want them to sit longer than their ability to pay attention. The poem for this week is:

1, 2 buckle my shoe,
3, 4 shut the door
(et cetera)

First I read it quickly, emphasizing the rhythm and pointing out the meaning of the words. It will reinforce the numbers in English, and they'll learn shoe, door, shut, pick up and several others. I have drawn illustrations after each line. One-to-one correspondence in numbers is new for most of them, that three sticks, for example, are one, two, three. So, with this poem I'll also be helping them to see the number—quantity connection they need for understanding math concepts.

Now I go over each line more slowly, making sure they can say it reasonably well; not perfectly, but comprehensibly. I look forward to a time when the children see words as building tools or colors that can expand their speaking and writing choices.

Although that time isn't now, I know that it's waiting. They'll write metaphors and use figurative language, and they'll easily recognize them. "One two, buckle my shoe" has meter and rhyme and is lots of fun to say, but it doesn't offer much to make them wonder. Its steady rhythm invites familiar body movement, while the vocabulary is concrete and limited. For its fun and accessibility, it's a good beginning experience.

A poem I will give them to learn in three months, "People" by Charlotte Zolotow, will illustrate what I mean when I say that I can use poetry with the children to show them some uses of language and its capacity to turn impressions into tangible, shared experience. This poem has limited vocabulary and poetic value, but the children really like it I think, because they can understand the words, and the meaning is accessible and within their range of experience.

PEOPLE

Some people talk and talk,
And never say a thing.
Some people look at you
And birds begin to sing.

Some people laugh and laugh
And yet you want to cry.
Some people touch your hand
And music fills the sky.

My English Language Learner students and I have had interesting conversations about this ordinary poem, even middle school ELL students. There is common experience to share, and the possibility of different interpretations due to different backgrounds. Because the words are basic, the meter straightforward, and the grammar regular, it's easily accessible for new English speakers. From a pedagogical point of view, it's interesting for the figurative language, although aesthetically I admit it's not very interesting to me. Middle school ELL students who read it with me once thought that birds literally began to sing, and that music literally filled the sky. The poem invited different interpretations.

Every morning this week we'll read "One, two, buckle my shoe" together, once again as I point to each word. The number words are useful, and so are the expressions, *Shut the door*, and *9, 10, a big fat hen*. For math today they will use yellow construction paper to illustrate the numbers with the words, digits, and quantities of objects, a project that we will post and use for reference all year. The number illustrations they make today will be opulent with color, and so unique that each one will invite the scrutiny from classmates that can promote learning.

This will be the children's first decorating project. They will prepare most of what appears on the bulletin boards in the room because of their partnership in what happens here. In my earlier years of teaching I followed the tradition I learned from experienced primary teachers, making an attractive setting for children, especially elaborate bulletin boards. The idea hasn't disappeared. A handsome setting is a cause for delight, but now the children participate in deciding what looks handsome. I have brought in large plants, bought a large and soft spring green carpet remnant, and put colorful paper on the bulletin boards.

Most of the rest is determined by the students. When the bulletin boards are covered with things they need or make, they pay more attention to them. For example, it won't be long before Etienne, without prompting, will make and post sign-up lists of who wants to play with blocks during recess and it won't be long until others imitate his idea for different purposes.

At the second recitation of the poem, they begin to bounce their heads with the words. Within a week the numbers from one to ten that are in the poem will be an internalized part of their new English vocabulary. They'll use them everyday for math and for their games at recess, and I'll lead them in counting objects and classmates whenever I see an opportunity. Etienne will count in English to form teams—and Jayson will be resisting his authority to do it. Already, after a few days of school, I'll be able to ask someone to shut the door, or to pick up a toy. Next week the poem will be a children's rhyme that will be useful for making choices, will reinforce the numbers, and will add to their fun with language:

ONE POTATO, TWO POTATO

One Potato
Two Potato
Three Potato
Four!

Five Potato
Six Potato
Seven Potato
More!

To learn the songs and poems students need to practice regularly. However, it isn't boring to them. It seems pleasant and natural when it involves a purpose, learning a good song or poem, and it increases the possibility that the words will be remembered, and will be remembered in the framework of natural syntax.

When they nearly know the work by heart, their performance is joyful—a group celebration of their achievement. Sometimes they'll nearly shout it: "One two, buckle my shoe!" Or if the song is sentimental, they will sing it seriously, but conscious of doing it well. From my point of view, I see the words remembered as vocabulary phrases, and the sight words accumulating for reading in other texts. I see that they are glad to be in school.

In two weeks, according to my yearlong plan to build their vocabularies, I will begin our first author study with Ezra Jack Keats. I will have a large sheet of butcher paper ready for the first book, *Whistle for Willie*. On it I will draw a graphic organizer and we will follow a soon-to-be-familiar procedure. They will have first used it with the story, *The Little Red Hen*, which I will read to them next week:

WHISTLE FOR WILLIE

Somebody	Wanted	But	So
Willie	To whistle for his dog	He couldn't whistle	

Keats' books have a simple syntax, authentic language and are consistently interesting to my students. They can understand them without much input from me. Soon there will be a collection of seven of these forms, one for every Ezra Jack Keats book we read, taped one on top of the other on a bulletin board, and ultimately stapled together like a huge book.

There will be an accompanying class book titled *Our Favorite Ezra Jack Keats Books*. In it the children will each draw a picture of their favorite Keats story, will write the title of the story and sign their names. A few children will be able to add a sentence about why they like the story. I will have it bound, and it will go into the class library.

With every Keats story we read, their vocabularies in English will noticeably grow, and in their daily writing I will see some of the new words employed. Every class activity offers a chance to learn words. By making the class book about the Keats stories, they learn the word "*favorite*" and the words in the title of their favorite story.

It's around this time, after three or four weeks, that they know enough words for elementary understanding. Now I can show them the collection of words I began ten years ago, words I didn't know when I first read them. These words are in a special notebook written with a fine-pointed pen. The word collection began with terms that boggled my mind in educational research when I first went to graduate school. Almost immediately it grew to include many other words I didn't know. I treasure this notebook, although I haven't thought about why. I feel good just looking at it.

I show the children how many words I've collected, even at my age and with my native-speaker status in English. I want them to understand that there are plenty of words to learn, and that when they don't know one, all is not lost; they can learn it in a methodical way. I agree with their surprise that as an adult I had so many words to learn.

"But" I will say, "I know them now! And I'm *still* learning." "Now, though," I tell them, "now it's hard for me to find a new word, at least in English. I'm always looking for good ones. If you see any, let me know."

I have similar notebooks for the children on which, once again, I've written their names with my best script. Although as a class they have collections of words on a bulletin board with alphabetized squares, and a copy of the Dolch one hundred basic words stapled to their writing folders, these new notebooks will be for the children's private word selections. If nothing else, if they don't all learn to love words, I hope that having the notebooks promotes the idea of words as valuable and learnable.

There are other word collections in the class. If we're studying something, like worms or the seasons in Kansas City, unfamiliar words are collected on the bulletin boards in separate categories: Autumn words, Worm words. When they're posted, it's easier to remember and review them for long-term learning. If I don't post them, we all risk forgetting about them.

Using words in class conversations increases their usefulness for language learners. They become familiar with the subtle variations of meaning that words can have and students are more likely to recognize them in their reading and use them in their writing and conversations. It's amazing how many meanings are identified for some of the most common English words, *give* and *see*, for example. It's automatic for me to use more common words with language learners. But if I can remember to use less frequent words as well, they learn them just as easily. But to do it, to say "This playground looks bleak," instead of "This playground looks plain and sad," I need a reminder.

I don't worry much about their learning common words. They'll hear them everywhere and will learn them, especially when they're reinforced in a classroom based on discourse. It's the less common words that are important for future academic success, and I want to do what I can to make sure they are exposed to them.

After they learn "Where's Ernie," I give the children the song, "Five Little Ducks," to learn. It's on a cassette and I've bought an inviting storybook version that's available in most bookstores.

FIVE LITTLE DUCKS
Author and copyright ownership unknown

Five little ducks went out one day,
Over the hills and far away,
Mother Duck said, "Quack, quack, quack, quack"
But only four little ducks came back.

With each similar verse another little duck disappears until all of them come back.

I teach them the song with words and gestures: "far away" by sheltering my eyes and looking to the distance, "hills" by drawing hills on the chalkboard. They know the numbers well now, so the song is easier for them to understand. The loss of the little ducks, one by one, is a good background for imminent lessons in subtraction. Once the language is nearly memorized, I see no reason why they shouldn't learn to read it.

So I let them illustrate books I have made for them. I have typed pages with the text, one idea per page. The typed 8" by 5 1/2" pages are covered with yellow construction paper, and bound with red plastic spiral binding. Illustrating them sounds easy, but at their ages, levels of literacy and early English language skills, it's a challenge. After a few days, I wonder if I made a mistake to start it.

I encourage them to work together and to help each other. I help a few as well by pitching in with some coloring to move the routine part of the job along. They like to gather with friends on the carpet to do this, so that's where I am.

Not all of their difficulties with this task come from challenges in literacy. Some children are perfectionists and won't be satisfied with their drawings—Mufdi, for example. Researchers say that at this age, about 6 or 7, children begin to want their work to look canonical, like grown-up's work looks. They want their ducks to look like the ducks in the book we read.

"Your ducks are great!" I tell Mufdi. But no. He still looks dissatisfied, even grouchy. I give up insisting that they do all the drawings themselves and help the ones who seem frustrated; I draw a duck for Mufdi, and now he's satisfied and draws the rest himself. They relax when I draw a duck for them, and draw the rest alone. I show them an easy way to get a credible duck with the webbed feet, oblong body and bill. I guess the hardly canonical duck I draw gives them confidence that they could draw their own. Their ducks are really cute.

Abubakar is sprawled on the carpet, oblivious to anything but his drawing. I sit next to him. On a page that says "three little ducks...," he is working on a fourth duck.

"Can you read this page to me Abubakar?" Immediately he nearly sings the page: "Five little ducks went out to play...."

"So, right here, this is five, with th?" Now he will stop to think.

"No."

"What is the first sound for "five?"

"ffffffffffff."

"What is this letter?"

"T."

"And the sound for /t/ is...?"

"T, t, t." I've tried hard to avoid any accompanying vowel sounds when I teach these consonant letter sounds. It's not possible, but I think I have managed to make any vowel sound brief and difficult to identify.

"What could this word be then?"

"Two?"

"Two starts with /t/, so your idea makes sense. And you see? You know it's not 5! Isn't that great? You used the letter sounds and found out it wasn't five. I'll tell you because you don't know this one yet. It's three," I tell him because he can't read the /th/ sound yet. "Remember how we stuck out our tongues?" He nods.

"So, instead of five ducks for your illustration, you need...?"

"Three!" He will say. This child is irrepressible.

Although he knows the /f/ sound, he hasn't used his knowledge to make sense of this text. That's what I will want him to practice—the ability to use letter sounds for deciphering text. It isn't a skill that most children learn immediately, but rather is one that grows with use and guidance. This print exposure to /th/, combined with the earlier pronunciation practice, increases his background knowledge for learning to read /th/ later.

Although they take a week and, in some cases, two to complete, illustrating the books will produce memorization of a few sight words, a number of new, solidly learned vocabulary words and a growing understanding of what words do in a text. The project is worth the trouble.

After the books are finished, I let the children take them home to show their parents because most of the children can read them rather well. The next day, I ask them to tell me how they've read their stories at home. "Were your families proud of you?" I ask. There were varied responses.

"She don't know," says Rosalinda. "She doesn't know English?" Rosalinda nods her head. "How about your mother and father Salam?" He smiles and says, "They like it." His parents were teachers in Iraq.

"My dad says, 'good job!' " volunteers Jayson.

"No one listen to me," says Etienne.

Shared reading of songs and poems is a daily activity. So is reading stories. If I pick literature that is well written, interesting and close enough to their language abilities to understand, they'll learn uncommon and superb words. Less basic but relatively common words like *scurry, scorn, flee,* and *frequently* occur more often in children's literature than in normal conversations as well, and introducing them as I read to my students makes learning them a pleasure.

Escape is one of these words. By the time I read a story titled *Harriet,* the children were fluently conversational and knew quite a few words that were beyond basic. They already had learned about similes and metaphors and could recognize and write them. Many were reading chapter books so sometimes I forgot that there was a level of meaning I should never assume.

"Harriet had escaped," I read. I stopped. It hadn't occurred to me as I planned before school that "escaped" might be a problem today. I don't know why I assumed they'd know it unless it was their level of fluency, but intuition and the habit of checking for comprehension saved me. I looked at the children.

"Can anyone explain that, *escaped*?" No one could. I tried an oral explanation, but it was unsuccessful. I switched to a reliable method. "Etienne, would you come here a minute?" He came up to the chair and stood by me. I held his arm lightly around the bicep and said, "Can you escape Etienne?" His face searched mine for a clue, and I gave it to him through my hand. I held it a little more tightly and indicated with a little jerk of my head the rest of the room. He was unsure for a minute and continued to search my face. Slowly the look of understanding began to dawn on his face.

"Go!" I said. "You can't escape!" and pulled him a little toward me, tightening my grip slightly. Aha! Now he knew what to do! Off he went, or tried to. I held him firmly as he struggled with increasing vigor against me. "You can't escape!" He was very strong and began slipping away from me. The children were cheering him on. I let him go.

"He escaped! Etienne escaped!" I cried. "He's escaping! Jayson! Don't let him escape! Catch him Jayson!" There's lots of space for the children to move in this room—I exchanged most of the desks for a few shared tables just for that purpose—and around raced Etienne, Jayson eagerly chasing him. Both of them ran as fast as their bodies would take them, and the rest of the children cheered. The boys had run enough.

"Bravo Etienne! You escaped. Come back boys." Jayson and Etienne exchanged a high five and sat down.

"I almost catch him!" claims Jayson, quickly denied by a triumphant Etienne.

Their faces were bright with humor. "Brenda, would you put *escape* up on the word wall?" I hand her an index card on which I had quickly printed *escape*. It joined *evening*, *effort* and others, and soon it would find a place in a story Etienne would write, where he would tell about a boy who "got escape" from a gorilla.

After a month and a half in school, the daily poem and song recitations, the daily read-alouds and the classroom procedures have stimulated confidence and basic language production in the children. Now I want to enhance their enjoyment of language and encourage more vocabulary growth, so we're going to put on a play. Plays are useful in the same way and for the same reasons that poems and songs are, with added advantages for reading comprehension. I introduce one as soon as I can this year, which is at Halloween. It's not exactly a play, but a reader's theater piece that required some characterization and could have masks. It was a simple play, but I needed to remove a few idiomatic expressions that I thought the students weren't ready to learn.

Theater productions will help them understand the importance of analysis in reading and will require, like the poems and songs they learn, repetition, but this time, repetition for creating a lively production that an audience will find exciting. To bring life to their lines, actors need to understand characters' personalities and motivations, helpful skills for reading comprehension in many texts.

This audience will be the parents, and the children are excited about inviting them. Since so many of the parents work, have little children at home or need to find transportation, we send them invitations a month before the show, and a reminder two weeks before so they have time to make arrangements.

Writing the invitations is another challenging literacy activity. We compose one together on a large sheet of paper and they copy it. They learn a little about the format of invitations.

We practice the play during reading period because it involves intensive reading. I ask those children who are not speaking and reading to follow every line so they'll know when their turn comes, and I explain that doing so will also help their reading.

"Pumpkin says 'Here comes the farmer!' Ingrid, is she sad?" I remind her of "sad" by wiping imaginary tears from my eyes. Ingrid has read "Here comes the farmer!" in a flat, halting voice.

"No."

"Is she happy?" I show a big smile.

"No."

"Pretend I'm the farmer, Ingrid. Here I come! Can you show me how she feels? How does Pumpkin say 'Here comes the farmer!' You are Pumpkin! I'm the farmer and here I come with a basket for juicy little pumpkins!" I approach her in the role of the farmer, looking scary.

"What do you do Ingrid?"

"Here comes the farmer," she tries, more fluently and a little more loudly, but still unconvincingly.

"Hurray! Interesting idea for Pumpkin's voice. You sound scared. Can you make it even more scared?" The children have just learned "voice" from doing this play. She tries again, and then again, each time with more emotion. By now she has memorized the line and is sure of what is going on in the play. She's communicating something with these words, and when she cries, "Here comes the farmer!," the other actors cheer her, and a few applaud enthusiastically.

And she's inspiring in the role; the other children want their parts to be as exciting as Ingrid's is now. They'll need help, but they will have grasped the idea that characters have emotions, and that these emotions can be found through clues that writers give in words. If they want to bring a character to life, the words, once again, are important tools.

On the day of the performance we have several rows of chairs set up in the classroom for visitors. The children and I are dressed for a special occasion, and the room is decorated with the children's latest work and some flowers. All the rubrics, checklists words, charts, poems and songs we've used so far this year are hanging on the wall and bulletin boards. The children have brought in some apple juice, and I've made cookies, everything set out on a decorated table for the reception that will follow the performance.

It's time for the performance. In groups and alone, parents come to the door and Sara, the hostess, accompanies them to their seats. It's exciting to see them come looking as animated as we feel, and like us, dressed for a special occasion. Ingrid's mother arrives to see her star. Ali's father comes; I've never met him. Laura's mother is there, and Brenda's, and here come Sara's parents and grandmother. No one comes to see Etienne, and he is trying to act as if he doesn't care, surreptitiously looking at the door from time to time, just in case. Elmer's father comes, and Vinh's mother. Tamathor's parents, elegant and reserved, enter quietly and sit toward the back where a few unoccupied seats remain. In all, more than fifteen family members have come.

I've trained the children to line up and walk to their places for the play, quietly and together, their hands at their sides. I've taught them to watch my hand as I direct when they sing and recite the poems, and to respond to signals for bowing, sitting down and standing up together. Before and after the play, the children will sing two songs, and after the play they will recite a poem. They look wonderful.

It's time to start. There is a quiet buzz in the room. When Jayson, our announcer, walks to the center of the performance space, everyone stops chatting and looks expectantly at him. I look at Jayson's father and see the face of a man loving his child beyond measure.

"Welcome to our class. First we will sing 'Five Little Ducks.'" He turns and takes his place with a quick look at his parents, confident that they would be proud. They look at one another and smile. Once the show starts, every parent watches intently. When their child reads, they look as if they are trying to hide their pride, as if it were immoderate to have such a child.

Their children are speaking and reading English, which most parents don't understand themselves. This is the first time they see how much their children have learned. I notice that Brenda's mother's eyes brim with tears as she sits there, for the reading, I eventually learn, because she can't read herself.

Studying the parents' faces as they watch the performance, I wonder if they have mixed feelings of pride, dread, loss. How would it feel to be in a foreign country and observe your children as they assimilate before your eyes? I try to imagine, but I don't think I can reach the full experience. Afterwards, they applaud enthusiastically and smile and hug the children. The room is full of high spirits and delight—exactly what I had hoped for on the first day of school.

I'm proud of the children. I'm proud that they're learning to read, write and express themselves in a second language. I'm proud of all the words they know already, so many in such little time. I know that they're learning about language more than they're learning about English. I know that with every word they've learned their ability to read and understand increases, and with that, their ability to write to express themselves. I hope for an end of the year that will show every one of them reading in two languages.

It wasn't hard to teach them to speak English and to help them collect words; it involved starting, plunging into the task and believing that they would grasp and hold onto words they wanted and needed. The important elements were repetition, comprehensibility, and finding subject matter that would be engaging at least and irresistible at best. To be sure that any work was comprehensible involved showing them multiple ways of illustration, like pictures, my physical movements, the children's physical participation and anything else that would lead to understanding, driven by keenness to communicate. The key was that all communication had to be for a purpose, connected to real life and not to a pretend world with fabricated life situations. It had to be critical to their real lives and survival in our real classroom, like sharing their names for example, or asking for things. Words and language made it possible for them to participate in our class.

And I also had to be fair. I didn't know all the children's heritage languages and didn't want to appear to favor one group; children are awfully attuned to fairness and to how much love they perceive they're getting compared with their companions. To some degree the relationship to attention and affection from the teacher is akin to sibling rivalry, as teachers are often seen in the role of surrogate mothers at school, especially by primary children.

I thought that it was important to speak only English to create their need and desire for the language, but there's a poem by Rhina P. Espaillat that expresses a different point of view, different and lovely:

BILINGUAL/BILINGÜE

... "English outside this door, Spanish inside,"
he said [her father], "*y basta.*" But who can divide

the world, the word (*mundo y palabra*)
from any child? I knew how to be dumb

and stubborn (*testaruda*); late, in bed,
I hoarded secret syllables I read

Until my tongue (*mi lengua*) learned to run
where his stumbled. And still the heart was one...

I'm not one hundred percent persuaded that what I did was the best way to teach a linguistically diverse group of children to speak a new language and to be literate. Someone sometime may find something better. However, I do know that what I did worked. I kept the languages separate, at least in class, and the children learned to speak English well and learned about languages in general through its study. They all became literate, and I showed them how to transfer what they knew about English literacy to their heritage languages, even the Arabic speakers, to whom I pointed out that the kind of thinking they did for understanding English stories could work in stories in their language as well. They learned that the signs on the paper meant language. I don't think I hurt my students or their identities because I made sure to value their heritage languages and promoted the development of all the languages they knew—I gave equal value to all of them. I feel confident that they could agree with Espaillat's words: "And still the heart was one."

Chapter 2

First Days: First Steps to Literacy

Mufdi arrived in our classroom on an already stifling morning several days after school began. He held the hand of a tall man, African I thought, who gave me a registration card and said in formal tones, "This is my son." Looking down at his sobbing child then up again, he held my glance and in a quiet voice added, "He has never been to school." His presence was imposing, but he spoke of his son with exquisite tenderness and I saw no need to put him at ease except to reassure him that his child would be safe.

"I will take care of your son," I said, responding with equal formality as I accepted the card. He bent down, whispered something in the child's ear, gave me a probing look and left. Mufdi remained at the door, his shoulders heaving, his eyes flooding tears and his nose running, a child more the size of a four-year-old than the six-year-old his registration card announced.

I put my hand on his shoulder and led him to the coatroom. With gestures to show him where he could store his things among those of his twenty-one new classmates, I said quietly, pointing to myself, "I will do it," and put them away for him. We moved back out into the room while his shoulders continued to heave with quiet but heavy sobs.

"Boys and girls, we have a new friend. His name is Mufdi. He will need our help." The children, seated on the carpet, looked worried as Mufdi continued to sob almost noiselessly, his eyes lowered, averted from all contact. Sara turned to whisper something to Ingrid, and then they soberly looked up together.

I looked around for someone I knew would be reliable. "Jayson, can you help Mufdi?" I gestured to show taking hands while I emphasized the word *help*. In the few days that school had been in session, Jayson had already shown his capacity for empathy, this boy brimming with enthusiasm, sensitive and quick.

"Yes, teacher." His face brightened with eagerness as he jumped up and came over to where Mufdi and I stood. He knew probably three words in English, but was eager to use them, foreshadowing his future pleasure in talk. Like all the children, he called me "Teacher," a transfer, I concluded, from a culture that calls teachers by their title. Most of my students and many of their parents called me this and I'd grown proud to be called "Teacher."

Jayson came up to Mufdi, took his hand and led him to his place on the carpet, gently indicating where Mufdi could sit, with gestures to explain. I know Mufdi could sense Jayson's kindness because he went with him and quickly sat down, although continuing to cry quietly. Jayson sat down by his side.

Some of the students sitting nearby inched away from him, among them Sara and Ingrid, glancing at one another with a conspiratorial air while stealing a glance at me. They had come to an unspoken consensus about Mufdi it seemed, a consensus that had the look of rejection. My heart sank. I stared at them and mimed shock as I gestured them back being careful that Mufdi, since he continued to look down, wouldn't see my quick motions. I hoped he hadn't seen the children's movements and what they seemed to signal. They inched back to their places, once again looking at one another as they did.

Mufdi's crying continued. While I tried to carry on as though nothing had changed in the room, the children looked between Mufdi and me with questions on their faces. "Who knows what day it is?" I asked while he sobbed. I hoped that by ignoring his distress we might give him the time and privacy to look around and see that he was not in danger.

But it did not help Mufdi to leave him alone and he continued to cry with the same distress. I moved to where he sat on the carpet and sat next to him hoping that my adult, governing presence could be comforting. He continued to cry with unchanged intensity. I lightly patted his hand, but what he needed was the arms of someone he loved and trusted. It may have been easier if I spoke his language, but I couldn't, and with the intensity of his anguish, it might not have improved anything if I did. Still, I continued the rest of the calendar activities from where I sat as I relied on what has been my most trustworthy support in the classroom, the teaching and learning processes. They bring reason and order to the worst educational circumstances.

Through them children understand and join the focus and purpose of the class. If Mufdi could see what was going on around him he might understand why he was there and become curious about it. His attention might be diverted away from his misery at being in yet another unfamiliar setting, to what we were doing. More often than not, this is how my students have reacted in the past, but none of them has seemed as distressed as this child.

Teaching language through the study of the first-grade subjects was the rationale that directed the teaching and learning in this class. This study was the source of reason and order in the year's plan, and was the structure that sustained us in these challenging early days. It gave shape to the effort to accomplish the goal of language acquisition for twenty-four young children. The content I would use to teach language would be the district's mainstream curriculum, especially literacy skills. That is, Mufdi and his classmates would learn English by learning to read, write, think mathematically and consider distillations of the fundamental ideas of the sciences and social studies. Included in every lesson would be informal and formal lessons about the language they would need.

At the moment, the first week of school, our class was devoted to the earliest English literacy activities: phonemic awareness, letters and their sounds, left-to-right sequence of English written text, the use of pencils and paper, and the connection between oral language and text. The effort to teach these concepts had led me to repeat and emphasize certain expressions, and the children could already say or understand a few of them. At the same time, we had begun the passage toward creating the intimacy and shared culture that would nurture the children's desire to communicate with me and one another and thus inspire their language acquisition.

I was using lively, simple activities that all my previous students had liked. In the area of literacy instruction at least, I had weeded away most unsuccessful, dull lessons and I hoped those we used would be attractive enough to draw Mufdi into them, or at least draw his attention. Apart from the activities, which I was fairly confident he would like, the children's early reception of him was troubling, a problem I would need to solve if he was going to learn at his potential.

He was from Sudan. As I later learned, from there his Christian family had fled to Egypt and from Egypt to the United States. At this point my understanding about the politics in Sudan was superficial, and I knew little about its geography or people. I found useful resources about the struggles in Sudan between Christians and Muslims on the Internet, but it was only at the end of the school year that I read a vivid essay in *The New York Review of Books* describing the special experience of the Sudanese refugees in Egypt—a chronicle of racism, abuse, profiteering and unspeakable physical misery—and could approach understanding what Mufdi and his family had endured.

Little wonder that Mufdi suffered. Now in our class, although it was composed of new immigrants, he could see no one from Sudan to be his immediate ally, and no one who could speak his first language, no one even vaguely familiar. In addition, school, compared with home life, is quite structured. Surely that was unfamiliar too—American public school, with its decades of tradition, myths and structure, especially visible at the beginning of the year.

While he would need support and guidance through a difficult time, he also possessed a dignity that needed to be balanced with his vulnerability: I could not seem excessively anxious in my concern and the real need to help him; the children would feel unsettled and more guarded with him, even jealous, and he would feel diminished. Yet I couldn't ignore his need for support; his distress was evident. While supporting him, I wanted to communicate to the children that here was a friend who needed help not only from me, but from all of them as well. By helping Mufdi, they could experience affecting the lives of others with their good actions. I needed to teach them how to help him, and to see him as a friend. They could learn to pay attention to the quality of others' experiences, further their own comfort in the classroom and feel empowered as members of the class. Without this kind of learning we wouldn't have the intimacy and shared culture we needed to promote an optimal learning environment.

During the early morning routines that took place after the calendar activities—shared repeated readings for a song, and shared repeated reading of a weekly poem—Mufdi continued to cry and ignored the students who tried to comfort him, once or twice sharply turning away from them. His crying was a prolonged, quiet sobbing, impossible to ignore or ever forget.

After the calendar and shared readings, it was time to begin the phase of the literacy period where the children worked independently. At the moment this occurred in centers. Once the children were ready—once they knew the letters and sounds and were trained to make responsible decisions for reading—the centers would be replaced by independent reading. This took one month, every year.

We always initiated the literacy period with a quickly read story to turn their minds to the pleasures of words, ideas and imagination. Today, I sat down and pulled out a big book from a large container that held many big books and was located right behind the reading chair. The book I chose was *Mrs. Wishy Washy*, which I had read to them on the first day of school. Its illustrations always prompted enthusiastic laughter for a truly modest story line—an optimistic farm woman bathes farm animals who joyfully embrace mud and dirt (the pig's big bottom is particularly successful). In the end, just after a bath, they roll in the mud yet one more time. It's a good book to read to young ELL students early in the year; the images are graphic and the children develop the supportive feeling of a shared experience, laughing together. In addition it has repetitive text that they quickly learn to repeat together, promoting language learning and active participation. When they saw it again today, a little wave of recognition and pleased sounds ran through the group.

When the children began to laugh, Mufdi quickly raised his eyes and examined them, his residual sobs broken now by a fleeting expression of curiosity. I kept reading, hoping he would see that the class activities and students were fun and that joining in would be his choice. The children's laughter grew. I resisted the desire to look at Mufdi with every sentence and instead focused on the story and the other students, trying to evaluate his mood when I surveyed the class for attention or response. Each time he caught me looking, he quickly lowered his head.

Our next focus in this literacy period would involve early alphabetic activities. In four stations the students would be learning letter names and sounds, and learning to associate them. They wouldn't need much English ability to learn them, yet they would be acquiring an essential skill for literacy. In addition, they would internalize the English expressions that accompanied the activities everyday. I had added a new station today—writing A and B, a and b five times each to reinforce the names of these letters with their sounds as they learned handwriting.

The centers were labeled and coordinated with the groups into which I'd placed the children; for example, RED GROUP: Ivan, Derek, Rosalinda, Salam and Etienne; BLUE GROUP: Ali, Sang, Ingrid, Mohammed, and Tamathor, etc. BLUE GROUP was the first to go to the new handwriting center. The members of the groups had mixed degrees of familiarity with literacy and school so the children could learn from one another and help each other. I also wanted to avoid any sense of a knowledge hierarchy in the class, or the perception that any privilege or extra respect was given to advanced learners. They would soon learn, with guidance, that everyone had something to offer, and that everyone excelled at something. Because most of our work would be individualized, advanced children would have an opportunity to work at their levels, and children with more to learn would have the time and opportunity to acquire the skills they needed. No one would be working on a skill they already had mastered, or a skill that they weren't prepared to learn.

Before sending the children off to the centers, I explained the new activity to them while they were all still on the carpet. On the dry erase board next to my reading chair I had posted a piece of lined paper for demonstration that was a large version of the one they would have at the center. It showed the first letters (A, B, a and b) they would practice. First, I demonstrated what I intended for them to do, saying aloud "Now I write A. I need to make ten of them." I held up ten fingers and counted aloud as I wrote. Then I asked for several volunteers to try it—Sara, Etienne, and Ingrid. One at a time they completed a few letters and I asked them to try to make each one better than the one before, and to whisper the letter to themselves as they make each one. Then I said, "Do you all know what to do?" They seemed ready, or as ready as they could be without trying the skill, so I said, "All right, go to your centers." They had little tags to remind them of the color of their group.

I put Mufdi in a group that would be with me first, a center where I promoted letter–sound relationships by tossing the children lettered beanbags from a distance of about three meters; the greater the distance the more the fun and motivation to learn the answers. To qualify for an attempt to catch the beanbag the children had to know the letter name and the phonemic sound of the letter I held up for their turns. Mufdi was seated between Abubakar and Ivan.

"Abubakar, what is this letter?" At this point no one knew the names of the letters or their sounds; they were learning the routine of the game and the vocabulary that went with it, although focusing on the letters. And they were only beginning to learn the vocabulary and syntax for the expressions required for the game: "I don't know," "It's _____. Listen to what _____ says. Then you will learn."

"Keep your eyes on the beanbag and then you will catch it," I say, pointing to my eyes and then to the beanbag. Part of the process was for me to act as if I thought Abubakar could have the correct answer.

"You don't know?" I asked, emphasizing my target words while I shook my head, and pointed to him.

"No." He shook his head for "no." I persisted, making a gesture with my hand to encourage him to repeat. I wanted "I don't know," to seem an acceptable possibility while they were learning, and tried to communicate this stance with the tone of my voice. I also wanted them to learn this useful expression.

"Say, 'I don't know.' " I made a kind of "come" gesture with one hand to communicate "say." He seemed self-conscious about it so I quickly moved my attention to the next child. I hoped that this activity would distract Mufdi, but it didn't. He looked up occasionally and sank back into his private misery.

It was his turn. Even though I knew he was distressed I held up a lettered beanbag to signal to him and to the other students his membership in the class.

"Mufdi, what is this letter?" He kept his head down.

"You don't know?" I asked in his direction, again exaggeratedly pronouncing the words so they could hear all the sounds and learn the expression, just as I had with Abubakar. I moved on to the next student. Finally, when by the end of the row none of the students had correctly responded, I gave the answer.

"It's name is A and the sound is /a/," (at). For my ELL students, distinguishing between some of the vowel sounds was always the hardest skill to learn, but this focused attention to them never failed to bring the desired results. Saying the vowels correctly would help them immensely as they began to identify the written words they could say or had heard. I asked for near-perfection with letter pronunciation, and had even studied standard American English pronunciation with language CDs in an attempt to eliminate my own personal or regional vowel pronunciation.

I held up a beanbag with Ff.

"What is this letter?" and repeated the process, careful to repeat the same wording so they would hear it over and over.

Then I returned to A and—a gift! Sara got it. Now I could throw her the beanbag and the children would see the consequences of Sara's success—she could keep the beanbag for the duration of the game. When they saw Sara catch and keep the beanbag, the children paid attention with increased excitement. This time when Abubakar saw a new letter he proudly said, "I don't know."

"Very good, Abubakar! You don't know. Let's see if Jayson knows it. Listen." I cupped my ear. Jayson didn't know it either, and said, also with some delight, "I don't know." I applauded his English and continued on to the next person. Now they all said, some of them a little self-consciously but still proudly, "I don't know."

Mufdi occasionally glanced up, but looked down each time it was his turn. Next to him Jayson and especially Abubakar were increasingly animated. Too bad for them; the time was at an end at this center. "Tomorrow," I said, and went to the calendar to point to the square for "tomorrow", repeating several times "to-morr-ow" (as if stressing the *mor* would make a difference!). There were disappointed groans all around.

I led Mufdi to his group's next work area, the handwriting center where the four other group members were already sitting down to work. I again modeled to all of them what they needed to do. With Mufdi in mind, I urged Sara to help anyone who needed help and returned to the beanbags. After a minute or two I checked around the room to see how everyone was doing, including a glance over my shoulder at the handwriting group. My attention froze.

Abubakar and Mufdi had grabbed their pencils like digging sticks—in their fists—and were attempting to stab marks on pieces of paper while Sara stared at them, paralyzed with fascination. I left my group for a minute after whispering to them to talk softly. I physically indicated that I would be right back.

Meanwhile, at the handwriting center Mufdi (whose remaining signs of distress were an occasional immense sob, a tear-streaked face, the appearance of apathy, and an expression of deep sorrow) and Abubakar were trying to figure out how to make marks on their papers, Aa, Bb surely forgotten. I stepped around to stand between them.

I gestured by touching my eyes that I wanted them to observe me and modeled how to hold a pencil. Then I placed a pencil in Abubakar's hand by arranging each finger, placed my hand over his and guided his hand to make a few letters. It required enormous concentration on his part—his hands resisted the unfamiliar movements. But we worked on until he finally succeeded in holding the pencil well enough to make short and undefined marks. The waiting children, I noted, were quietly chatting. I gave them a look of approval to encourage their cooperation for one or two more seconds.

Mufdi watched listlessly. When it was his turn he accepted the same kind of help I had given to Abubakar with the same difficulties in holding the pencil and making marks. I was pleased to note that he began to show mild interest. The attention that the writing required seemed to distract him from his suffering for awhile, and his partner Abubakar's humor and ardent embrace of anything new had to have been contagious.

"A" I repeated as he and I formed circles. "Good job." I patted his shoulder, gave Abubakar a nod of approval, glanced at Sara, Ivan and Jayson's work, and returned to the waiting children.

Before going to their next area the children at the handwriting center brought me their work, Mufdi with his tear-stained paper following Abubakar. The two boys' papers were covered with random, dark marks which I praised lavishly. Abubakar beamed; Mufdi remained apathetic.

They moved on to a listening center where a song I recorded was in a player. It accompanied an alphabet book that I had copied so that each child at the station would have one. The tune was exceedingly simple, created to be easily memorized and understood.

"A is for alligator, ah ah ah (ă). B is for butterfly, b, b, b," I used the same notes and rhythm for each letter. They all had smiled and laughed when they first heard it, pointing at me and laughing again. Rosalinda and Sara, who knew rudimentary English, saying what the others couldn't.

"That's you teacher!" as if they had made a great discovery. And they liked the animals. The novelty would wear off, but as they memorized the letter sounds the activity would lead them to learn the animals' names as well—a bounty of twenty-six new vocabulary words. The tune with the animal names would prove to be an effective mnemonic for letter sounds when they began reading.

"What's the first letter for this word?"

"A."

"How does it sound?"

"I don't know."

"A is for alligator..." I would sing to the student who needed the clue. The song became so familiar, so automatic, that without fail the sound would follow.

"a, a, a—After!"

They would be so amazed at how sounds could help to produce a word that even when they had free time they would gather in small groups to figure out the words of a familiar big book, a posted nursery rhyme or a song together, applying this new tool to get them started.

I quickly showed Mufdi how to use the headphones by putting them on my own head and then his, as gently as I could. But he immediately removed them with some distaste. I left him alone, expressed my sympathy for his situation with a light pat on his shoulder and returned to the next beanbag group.

Mufdi physically turned away from the activity—he remained seated but his head was turned away from the group, his head resting on his arms on the table—cooperating in a sense; other children might have wailed or run around the room, or even out of it, but instead he showed his participation by mute and doubtless uncomprehending compliance. Or was it resignation?

As we were preparing for lunch I asked Abubakar to be Mufdi's helper. He turned away from Mufdi with an expression of aversion. When I mimed puzzlement and mouthed "Why?" he shrugged his shoulders and again looked away. Etienne also refused with a shake of his head. I looked at Jayson with a question on my face, and he answered this with a bright, "Okay, teacher." Jayson put his arm around Mufdi's shoulder and led him to the line, where he stood with him.

I led the children to the cafeteria and stayed with them as they picked up their trays and tried to understand the cafeteria helpers' questions about what food they wanted. During the early part of the year they needed my help to negotiate this part of the day. Like children in other years, they were frightened by the unfamiliar staff, the need to respond to questions they couldn't understand, the choices, the food, the need to move quickly, the precise routine for picking up milk and tableware, the rules for seating and the procedures for indicating that they had finished eating.

We had practiced this on the first day of school, but I usually needed to stay with them for a week or more. We went through the line together and headed toward the tables. Some of the children didn't recognize what the food was. I was in complete sympathy; it was a meat and noodle dish floating in grease with tomato sauce and a thick layer of cheddar cheese. "Spaghetti" the menu said. I sat by Mufdi and Jayson for this spaghetti lunch.

No talking whatsoever was allowed at lunchtime, either in the food line or at the tables. This requirement was expedient for the supervising adults but difficult for the children and precisely the opposite of what my students and most of the others needed for their language and social development. However, I understood the impulse that led to the rule. Student cafeteria talk in past years had escalated to nearly uncontrollable shouting and disorder that included throwing food, so the quick solution had been "no talking." It calmed everyone. After they ate, the children were required to return their trays, go back to their seats, remain speechless and put their heads on their tables. Later in the year this requirement was negotiated to "quiet talking" that would be stopped if after a warning it became too loud. When this approach became too difficult to monitor, the "no talking" rule returned.

It was awfully hard. I was convinced that children could be taught to speak quietly with consistent reminders, but it would take an effort by the entire staff, and with busy teaching schedules and a heavy load of paperwork, teachers had many other priorities. In addition, a number of staff members didn't think the children would learn the quiet talk and cooperate with it. Others didn't see the need for talk. I didn't agree, but at any rate, today as soon as I saw that my students had finished eating, I got them into a line and took them out early. Mufdi had cried during the entire lunch period and had eaten nothing.

I led the children to the playground where I began turning a jump rope with Sara. Without yard duty today I could focus on my students as they adapted to life on the playground. I especially wanted to be sure that Mufdi would be comfortable and safe.

Once the jump rope game had begun, I left it to walk around the playground and see how my students were doing. My first move was to stand by Mufdi. Salam was standing nearby, hesitant to join in the play and looking lonely, but not upset. Mufdi was crying. I tried to talk to them and succeeded somewhat with Salam—he responded and became more animated, but Mufdi seemed not to hear.

These first days of the year were always hard for my immigrant students, and although I expected many of them to be lonely, or to feel sad or lost, I never could be completely objective about their suffering, and in this sense the early days were hard for me as well. The answer to this was to make a home of the class, and I would soon increase my efforts to ensure that this happened.

When the bell rang to end recess, I gathered the children around me and led them back into the classroom. This took some time; many required special invitations from the classmates I sent to find them. Although they had quickly learned the terms "line up" and "recess is over," walking into the classroom at this time of the year was not as straightforward as it sounds: some children wanted to keep playing, some wanted to linger and explore found objects on the ground and others wanted to continue talking to family members from other classes. If they were talking to classmates in line they often didn't notice that everyone else was moving along, and they would be accidentally bumped by other students, causing a mild uproar. We were twenty-two people, soon to be twenty-four in all—twenty-two children and I, with nearly as many agendas.

Inside, I invited them to sit around my reading chair where I now was seated. With some ceremony I reached into the big-book bin and brought out a book, *The Little Red Hen*.

"Does this look like a good book to you?" I asked, nodding up and down with a question on my face as I showed them the cover of the book. Because this simple story lends itself to discussions that can go beyond recall of what happened, I wanted to use it to begin a class tradition of book talks. It also had the large and colorful illustrations and repeated text that is attractive to early readers and comprehensible to beginning English learners. They quickly agreed that it looked like a good book with the kind of unconsidered consensus that would disappear once they were more critical thinkers and could understand English.

I had brought some wheat grains to show them, and samples of different kinds of bread for them to taste—naan, flour tortillas, pita bread and a loaf of French bread. In these early stages of their language and literacy learning, understanding was quicker when they could see and touch objects that were discussed in books. If I couldn't get the items, I used pictures. I set the bread and grains out on the table behind the reading chair, ready for use when the words appeared in the story. Sometimes I showed objects and discussed vocabulary before reading, but not for this story, and not for these circumstances.

I looked at the cover of the book with a puzzled look on my face.

"Hmmm. Here's a hen!" I said, as if talking to myself. I pointed to her. "And here's a cat, a duck and a dog! What..." I looked even more puzzled. "... are a cat, a dog and a duck doing with a hen!?" To clarify, I said, "A Cat!? A Dog!? A HEN?" Some of these words were already becoming familiar to many of the children from the alphabet song. Most were also in *Mrs. Wishy Washy*. I pointed to each animal and looked at the children. "Won't the dog and the cat hurt the hen? Do you have an idea?" I pointed to my head and then to them in invitation.

"Friends?" suggested Elmer.

"Hmmm," I said. I brightened. "Maybe! Does anyone else have another idea?"

At this point no one offered another idea—the concept of extended conversations was new and limited by their beginning levels of English language. I knew from past experience how skillful they would become as the year went on and so kept asking questions. It was the process I was teaching now, and I didn't expect much language use.

I opened to the first page and talked about how it looked, what might be happening. I moved to the next one and continued with an exploration of the illustrations on each page as a preview of the book. Then I began to read. As I read I stopped to wonder aloud about the fairness of friends wanting the benefits of Hen's labor without sharing in the work. I asked the children what they thought.

When the story was finished I went to the board where I had posted the graphic organizer template I would use all year. Today's version was made with yellow butcher paper, empty except for the headings: Someone, Wanted, But, So. One by one we added the characters' names:

"Who are the characters in this story? The little red hen is one," I say to illustrate. And they understand as I look at them expectantly. "Are there any more?" After simple discussions, with my guidance they filled in the rest.

THE LITTLE RED HEN

Somebody	Wanted	But	So

I intended for them to see how characters interact with one another in stories, and how important they are in the movement and outcome of a story. That characters' purposes could be in conflict was clear from the chart. The visual representation time after time would finally help to provide insight about this complex idea. I hoped also to see this growing understanding of character motivation reflected in their writing once they acquired the English facility to write with a little complexity. Later in the year I would add another heading to the chart: What Was the Most Important Idea?

We filled the chart out together, and with this basic tale the conflicting motivations and desires weren't hard to see. When the children seemed to have forgotten what an animal wanted, I brought out the book and found the page as a reminder.

"Let's refer back to the text" I said, without an explanation, but at the same time I turned back pages of the book, looking for the picture of the cat and what she wanted to do. I knew that my many repetitions of these words paired with these same gestures every storytime would soon make the meaning clear. I found the illustration.

"Sleep!" said Rosalinda. She had had a few months of English in kindergarten.

"Does everyone agree?" I shook my head up and down with a question on my face. "Does the cat want to sleep?" I closed my eyes and pretended to sleep to illustrate. "Raise your hand..." I raised my hand "...if you agree." I nodded, exaggerating "yes," and shook my head left to right to show "No." Everyone raised a hand for "yes" and I wrote it on the chart.

"That's it? That's all she wants?" I examined the chart as I kept my tone neutral so I wouldn't lead their thoughts. The children didn't react. "Does she want anything else?"

"Bread?" asked Sara. She was unsure of herself with this open question.

"Sara says the cat wants bread too. Does anyone agree? Does the cat want bread?" I pointed to each child so they would know I expected them to be thinking about the question. I illustrated "want" by pointing to bread, saying, "Mmmm," while hoping the look I gave toward the bread looked wishful as I made repeated gestures from bread to my chest. They named the characters appropriately, and I assumed that they understood my meaning.

"What would you do if you were the Little Red Hen?" I asked. "Share?" I take some bread and indicate giving it out. "Say, 'No?'" I pull the bread in close to me. At this beginning point, the discussion was basic and involved a lot of physical modeling.

THE LITTLE RED HEN

Somebody	Wanted	But	So
Little Red Hen	To make bread. Dog, Cat, and Duck to help her make bread	They didn't want to help	She made it herself and she ate it herself
Dog	To dig and eat bread	He didn't help with the bread work	He could not eat bread
Cat	To sleep and eat bread	She didn't help with the bread work	She could not eat bread
Duck	To swim and eat bread	He didn't help with the bread work	She could not eat bread

Opinions about what the Little Red Hen should have done were varied: share, share a little, and share not at all—just what I hoped. I wanted them to appreciate that a variety of opinions are possible and desirable in a discussion. I quickly wrote what they thought on the board next to their initials:

Share: R.S., I.S., S.A., E.L., J.S.

Share a little: K.M., I.P.

Don't share: C.S.

They were learning an attitude of "there's not always one answer," but they were also learning share. It was a word that would be useful in class and on the playground.

"Interesting, no?" I asked them. "Five say 'she should share'; nine say 'share a little'; four say 'don't share'...." I had some simple graph forms on the table behind me, prepared for next week. I was going to begin daily graphing of opinions and preferences as a regular morning activity: "Which color do you prefer, red or blue?" "Do you prefer cake or ice cream?" One graph form would be posted on a chart stand by the door, and when they first entered in the morning, each child would either initial or color in a space under the illustration that represented their preference—I hadn't decided how I would do that yet. The forms I had prepared were enough for one every day for two months.

It was probably because I had been thinking about graphing and had the forms close by that I was inspired to graph their Red Hen opinions. The process could provide background information to them for the new graphing activities. I drew a graph like the forms they would have and noted their options—a bar graph of one child, one vote: share, share a little, share next time, don't share. On each space of the graph I put a child's initials to point out the one-to-one correspondence and to let them know that what they thought individually was important. It was helpful to integrate math into other activities throughout the day. It enabled them to understand that math had a role in our daily lives and to reinforce difficult concepts. Today's graphing not only was an appropriate integration of math into social studies and reading, it was a perfect segue into the next scheduled activity, math.

They looked forward to math because they thought it was play. Hector even said one day, "Can we play math?" During the day they would ask, "Is it time for math?" We used an active math program centered around explorations: they investigated questions, worked together, and always used objects they could manipulate for their work.

The program required original thinking and problem-solving—instruction for formulaic responses was avoided. The students made original solutions and learned to show and explain their thinking and solutions with models, graphs and drawings. Later, they would have to write explanations to accompany their illustrations. I liked it as well as they did—it reinforced the importance of the original thinking I wanted to promote.

One thing I uniformly did expect and teach them was that their work should be neat and organized to communicate, an expectation that took nearly the whole year for every child to achieve, and was a considerable accomplishment for young children. Part of the difficulty in teaching and learning this aspect of their math work lay in the children's developmental levels; at their ages it was difficult to consider someone else's thinking, to know what information another person needed to understand.

They were successfully learning challenging math concepts with this program and at the moment, the beginning of the year, they were learning how to count objects and to assign the correct numeral for the count, an association called one-to-one correspondence. It was a perfect way to learn the language of numbers—counting as the concept that supported the English-language acquisition.

First I asked them to sit together in a circle on the carpet so that I could show them what they would be doing today. As they sat I had Ivan and Rosalinda pass out ten colorful, interlocking cubes to each child. One by one we counted out loud together. I showed them how to move each object to another spot so they would know it had been counted.

"One…" and I moved my object firmly and clearly, forming a new set of the counted numbers.

Understanding the relationship of one object and one number together is a great leap for some children, especially for those whose cultures aren't as quantifying as ours, or that don't measure everything as ours does. In the beginning we counted everything. As they improved, I moved them toward noticing how many tens were in everything, a practice I continued all year and that evolved to hundreds and thousands.

They had already played at length with these cubes two days ago. It has worked best for my classes if I let them play with the objects for math, especially these cubes when they first get them, so the novelty will wear off and the challenge and pleasure of using them to solve math problems will take over. There always seemed to be a gun problem to solve. If one boy, and it was always a boy, made a gun, most of the others immediately followed suit. It happened every year, and was the one object I explicitly forbade them to make. If I could have remembered ahead of time that they would do this, I could have avoided having the guns introduced, but I never did.

For today's counting activity they sat in groups and counted together, drew quantities of self-selected objects and numbered them. They chatted loudly, were excited and yet challenged. I moved from group to group, and then sent them off to their assigned places at the tables for independent work. Only for math did they have assigned seating. I arranged the members at each set of tables so that there would be a balance of children for whom math seemed easy, and others for whom it was harder. Later, when their language abilities grew, I would teach them how to help one another, including what to say and not say as coaches.

I passed from table to table, child to child to check their understanding and to guide them individually. Many times that day, I guided a child's hand and counted objects, moving the objects with them each time. Without guidance they would count "One, two, three" while touching any number of unrelated cubes, their hands bouncing off the cubes in an attempt to copy my example without understanding the meaning of the movements.

"One," and with exaggerated attention, my hand with a child's hand, moved one cube aside."Two," and we placed another cube. Now, "One, two" and we touched each cube, moving it aside with exaggerated attention. Then I watched as they tried it. The connection between spoken numbers and quantity of objects was simply not apparent to most of the children, and they were learning the language as well, a lot to learn.

When I came to Mufdi, who was with Abubakar and Jayson, I crouched down and looked into his face. It had the white traces of tears and an expression so sad that I stroked his hand and said so that no one but he could hear, "It's hard, isn't it Mufdi?" He looked away but his body relaxed a little, and he seemed to feel better for that single moment, without knowing what I had said, but sensing it, I'm sure.

I took a few of the connecting cubes from a box on the table and counted them quietly, exaggerating each word as he watched with an unchanged expression.

"One cube, two cubes, three cubes...." Then I thought, "He hasn't had a chance to explore these cubes yet. Maybe he'll be more interested if he had a chance to play with them and make discoveries about what they do." I showed him how he could make interesting things with the cubes, like airplanes and a giraffe, looked into his eyes and said, "Now I need to see what Abubakar is doing," and left. A few minutes later when I looked over to his table, I saw him putting a few cubes together, apparently making something, although with little sign of enthusiasm, and less of feeling comfortable.

The day was nearly over. The children and I cleaned up after math and gathered on the carpet again where I read them a simple nonfiction book which explained the seasons through the life cycle of an apple. It was perfect. A pending trip to an apple orchard would bring the idea to life, and the book would make the meaning of the language they would need during the trip more accessible. Sometimes one is lucky enough to find just the right fit between the curriculum, the language and a book, and for this topic, apple growth, I had several.

On the field trip not only would they see apples on trees in an orchard, but the bus would pass through farming country on the way and they would see fields and some of the animals whose names they were learning in the listening center and at storytime. They would pick apples, and put them in baskets. They would pet the farm animals and talk about them by name; animals that were strange to some of them. I would talk with them about autumn as we moved through the day, and point out signs of the season's change. If ever I could find the money and get permission, I would take them on at least one field trip a month, or even one every week, but unfortunately, this was a dream. Taking numerous field trips could have been so valuable for the increase of their language and background knowledge. Both would have benefited the children's reading comprehension.

They were excited about the pending trip but they were sweating and looked wilted. It was hot, and I thought they'd had enough of this school structure. I gave them fifteen minutes to relax and be free of planned time and English, and then it was time for getting ready to go home.

Mufdi had stopped crying, but he was still a very sad and lost-looking boy, with a face streaked with tears and dried mucous. He sat alone while the children talked and played, his head lowered, his shoulders slumped in a private world. I asked everyone to come together on the carpet and in groups of four sent them into the coatroom for their belongings while I chatted informally with them.

When the children were ready, I walked out to the busses with them. In the halls filled with classes headed toward the doors, several children were running, and many friends were calling to one another, "Wait for me!" so they could walk home together. It was quite noisy and a little chaotic, but happy.

As we approached the busses, I saw Mufdi's big brother, the fourth grader listed on Mufdi's class assignment card, standing outside with other excited and bustling children from bus 6. I knew who he was because he looked like a taller version of Mufdi. He was alone and as he stood his eyes keenly searched with an anxious expression. When suddenly he saw his brother, he stopped looking and watched, waiting with a smile that was understanding and kind, like his father's. Then Mufdi saw him. His face lit up, and although he still didn't smile, he rushed from his classmates to his brother's side and started to talk.

I thought of my promise, "I will take care of your son," and knew it was going to prove a challenge to keep. When I say "I will take care of your child," I mean that the child will be happy and learn. If I couldn't find a way to make Mufdi happy, he wouldn't learn, and I wasn't taking care of him.

These first days of school are among the most important of the year as they set the tone for the entire year and establish procedures: what is the purpose of our being together, and how will we treat one another. I had decided when I began teaching in the Sheltered English program that my personal purpose for being with the ELL children would be to focus on their academic achievement, not their English acquisition. English would be the essential tool that would lead to the academic achievement, and obviously couldn't be ignored, but it was the children's academic achievement that would drive my work. I knew that if I used English exclusively and taught the subject matter intensively, they would learn English. My effort to communicate would lead me to employ all the means I could to make them understand. Their effort to understand and respond would lead them to listen intently and to listen and watch for clues.

That's why I began the year by focusing on literacy, the prime academic goal of first graders in nearly all classrooms. The effort to teach the beginning tools of literacy led the children to learn elementary English. By the time they spoke English fluently, they already would have had the knowledge to read and understand well beyond what they would have if I had waited for English to be solidly in place: the learning led to the language. Besides, these early reading skills—letter recognition and letter sounds, left to right, top to bottom directionality in English reading, book handling, printing—didn't require much language to learn, just enough for beginners.

I also knew that the children would have to be relaxed and motivated to learn. This meant that they would have to treat one another well; everyone would need to be included equally in all classroom activities, and they all would have to believe in their capacity to learn. I could see from the children's reception of Mufdi that these conditions were a long way from being established. Inclusion and confidence would require my input, as they had every year that I taught, and in every grade level. Every year there was something to remind me.

It is plain to me that teaching is infinitely more than the transmission of information and skills, especially if the intention is to teach all of the children and not just the few who might learn without much help. Teachers' imaginations, enthusiasm, empathy and education—all that they are—are interwoven threads, functioning in combination with all that the children are, to create the only satisfactory end: that all children have learned at their full potential. Our class was on its way toward that goal, but it was clear to me that there was a lot of work to do before it would happen.

Figure 2.1: On the floor with Mufdi

Chapter 3

Under the Skin

On his second day of school Mufdi came to the door accompanied by Dang, his brother. His small body was heaving with the same sobs and distress we had seen the day before and his dark face recorded the duration of his suffering with traces of dried tears and mucous, which mixed with the new. Dang, who was tall for his age and quiet like his father, gently tried to console Mufdi, but without success. As soon as I saw them, I went to the door and waited until Dang finished. Children passing in the halls and entering the classroom paused curiously to watch us and then moved on. When at last Dang looked up at me for help, I took Mufdi's hand, bent over and said quietly, "Let's go Mufdi." He came along with apparent trust, but his shoulders were still heaving with sobs and he now covered his eyes with his left arm as he walked. I led him inside where Jayson approached with a silent offer of help.

His new classmates were putting their things away and joining prospective friends on the carpet. Mufdi went with Jayson to the coatroom and then to sit down where he was met with the same shunning that Sara and the others showed toward him the day before. But yesterday's obvious rejection—the complicit glances, the refusal of Abubakar and Etienne to help him, and the movements away from where he sat—was replaced today by a subtler one: slight shifts of their bodies away from him, and quick glances at one another. Since they didn't know Mufdi, they could only be reacting to his appearance and signs of feeling desperately alien. In a way I was grateful that he was too buried in his own world to notice what the children did. At least for now they wouldn't be adding to his grief.

If he had been greeted by the comforting sounds and touches of sympathetic voices and hands, I wondered, would he have had a different reaction?

If they had all been Sudanese? And what would happen if he started to adjust to the surroundings, if he wanted to play? Would they continue to reject him? I was unsure about the answers to these questions, but I was sure that if the children learned to see him as a playmate and to invite him into their play, they could help him feel safe and wanted in the class. At least then talk and relationships would have a chance to develop, and he might understand that he belonged here.

He wasn't the only one whose well-being seemed threatened by their classmates. Within a few weeks I noticed a disturbing pattern: Glenda, more quiet and mature than the others in the small circle of Spanish-speaking girls, was excluded when they gathered to talk or play quietly. The same thing happened to Tamathor, who was more exuberant and active than they were, and didn't speak Spanish. Vinh was ignored or firmly told "No," as he awkwardly tried to join in play. It affected all of them: Tamathor came to me in tears, Vinh looked perplexed, Mufdi still cried constantly, and Glenda looked lonely and unhappy. The other children were cautiously getting to know one another.

In addition to the emotional cloud this behavior brought to our classroom, it created an environment that compromised the children's education. Feelings of loneliness and exclusion are a death knell for individual happiness at school and consequently for learning and healthy emotional development. Furthermore, if shunning and rejection are allowed, it isn't just certain children who are affected; it's all of them, because in this kind of environment anyone might be vulnerable to exclusion when the winds of acceptability change. The defense is to be alert and ready to defend oneself, always to be acceptable, an anxious state as harmful to healthy development as loneliness and exclusion. For optimal learning we needed the opposite, a classroom where everyone knew they were physically and emotionally safe, a joyful place where creative thinking and curiosity could thrive.

Optimal learning requires an environment where students can relax and consequently dare to take risks as they explore. The confidence to risk being wrong is important in many areas, but for language development it's indispensable. Daring to engage in spontaneous, purposeful talk without worrying about mistakes and the need to search for words is important for language growth. I wouldn't be encouraging this or any other learning if my students were afraid to speak in the classroom for fear of being scorned or ignored. On the other hand, if they could relax they could turn to their real work: finding out about their world through play and exploration.

I could force them to include everyone in their play, but imposed behavior wouldn't create permanent changes in their understanding or the mutual respect that would lead them to treat one another well without my authoritarian presence. And it wouldn't encourage the confidence that each child needed through knowing they belonged and were likable.

Rather than forcing them to include everyone, I preferred to help them learn to respect one another. As the antithesis of contempt, respect makes bullying unlikely if not completely impossible. Respect would develop if they could recognize the basic humanity they shared. It was my job to help bring them the knowledge they required; the opportunity for exposure to a diverse population was a blessing of our situation. If I could find a way to change the classroom environment, a way to help the children understand one another, then all the children would be safe even when I wasn't around. Perhaps deeper understanding couldn't guarantee that the children would respect and enjoy one another, but it would increase the chances that they would. Besides, I couldn't bear to see them unhappy. It was as basic as that.

I continued to intervene as needed, the strategy I'd always used, but Mufdi's prolonged suffering was troubling; it wasn't going away even after a few weeks. He seemed more seriously at risk than Vinh, Tamathor, Glenda or, in fact, any other child I had ever taught. My perception may not have been accurate: other children might have hidden their emotions, but because Mufdi's pain was so obvious, it was impossible to overlook. As days went by with little change in his distress or his acceptance by classmates, my concern for him grew. He cried and stayed to himself. I thought that exclusion wasn't entirely responsible for his anguish at this point; he seemed too self-absorbed to be aware of it. However, the children's behavior toward him would not only delay his recovery but make it less likely to happen at all. As things were now, they only let him join in the shared play with blocks, marble mazes, or little toy cars if I intervened, and even then, he wasn't playing with them, he was playing by them without interaction.

The exclusion wasn't caused by their language differences. These children and most others I had taught could play and communicate when they wanted without a shared language. No, there were other reasons. They were discreet when I was around; they would look at me as they were about to say something they suspected I wouldn't like, and stop. Although I don't remember doing it explicitly, I apparently had communicated that I wanted them to include everyone—perhaps the genuine feelings of surprise and disappointment had leaked onto my face.

There were tiny glimmers of hope. We began to see signs that Mufdi might be interested in either the children's or the classroom's activities. During indoor recesses he began to move to the carpet where the boys' favorite game at the time was to operate miniature cars on roadways, garages and castles they had built with blocks. He would find a car and silently maneuver it on the carpet near the other children. Whatever the reason, either wanting to join in their play or curiosity about the toys and what he could do with them, support of his steps away from misery and toward a child's normal life of play and discovery was vital. If the other children could learn to invite him to play and learn the language to do it, it would be helpful for Mufdi and helpful for them. If he only wanted to play with the toys, being invited to play might make him aware of a new possibility.

"Why did you take the car from Mufdi?" With the tone of my voice, I made an effort to form a question, not to make an accusation.

"We need that car for our game."

"If I need your car, should I grab it from you?" I make a grabbing movement to illustrate, and Elmer returns the car to Mufdi looking ashamed. He's a sensitive, cooperative boy and this behavior isn't typical of him. Without my intervention I wonder, would this atypical behavior have become typical? "Thank you, Elmer." I pat him on the back; I want him to feel good about giving the car back and to forget the shame. It seems to work because his face relaxes and he goes back to his play. Mufdi's crying lessens, and he also resumes his play. But the outcome I hope to see is more complex. I want to see him relaxed and confident.

"Can Mufdi play too?" I asked the boys on the carpet one day. They looked at one another. "Okay," said Abubakar, without looking at Mufdi. They knew what the right action would be, but didn't really want to do it.

This kind of question would be received with silence or denial and then reluctant inclusion; Mufdi got the car for example, but not joined play. The same was true for Tamathor, Glenda and Vinh. A solution for changing this behavior didn't come easily because the causes were ill-defined and varied. Tamathor, Glenda, Vinh and Mufdi had little in common except that they were more obviously different from the other children in behavior or appearance. Once I realized that the common thread was difference, an insight that took several weeks to appear, I saw that the informal interventions I'd been using were not adequate for this class. I needed to focus on teaching about attitudes toward differences and not spread my time and energy throughout each day on seemingly unrelated events.

I decided that I wanted to try a programmatic approach instead of the "as needed" one addressing each incident as it occurred. As the kinds of lessons I needed became clearer to me, I looked for inspiration everywhere—teachers' guides, books on multiculturalism, teachers' workbooks—without success. This time I needed tactics, not theory, and couldn't find any to fit our situation.

I knew that they would have to be the kinds of experiences where they would see and feel a social life that included everyone. I didn't find a way to do this for several weeks while I continued to worry about the children and how I could help them. There was a reason for my hesitation. I was highly concerned that with a direct approach I might risk making the problems of apprehension toward differences worse by translating what was unstated into a subject for discussion. I wanted to help the children see their classmates as interesting individuals while avoiding hurt feelings.

Then one day I observed something in class that suggested a concrete area of difference I could use: skin color. It was an obvious difference between people that I knew was important to the children from comments they had made, exemplified one day during an indoor recess when they compared skin colors by holding their arms together to see who was the lightest. It began with Ingrid and Sara, and soon others were following suit. I'm not sure what prompted the comparisons; I looked up from my work with a student one day and saw them. At the time I didn't say anything; I watched and listened.

"We're the same," Sara said, holding her arm next to Ingrid's.

"No! Ingrid's white!" said Etienne loudly, and then at least half the class gathered around to see and to compare their colors. Sara said nothing.

It seemed to have something to do with trying to figure out why the boys liked Ingrid so much and so openly. She was Italian-Mexican with blue eyes, medium honey hair and lighter skin than the other girls. She was the girl whom all the girls admired as well. It's hard to tease out the exact reason; she was also confident and flirtatious, and the girls wanted her friendship and approval. No matter what the reason, it was a fact that they were comparing skin colors, and Ingrid's was the ideal. She was different too, as different from the other children as they were from each other, yet she was admired and respected, almost because of her kinds of differences.

It was possible that Mufdi's exceptionally dark color was one of the factors that set him apart as too different to understand. If the children indeed considered light skin as desirable, how would they view Mufdi's, and Mufdi? Skin color is a concrete difference between individuals, and if I could successfully exploit their interest in it, then maybe as a class we would have the concepts we needed to explain other less evident differences.

There was a risk that I was wrong, that I was looking at the children's behavior through my generational eyes, with my own possibly incorrect fears and points of view. I wanted a way into the topic of skin color that wouldn't reveal my thoughts, that would be neutral in case I was wrong. I especially didn't want to introduce ideas of race if there were none to begin with. I kept worrying but I still couldn't find a satisfactory approach, although I felt I was getting closer. At least I had a place to start, differences explored through skin color, and involving lived experiences.

Then one morning I opened my eyes at 3:00 and had an answer: I could give a lesson on skin and its melanin which on the surface would be a science lesson. It would begin a broader project to show them that the differences between individuals are interesting, useful and normal. There would be no lectures about rejecting people on the basis of appearance, just a lesson about how our skin colors are different and why. I began to plan, hoping that the project would do what we needed.

I looked for resources about skin and found a science kit for older children that included slides showing skin cells and the melanin in them. It was too complicated for my students' ages and language levels, but it would be easy to adapt, and it had the illustrations I always needed for linguistic support. As usual, I would have to establish vocabulary and concepts before I could begin, and I would need to do a lesson or two about the cellular structure of living things before they could understand the skin-cell lesson.

So I looked further and found some resources for teaching about cells to elementary children. Because of my students' beginning language levels, the teaching objectives would be the most basic: that living things are made of cells, and all cells are not the same. I brought in a physician's microscope with borrowed slides of blood stains. I brought in onion skins for them to examine. They explored onion cells with hand- held lenses, drew what they saw, and labeled their drawings. With my supervision they compared the blood cells and the onion cells under the finer lenses of the physician's microscope. As usual, with our lived experiences there were plenty of expressions and vocabulary words to learn.

The day after this lesson I put up a retro-projector so we all could see the same slides, magnified on a screen. Then I introduced the skin cells and talked about how tiny they are. I asked the children to imagine how many there could be in one person's skin. "Does Ivan have as many skin cells as I do?" I asked.

When I showed these slides, I pointed out melanin and suggested that because all skin had melanin but in different quantities, we could all be said to be brown in one degree or another; the same but different too. I drew a cell and added a few dots to represent melanin, and then drew another with more dots. The subject of excluding someone from friendship based on these differences remained unspoken.

"We're all brown. Some people are light brown like me, and some people are darker brown. Melanin helps us be safe from the sun in very sunny places," and so forth. I talked about sunburns and the protection of melanin. We concluded that people who lived where there wasn't much sun wouldn't need as much melanin.

"Isn't that interesting..." I said, "...how we're all the same?" This lesson, even though simplistic, was close enough to the children's concerns and levels of comprehension that they could become engaged.

"I'm not brown!" states Sara,

"Sure you are, just like I am. We're brown," I said. Look at this white paper. That's not our color, is it?" She stopped to think about this. "I think if we put a little brown on this paper you will find our color."

The next day, following my plan, I gave a lesson I had read about several years ago and rejected. It involved using multicultural crayons to create self-portraits. As written, the lesson suggested talking about race. I rejected that; I wanted to stick with "differences as interesting," "differences as explainable," and "differences as the normal state of life." The idea of portraits with multicultural crayons seemed promising, but it also had the potential to produce hurtful comments when children began chatting among themselves. They might feel free in their inexperience to say whatever entered their minds first, and I was afraid about what that might be in view of the previous comments I'd heard from children. I'd grappled with this concern every year, and every year I had rejected an explicit approach to skin color because of it.

It wasn't the uncensored nature of their talk that I wanted to change, but the bases upon which they judged people. This is a huge change to hope for, and a job for anyone's lifetime, but if I sowed the seeds now when my students were young, maybe they would have a foundation for thinking as they grew up. Only the development of deep roots of knowledge could create a permanent change in their evaluation criteria and lead them to judge others by, as Martin Luther King, Jr. said, "the content of their character." To develop those roots I would have to follow the concrete experiences with consistent guidance all year. And that would be just a beginning. As for skin talk specifically, it's harmless as long as there's no hierarchy associated with it.

I took the leap and decided to try the lesson. I bought thirteen boxes of multicultural crayons, tinted in various shades of skin colors. I would see how it went as I worked with them. If it looked as if negative results might develop, I would change the lesson and move it in another direction. The children sat in a circle with me, excited by the sight of new and curious boxes of crayons in tones of only brown. I distributed the boxes to pairs of children.

"We're going to make self-portraits today—pictures we make of ourselves. I make a picture of Ms. Stark, Ivan makes a picture of Ivan, Sara makes a picture of Sara... pictures of us. We all make pictures of ourselves. We need them to put on the walls in the halls so people in school know who we are." I repeated "self-portrait" as often as I could. As I pointed out partners and passed out the crayons, I added, "You need these to get the right colors for your skin in your self-portraits."

I also made a self-portrait and consulted them about my skin color. Soon they were busy comparing colors and helping one another find the crayon that best approximated their colors; their natural colors were far too varied to fit exactly the sixteen shades available. Some pairs of children cooperated with other pairs over which color to choose if a color couldn't be matched. Sometimes colors were mixed. They relied on each other, and no one was left out.

This lesson turned out to be a godsend. During their eager and animated work on this project, I saw the judgmental nature of color talk evaporate. Crayons of approximate colors were held up to arms and faces without a sign of self-consciousness, signs I had seen at the beginning of the year. A few times I helped by getting a consensus from the whole group on a color choice. Mufdi, whose skin was the darkest, chose his color with his partner as easily as the others, still not speaking, but listening to suggestions and participating.

There was a suggestion from Sara that the appropriate crayon for Mufdi would be black, just the kind of comment I had feared, knowing their preference for light skin. Yet it was the very kind of moment that could change their minds. Much would turn on how I handled the remark. If I acted as if it might hurt Mufdi, I would be denying the beauty of his skin and would be reinforcing their color biases. I chose a matter-of-fact tone.

"Mmmm," I said. "I don't think so. Remember about melanin? That it's brown?" The black color wouldn't do. "Mufdi and Elmer, what do you think would be good for Mufdi?" They were partners, and together decided on a crayon for Mufdi, just as Mufdi had helped Elmer find his crayon. Sara's interest returned to her own portrait.

For all his distress and original lack of experience with pencils and paper, by the time I did this lesson with the children Mufdi had become a confident artist. The drawings he made of his family and himself were exceptionally happy looking and he always had a slight smile on his face as he made them. The people he drew had the details and proportions that more sophisticated young artists used, with ears, noses, faces with large smiles and hands with rounded fingers all placed in natural human proportions. Many children place eyes in the foreheads of their face drawings, but not Mufdi. And his self-portrait was as fine as anyone's. I was glad to see the peace his drawings revealed, but I can't presume to make psychological conclusions about them. I confess that I thought, "He must have a wonderful and loving family," and I keep this impression.

There was no ridicule or lack of seriousness with our lesson. It was as if they were excited to talk about this topic that had become troubled with cultural biases, probably before they came to school. The curiosity about colors made every color viable and interesting, so the talk was a stimulating exploration, not a production of comments based on stereotypes. Maybe I had underestimated the children and myself. Maybe the development of their attitudes was shallow, too new to have deep roots. And maybe the series of lessons was effective because it had released the subject of skin color as a topic for study and relaxed the children's attitudes toward one another as they explored it together. After these lessons talk of skin color disappeared from the class. They moved to other interests.

I knew that wariness over all differences wouldn't disappear with a few lessons about a single difference, but now we could talk about them—they knew the vocabulary and concepts, and their caution was gradually transforming into curiosity. The lessons began a yearlong effort to erase beginning racism and cultural bias and to work for the inclusion of every child into the class culture. After these lessons with their emphasis on our natural differences, the shunning disappeared. The remaining work would be on reinforcing the principles that had been established.

As far as I could tell, their attitude toward Mufdi had permanently changed; he was one of them. For that matter, his attitude began to change as well, because he seemed to feel that he was a member of the class. What did he think of the children when he first came, I wondered, and of me? For now, he remained silent most of the time, but cried less every day and participated more. He smiled occasionally, a shy smile, even though he still didn't speak except for one-word responses to my questions. He was now protected by the children. They watched out for his feelings and were disturbed when he cried. When he did, someone would always put an arm around him and ask him what had happened, or come to me to say, "Mufdi's crying." He never told what had happened, but always seemed to feel better.

The work to help the children understand their differences and be kind to one another was an important part of establishing the basic conditions of a classroom where all children would learn at their greatest potential. This understanding was as basic as having a place to meet, or having a large choice of books in the class library. Without it, none of the children would have learned as much about any of our subjects as they did. I'm hopeful that by the end of the year the children not only had succeeded academically, but had left first grade with permanent mental traces of how people can live peacefully with one another. I hope that they learned to be curious about people who are different from themselves, not suspicious.

The effort to create an emotionally safe classroom, an inclusive classroom, has become an essential part of my role as a teacher. When I first thought of entering the profession I thought of academic goals—how my students would all read, write and be thinkers, etc.; my thinking didn't include playing a role in children's well-being. Not that I didn't care about such things, but I simply hadn't considered them. I assumed a group of children, eager to learn.

Yet from the first day I taught, there they were, the real children in the classroom whose well-being wasn't at all a given: the brilliant, obese child of five; the children who cried for their daddies; the child who spat on classmates when he was angry; the child who, unprovoked, stabbed someone with a sharpened pencil; the ones who cried because they were excluded; the children who bullied; Mufdi and his anguish; Sara, Jayson, Glenda.... No one mentioned them in my education classes. We talked about students, not individuals.

I couldn't make fathers come back, help mothers stop taking drugs, cure an eating disorder, or bring grandparents to the United States, but I could make the classroom a socially and emotionally safe place for the children. I could end bullying. I could show students how to be curious about one another because of their differences, I could show them how to support one another's learning, and I could give them some social tools for survival.

There was no choice. It was clear from my first day as a teacher that before anything significant could occur in academics, the social and psychological elements had to be put in balance.

The best way to do this, I have realized, is to help students understand and respect one another by helping them to expect that they will be different from one another, and that their differences will make life much more interesting than if they were all the same.

With the tactics I used, letting the children discover together the real-life effects of their differences, they shared a mutual discovery—that their different appearances didn't interfere with the work they needed to do together; they didn't matter. Incidentally, their similarities facilitated their discovery—they all had arms to hold out and compare, they all had families although they might be different, they all had skin with brown tones, they all had hair to draw, likes, dislikes, sensitivity to comments—and their similarities prevailed over their differences. The fact that they worked together so much, and had to help each other and think together in purposely mixed groups, caused them to learn to respect one another and created a feeling of fellowship.

Classrooms have always been diverse; no one child is quite like another even when they all speak the same language and have the same skin color. The added diversity of languages, cultures and skin colors only strengthens the argument for teaching children to see one another as unique, to be curious about one another, and to treat one another well. Students aren't religions, cultures, language groups or types of anything. They are themselves only. In fact, Mohammed, when he proclaimed "That's my Somalia," innocently expressed the unique experience of an individual in a culture. It is his Somalia, and Abubakar's too, in another, different experience of it. I have learned that it is wisest to avoid generalizations or assumptions, and to teach individual children.

Because of this very uniqueness, children may want or be able to participate in class life with varying degrees of enthusiasm, like Mufdi or his counterpart, Abubakar, but we can help them be as comfortable as possible at school, free to be themselves. And there's no need to worry that the poetry of loneliness and isolation would disappear from human experience because schools are welcoming places; no such brave new world is likely to appear in the near future. The isolation some children endure goes beyond what they should have to endure when there are adults in charge who can make them safe. It is the kind of experience we can eliminate from our students' school days.

The justifications for paying attention to children's social and emotional states are both practical and humane. For the teacher interested in bottom-line test scores, children achieve more when they feel safe, and if they come to school. It is estimated that 160,000 children stay home from school everyday for fear of being bullied. Honestly, I would wager anytime that this figure represents only the tip of the iceberg. I think it's an underreported problem. There won't be much learning if children aren't present, or if when they come, they feel left out of the social life of the classroom or school. If instead they are welcomed everyday, see themselves as interesting and capable, and are encouraged by their classmates, the gains in learning can be even greater. In addition, the ability to be comfortable with people who are different from themselves eases children's capacity to work in groups in both cooperative and supervisory roles, a benefit when they are grown and living in increasingly diverse communities throughout the world. The time it takes to pay attention to affective matters in school doesn't dilute rigor; it makes it possible. Besides, who knows? The value to the world of kindness may be more important than any academic curriculum.

Chapter 4

Helping Friends

"There is a courtesy of the heart. It is akin to love. Out of it arises the purest courtesy in the outward behavior."

- Johann Wolfgang von Goethe

Although the skin lessons had helped Mufdi and relaxed the children, the differences in the ways and rates at which they learned and a few differences between the etiquette needed at home and at school required attention. Without consideration of these differences we couldn't establish the comfortable and encouraging class atmosphere that productive study required. I would address learning differences first since they were interfering with the children's growth at school.

The children's early reaction to their learning differences was problematic but expected. They began to notice that some of them were quicker to read, write, spell or do math operations than others. In other words, they were comparing themselves to one another. The tactless comments they made—"Ingrid's only on level one?" for example—even though they were common for children their age and not intended to hurt anyone, were disheartening to the slower students subjected to them. I cringed when I heard them because they undid the motivation I was trying to develop, and I knew how the comments hurt the children.

To eliminate these comments from the classroom, my students needed to understand that it was normal for them to be different in their learning, and that their differences were not signs of inferiority or superiority. In a way I was dealing with prejudice in this area, just as with physical differences. The very idea of schooling as it usually operates compares learners. The "good" learners are in the Honor Society. The "poor" learners, it is whispered, might be in Special Education. Adults will be proud if children excel, tell the children so, and will beam when they show signs of excellence. Slow learners cause worry and sometimes are asked why they don't work harder. Children seem to absorb these attitudes. It may be the very act of encouraging them with the normal comments parents and teachers make: "Do a good job today." Or, "You're going to learn how to read in first grade!" In light of these comments, it seems to follow that in school the child who learns first and fastest is the best student, and the one who is the slowest and least apt is the worst student. "Do your best!" might be a good substitute.

Encouragement isn't the problem; it's normal for parents to make such comments. But since children acquire the attitudes implicit in them, it helps their confidence and motivation when they become aware of learning as a process, and to save them and their friends from comparisons, how it's natural for learners to be different. Otherwise, education becomes a race between unequal and dissimilar competitors, an illogical and ultimately disheartening race.

What I wanted for my students was for each one to learn as much as possible, a slightly different focus than for each of them to excel, which hints at being better than everyone else. I knew that all children wouldn't achieve the same thing in the same way, in every area of the curriculum, no matter how much I wished they would. Perhaps a dream class would have all fast learners without any differences to slow them down or to require special attention, but I've never seen this class in real life, and I doubt if anyone else has. In fact, in my dream class, or better, in my dream world, all students would progress as much as they could, guided, urged and nudged, and everyone's face would beam at their individual, incomparable victories—surpassing their own past performances. Fast learning wouldn't be prized over others, but all learning would be celebrated, the idea of doing one's personal best and the celebration of success in taking one more step toward a learning goal, the idea that many kinds of skills are valuable.

If I help every child on their personal way to the competencies the district wants, those enshrined in curriculum guides and lists of standards, I think I've met public expectations as far as they can be met. If children can surpass these expectations, that is what they will do if they are working at their potential. No child can do more than her best, but I want to be sure that I've done my best for him/her. If I then find ways to enrich the class work beyond what the district wants, it's to fulfill my private dreams of what children's education can be. What I actually worry about is happiness at school, eagerness to learn and the urge to do one's best. These are what lead to high achievement and personal satisfaction in any area, and I admit to wanting that for my students. Does this mean that my expectations are lower because I'm urging all children to do their best instead of urging them to meet general standards? I don't think so. Rather, it means that no child will have imposed limits of any kind, and no child will feel like a failure. It really means that the expectations are higher because the students will keep moving on to new challenges, not stopping because they lose faith in themselves, or because they've reached a state-mandated goal. If someone can read sixth-grade books in first grade, he will have those books because they are the books he should be reading. If another makes progress in first grade books but doesn't finish them all, her victories will be just as those of the more proficient readers, because she will have done her best and will have achieved as much as she could. If the class math is too easy for a child, that child needs enrichment. Each child urged and helped to do his/her best, that's what is possible, and that is what will nourish students' finest development.

Focusing on individual achievement doesn't mean that because children learn differently they are less capable of mastering the subject matter. It means that the time they take to do it might vary, and the kind of guidance each requires might be different. Their learning differences often are decided by their interests and past experiences with the material, and according to some theorists, by the structure of their brains. If a child is enchanted with movement and the body's ability to bend, twist and leap, special effort might be required to help this child discover the enchantment of stories, the fine discrimination between sounds, whereas a child already delighted with books and stories might learn to read quickly but need special urging to get up and move. The solution for educating all children to their capacity is to keep believing in each child's ability to learn, and to continue through every grade giving them the individual attention they need to do it.

Therefore, to encourage the children's optimism about their abilities and their eagerness to learn, it was important to make sure they didn't hear discouraging comments or feel compared to anyone else. The only comparison they needed was to their own past achievement.

I hoped it might be easy to show the children that differences in skills and interests are as normal as the differences in skin color. With the concept established that skin-color differences are normal, and the vocabulary for talking about differences already growing, the groundwork was laid for talking about learning differences. Understanding this concept would reassure the children that they are all right just as they are; they are perfect if they learn in their own way, at their own pace, and in their own time. In my experience when learners aren't compared their motivation soars and consequently so does their achievement on an individual and class level. By removing the relative values assigned to rates and types of learning, an academic aristocracy, we had a chance to create the learning environment we needed—all the children enthusiastically working as hard as they could to achieve individually determined goals.

I say this assuming a classroom where gender was not a difference accepted as a cause that explained or limited anyone's skills or preferences. Just like most, and possibly all the other differences, the range of abilities between the boys and girls was too great to generalize credibly with comments like: "Girls can't...," or "boys don't like...." We saw with our own eyes that some girls can, and some boys do. We used none of the gender-related, gender-limiting class management techniques that Mrs. Vega and I experienced as children. There were no boys' and girls' lines, no comments about what boys and girls do or don't do, and we did not address the children as "Boys and Girls...." The children occasionally did make biased remarks, but Mrs. Vega and I contradicted these comments right away by pointing out exceptions and exposing the abilities and interests the children had across gender lines. In addition, I expected that if we succeeded in helping the children see themselves as individuals in every way, with a full range of possibilities opened to each of them according to their abilities, gender considerations would seem out of place.

There were some children whose talents were already emerging and being noticed by their classmates: the fastest runners, the most thrilling writers, illustrators, intricate block-castle builders—all were given attention for their achievements, and this was wonderful. It was generous and encouraged the masters in their achievements. What I didn't want, but what I began to see, was the slowest achievers being judged as lacking and then becoming discouraged. I especially didn't want to see this in reading. What can keep slower readers on the path to learning is their pleasure in the process and their confidence as learners. Unfair competition will drain that away.

If the opposite could happen, if my students could be comfortable learning at their own rates and on their preferred pathways, who could predict what talents might appear? Just because in first grade some children didn't have already developed talents didn't mean that the talents weren't there, hidden and waiting for experience and practice in order to surface. That included literacy, where, as with many other skills, some children began school with a head start from home exposure. We wouldn't allow lack of previous exposure to become a limitation through negative comparisons. Understanding learning differences, children don't scorn or judge one another, they encourage one another, and rather than becoming discouraged, the children become more motivated. In a classroom, high achievement is driven by motivation, and confidence is its motor.

Although their early observations were innocent, the children subjected to them wilted on the spot and lost confidence. Afterward, instead of teaching or encouraging a child to take a new step, I would have to take time to motivate the child again, and restore confidence. In this way, the children's lack of sensitivity was inhibiting learning. Their comments could be expressed either in amazement or matter-of-factly.

When Ingrid heard "Ingrid's only in level one?" she lost for a moment her remarkable self-confidence and looked ashamed. The generosity of heart it would take for them to encourage each other, including friends who had better math proofs or were reading more difficult books, would only happen if all the children knew deeply that they were valuable in some way, and that one person's success didn't mean someone else's loss. Frames of mind like these are complex but they can be taught to children if they are presented in concrete experiences, and if they are lived and practiced. Nine months, especially in the first year or two of children's education, is a long time, time enough to convince them that they won't all learn the same way, and are all capable in some way.

As I had in past years, I decided to begin showing what I meant by individual talents and differences through relay races. The competitive essence of racing would produce the kinds of thinking and comments that I wanted the children to examine without preaching at them; they needed a tangible illustration of the ideas. Instead of an abstract sermon they would be having fun. My students have always loved relay races: they've always jumped up and down and cheered whenever I've said that I would referee them. I also like them for the effects they have on their physical fitness; children who normally weren't active at all would eagerly participate if I could make it emotionally safe for them, and they would run as fast as they could.

The races can show children the effects of encouragement. Faster runners can encourage slower ones and see the happy results of the encouragement. Slower runners can encourage the fastest runners. The same ideas will be extended later to encourage academic achievement. Some children will learn more slowly than the others, and some faster, just like runners. But they all can run, and they all can improve. The knowledge that they will be supported and helped to improve as readers, mathematicians, speakers, etc, has an unstated assumption—that everyone else in the class has confidence in their ability to learn. The acts of running and sharing friendship I hoped would prove more satisfying than winning.

When I first started having relay races with students it was immediately clear that I had to show them how to welcome every runner to their team. As conversations with children about this evolved over the years, its links to other school situations grew increasingly clear to me. The talks were so effective, the revelations they produced so important, that I began to plan for them every year. I was sure the same opportunities would appear again this year as they had in the past.

Some of the children would be fast runners, and others slow. The competitive players (most of the children) wouldn't want the slow runners on their teams, and would show signs of their preferences. In this would lie my opportunity to make a point or two about individuals helping the team, encouraging one another, about differences, and about a role for everyone. Among the fast runners would be Mufdi, Tamathor and Jorge, children whose confidence and value I wanted to promote. It would be easy to form balanced teams since I decided who would be on most teams or groups, a practice I adopted to keep children from feeling excluded at school, especially in first grade.

It would be most effective to let them experience a game of races and its dynamics before doing much talking, except for intervening with negative comments, which would be cut off immediately. The children would learn what a race is and how a relay race works, and they would begin to learn the particular vocabulary for the process.

"Line up," I said to the children as we finished the calendar work and shared reading. "We're going out to play." An excited buzz immediately filled the room for this unexpected change in the daily schedule, a playtime that wasn't at lunch recess. They quickly gathered at the door. Once we were on the playground I chose a small demonstration team, four children for two teams that would model what the others would be doing. Etienne was my first choice for the model team because he was always eager to move, quick to understand language, and physically talented. Then I chose three other good runners: Abubakar, Tamathor and Elmer.

DEMONSTRATION TEAMS

Etienne, Tamathor	Team A
Abubakar, Elmer	Team B

I used the words I wanted them to know: "Teams, hold out your hand," I said, showing what I meant. "Touch the wall and come back. Run as fast as you can." *As fast as you can* incidentally is a nice grammatical construction with transferable uses that they would hear many times today and later could use in numerous other situations. Every aspect of the relay racing was new, so I showed them the starting point, turning point and end point of the race. I mimed running (in place) and said, "You will run, fast, fast!" With my hands and legs I modeled what I meant, running in place. "Touch the building," I said, touching it. I walked to the turning point, the children following. "Touch the fence," and I touched it. "Touch the next person's hand," and I showed them what I meant, pretending that I was urgently running the whole time. With, "On your marks! Get set! Go!" I set them off on their race, which they ran eagerly. The other children were immediately captivated and cheered for the runners.

When this basic demonstration was over, I called out the names for two complete class teams, A and B. How eager and excited they were! I had firmly explained my requirement that they welcome every runner on their teams, but sure enough, there were quiet mumblings about the slower runners and enthusiastic cheers when a fast one was assigned to a team. A cold stare was enough to stop them. When everyone was in place, "On your marks. Get set! Go!" and the first whole-class race began. The fast runners on opposing teams passed the slow runners but the teams were balanced and would finish in close races. I expected that the children, as always, wouldn't be conscious of anything beyond the two runners who ran at the same time.

In this first whole-class race, some fast runners were discouraged by some of the slower runners and only jogged to show how they didn't care, and some slow runners stopped running altogether. This was supposed to ease their embarrassment, but it devastated their teammates who groaned in disappointment. In past years and already this year I had seen the same dynamic for academic subjects; some children stopped trying altogether when they felt discouraged, hiding their inability and embarrassment as if to say, "The reason I'm not doing well is that I'm not trying. I could if I wanted, but I don't want to." This was Ali's solution in reading, for example. What they needed in this situation was encouragement and training so they would develop the confidence to try. Without work and effort, which comes from motivation, the children's hidden talents wouldn't be uncovered, and there would be no improvement. Through the relay races they would have a visible model for the rewards of work, practice and encouragement. They could notice that although they are differently talented for running, with encouragement they would do their individual best. I called for them to gather around and listen to me.

"Some runners are fast and some are slow, right? And some are medium, no?" I used my hands to show fast, slow, and medium.

"Yes teacher." I had put together obvious facts, and they easily agreed to the rhetorical question. "So, everybody's a different runner, right?" They were following the argument. It was obvious that some of the most respected readers in the class were slow as runners, and some of the slowest readers were talented runners. I would point this out explicitly but in a different and comfortable context when I could use the support to point out learning differences.

"Let me show you something. Are there any slow runners who will help me?" Glenda, a leading reader, volunteered, and then Saul threw his hand up with a laugh.

"Thank you!" Both of them had a good sense of their abilities and could be self-deprecating. It would be wonderful if the entire class could develop this sense, every child recognizing what they did well and what they didn't, yet motivated to work in their areas of weakness, and strength.

I added six more runners to form two smaller model teams. The children watched as I placed the runners in different positions on the teams. "Watch this!" I said.

I placed Glenda at the beginning of a team, and Saul in third position on the other team. Otherwise the runners were fast.

"We have some really fast runners on these teams, right?" They agreed. "Is everyone fast on these teams?" The obvious question, but I asked it to make sure a point would be evident to them.

"No," they responded. The children prepared to run, lined up with their teams:

Team 1. Fast, fast, fast, Glenda

Team 2: Fast, Saul, fast, fast

Since there was a fast runner at the beginning of Team 2's lineup, the other children were sure that Team 2 would win. Team 2 thought so too. As they ran, I cheered for all the runners, including the slower Glenda and Saul, and the watching children immediately copied me. Glenda and Saul ran as fast as they could. What a surprise for everyone! Teams 1 and 2 finished neck and neck.

"What happened?" I asked them.

"Everybody run hard!" said Etienne. Mufdi looked alert and fascinated, and everyone watched me intently to hear what I would say.

"Suppose we put all the fast runners on this team and the slow ones on that one?" Using this and that allowed me to indicate the teams physically. I looked at them as if I were thinking.

"No!" said Abdulrahman. He was an average runner, neither fast nor slow.

"Why not?"

"It's not fun."

"Why not?"

"The fast runners win, all the time win." And he repeated, "It's not fun."

I looked at the others. Etienne and Abubakar seemed to think that it might be fun to have all the fast runners on one team, but no one else did. The best races, the most fun and exciting they agreed, would be when there was a fair mix of abilities.

"All right. Is everybody ready?" It was time now for the entire class to race again. I chose teams and they lined up, eager to start. When I assigned Saul to Abubakar's team, he started to groan, but I saw him stop himself and welcome Saul with an enthusiastic arm around his shoulders, a little forced, but also a sign of changing behavior and consciousness. A few other children—Etienne, Sara and Vinh— had similar reactions to the arrival of slower teammates, and I saw them consciously stop their beginning negative comments and welcome the runner instead.

"Everyone needs to go as fast as they can. Really try!" I looked at them for signs of understanding. "Right?" They nodded eagerly, ready for the race to begin. "On your marks! Get set! Go!"

Off they went. Predictably, the team with the fast runner in the first position initially pulled ahead, Jayson leading. The opposing team with a slower runner in the lead position began to deflate.

"Come on Ivan! Run! You can do it!" I urged. Immediately the children copied me.

"Run!" they shouted. Ivan perked up and although he was slow, must have doubled his speed with his effort. Everyone was jumping up and down. When he came back to slap the hand of the next runner he radiated happiness. Etienne was wild with excitement. He shouted and leaped into the air. When any runner came back, he gave them a high five. Soon the others were doing the same— encouraging everyone became part of the fun and added to the excitement.

The slow runners, when they were cheered and the center of positive attention, perked up and ran with restored confidence. The children's enthusiastic support of the slow runners and the effect it had on them—they really tried and believed that they helped their teams—came more naturally and quickly than I anticipated, and I was gratified by it. Glenda's face beamed as she raced to the line and slapped the hand of the next runner, his signal to begin running. She had run faster than I had ever seen her run.

Then two fast runners followed Glenda, Abubakar and Tamathor,—and their team caught up! At the end it was another neck-and-neck finish. The losing team was only mildly disappointed, focusing instead on the powerful race and the "almost won."

"You see! You see? Did you see how both teams ran fast, everyone at different speeds? Did you see what a good race it was? Everybody did their best." They gathered around me excitedly, their faces looking up with happy anticipation, literally jumping up and down. They wanted to race again.

I wanted all the children to get a chance to run again with the new ideas in place. I assigned members for the new teams. When Etienne forgot and groaned once, I said, "Etienne, you will help him. You're so fast; you can help the team catch up!" The other children actually reminded him to encourage the others. "We have to cheer! We help them."

"You all will have to run your best to help your team," I reminded them. "On your marks! Get set! Go!"

"Run!" they yelled, or, "You can do it!" They joyfully patted these runners on their backs when they finished. The slow children's expressions were as alive with excitement as the others'.

"Did you have fun?" I asked, once we were back inside. The important conversation began. They talked at first about running, and who was a fast runner and how each race was won. This seemed initially to be the most important feature to them.

"Didn't they run fast? And did you see how everyone ran!" I asked.

I guided this to the idea that we are different from each other in our skills, in the way we do things, and in the way we learn. They understood: everyone can learn something, but they learn it at different rates and in different ways. We help our friends with our strengths, they help us with theirs. The good-natured competition during the races was for fun only, and understanding that some children will excel at running, like reading, math, singing, compassion, and leadership, etc., didn't diminish anyone else's light. They grasped the central message, we are different, and it's normal that we are.

I modeled encouragement in class: "Do you see what a wonderful artist Derek is? Now he's starting to read too! He can read *Walk the Dog*." I said. The children cheered, Derek beamed. Or about Ingrid: "Everybody, Ingrid just finished *Clown Party*!" Once again, the children cheered, Ingrid smiled a happy, restrained smile. The children began to do the same. Elmer came up to me to say, "Abubakar was doing a good job today!"

"Good job!" I overheard Sara say to Brenda.

"You can read it, Ali!" exclaimed Abubakar a few days later.

After the lessons of these several days the gradual changes began that would shape the members of the classroom, including Mrs. Vega and me, into a cohesive band of teaching/learning friends. They enjoyed encouraging one another, and it became part of the class's culture. The beginnings of an environment friendly to learning had been established. They stopped comparing themselves to one another, or at least stopped thinking that differences in learning were worth mentioning. I never heard another word. They had learned to encourage and help one another, and the concept of not giving up, of doing one's personal best was successfully established as one of our class values. The role of this encouragement in their motivation and self-confidence was priceless.

There remained one more aspect of social behavior that urgently needed to improve to make the class function harmoniously: arguments between classmates and among individuals and groups who were not in our class. Arguments and bad feelings spilled into the class environment as students reacted with anger or sadness—just what we needed to eliminate from our school day. Some children retained these feelings for hours. They interrupted the students' learning much as negative observations about learning had, and so for the same reasons of motivation and classroom environment, they needed to be examined and, ideally, eliminated. It is normal for children to argue and disagree, but the arguments and unpleasantness that erupted from cultural misunderstandings could be reduced with some lessons on playground and school etiquette. Some etiquette—how to talk and behave with the teachers and children at this school—would be local.

Specifically, the children were having some problems with each other and the rest of the school population, including teachers, when they were on the playground, in the cafeteria and in the hallway. They were innocently breaching the school's expectations of courtesy patterns, and their mistakes were causing problems, mostly for them. The majority of the missing manners were for situations that would not arise at home or in most places typically visited by families.

Where else but school are age peers grouped by twenty to thirty in one room, and by the hundreds in a building? They couldn't have learned how to act in these situations if they hadn't been exposed to them. In most situations they had what Goethe described as "a courtesy of the heart." They were very nice children. I believed that they wanted to do what was kind and best, but didn't quite know how.

They were not saying "Sorry," when they bumped into other children, they were not saying "Thank you," and some teachers complained that my students were not listening to them. In my students' defense, they didn't speak English, some were intimidated by the American-born students, and most of the time didn't know they had done anything wrong. When teachers talked to them, some of my students didn't realize that they were being addressed, and many who did, didn't know how to react. Abdulrahman always grinned, but it was a nervous and embarrassed grin that several teachers had interpreted as a sign of disrespect. My students needed a few lessons and classroom practice sessions about the etiquette for school situations.

Like most teaching, instruction about etiquette and courtesy is sensitive. The idea is the same as with teaching language: I don't want to take away or disrespect already existing customs or etiquette patterns, only to add some useful ones for a specific place and/or situation. I always make sure my students know that the patterns I'm teaching them are what other people expect in this place and time. The reason for teaching them is to help the children live harmoniously with their schoolmates. I wanted the other teachers and students at the school to respect and enjoy my students. Then they would treat them well, my students would be happy, and they could relax and learn.

Inspiration to start came one day after an especially contentious period on the playground and in the cafeteria—I had spent the recess break helping one child after another solve problems with other children or teachers in the school. We came back into the room and immediately had a talk about what to do on the playground and in the cafeteria.

"Should we throw a ball around the heads of people who are sitting in chairs?" They looked at me blankly. This was after a recess incident where Jayson, Abubakar and others had been throwing the class ball near some teachers seated outside. The teachers had yelled at them and the boys hadn't paid attention until the teachers stood up and pointedly scolded them.

"I'll show you what I mean," I said.

I asked Ms. Vega to help me as two children sat down together in chairs brought to the carpet for the demonstration. Mrs. Vega and I threw the ball to one another.

"Oh oh! I hope I catch the ball!" The children looked at one another with deadpan humor. The point was so obvious and the ball-throwing looked so perilous that it went beyond manners and courtesy. But they understood the point. Tomorrow I would take them out early and show them: "Here. Here is how you can play with the ball without bothering anyone."

That was enough to absorb about playground etiquette in one day. I moved on to an easy language lesson for manners, *thank you*. To address negativity toward the children from cafeteria staff members.

"Sara, will you help me? Ivan?" I gestured to him. He was shy and completely new to English, while Sara could understand at a basic level. "Here, Sara." I handed her a dish. "Sara, what should you say now?"

"Thank you?"

"Yes! Good Sara. Now, you give it to Ivan."

"Ivan, what do you say?" Ivan said "Thank you," perfectly. This was an accomplishment for him, and as he sat down, several children patted him on the back in congratulations, making his smile bigger. He always would remain quiet, even when his level of English advanced. It would help him to have a formulaic response for some situations. I asked several more pairs to come up for the practice so that everyone could feel comfortable with these words and circumstances, and then we (because I generally said it with them to lead and model) all repeated it several times as I handed some object to different children.

"So tomorrow," and I pointed to the next day on the calendar, "you will say *thank you* in the cafeteria, no?" If they understood *thank you* and *cafeteria*, they would have the essence of the lesson. And I would be in the cafeteria to whisper a reminder in their ears. They all agreed, so if appearances meant anything, tomorrow would be a big success in the cafeteria. "Much better" the cafeteria milk server told me when I asked.

One day I was surprised by the need to teach another important social pattern and its vocabulary—*excuse me*, or *sorry*. At recess, Jayson and a boy from another class were angrily beginning to push one another. The boy from the other class was furious and Jayson was bewildered but unwilling to back down. I hurried across the playground to them.

The boy from the other class, Justin, said: "He pushed me!"

"I no do nothing," responded Jayson. "Nothing!" he dramatically spread his hands open for added emphasis.

"Yes he did!" shouted Justin.

It was completely uncharacteristic for Jayson to push anyone, and Justin looked genuinely offended, so I suspected that there was a misunderstanding between the boys.

"What happened? *¿Que pasó?* I asked both of them, to see what their points of view would be.

"He came and shoved me," Justin said.

"What were you doing Jayson?"

"I was runnin' and we was playin'," he said with the abbreviated endings he used for certain words. He had been playing with Etienne and Tamathor, and I thought I had figured out what might have happened.

"Did you bump into Justin like this?" and I lightly bumped into him but moved broadly to indicate a rough bump.

"Yes."

"Was it an accident?" He understood this since it's a cognate in English for the Spanish, accidente.

"Yes."

"What do you say when you bump into someone?" *"¿Qué dices?"* I asked both boys, translating for Jayson. Astonishing to me was that neither boy knew the answer, and they both looked at me fascinated, as if I possessed a fantastic secret.

"What?" asked Justin, his eyes bright with curiosity.

"You say 'I'm sorry!' Then the other person knows it was an accident. Let's try it." I bumped into Justin and immediately said, "Oh! I'm sorry!" I added, "Justin would you be angry at me if I said 'sorry?'"

"No," he said sincerely.

"Jayson, bump into Justin and then say, 'Sorry.' " I made motions to show what I wanted Jayson to do. The boys laughed and complied. Their curiosity and the entertaining act of bumping each other quickly diffused their anger. They continued to smile broadly and, at my suggestion, shook hands.

After recess I introduced this subject to the whole class and again was surprised to find that not one of the children knew what to say after accidentally bumping into someone, not even in their heritage languages. I imagine it was because there were few situations at home or in the community where this would happen with a stranger. Mrs. Vega and I performed one of our goofy role-plays. I exaggeratedly bumped into her while the children laughed.

"Hey!" she improvised. She pretended to get ready for a fight.

"I'm sorry," I said. "I didn't know I bumped into you."

"That's okay," she said, lowering her fists.

Lessons like this about playground manners with the reminders that followed did reduce unnecessary conflicts in the class and especially outdoors. The social formulas clarified intentions so the children didn't feel disrespected;

they were a means to save face. "Then the other person knows it was an accident," was probably the most persuasive and logical explanation I gave them. The cafeteria staff even commented to me about the children's good manners, and I could see in the workers' faces their changed attitudes toward the children. I overheard the students saying, "I'm sorry" to one another, or explaining that something was an accident. Their expressions showed a feeling of triumph at the practice of these more adult habits and useful English expressions. When they needed reminding, the point had already been made with this lesson and so no new discussion was required:

"Vinh, what should you say?" was enough.

The training to understand one another, although not a part of the curriculum, had everything to do with teaching and learning. As a result of attention to this part of classroom relations the children felt comfortable in class and free to focus on their work. The brief lessons on etiquette helped smooth relations in class and out and in their way also led the children to understand each other more than they had; they had a way to explain their social errors. Their individual motivation was noticeably increasing: they worked with focus, enjoyed sharing their work and hearing their classmates' comments. I was free to help them individually without worrying about the rest of the class. In the end we had a happier class and higher individual achievement than we would have had if we had ignored comparative comments about achievement.

The relay races produced a visual analogy that the children could understand. Running unfair races, the fast against the slow, the trained against the untrained looked unfair and wasn't fun. It was more satisfying to work together and to do a great job together, each one doing his or her best. That's what was needed in class work as well—each child working to do his/her best. Having children learn in a competitive environment where players come with mixed preparation and perhaps different talents turns learning into a game that's unfair and defeats the players before they start, like matching a welterweight wrestler with a heavy-weight, or a team of fast runners against a team of slow ones. As Abdulrahman said, "It's not fun." Learning achievement isn't about "age-appropriate." It's about prior knowledge, maximum individual accomplishment and differences in maturation. A fair chance and fun have everything to do with learning.

Attention to children's understanding of differences is a vital part of helping them believe they can learn and that school is a valuable place where they can be successful. Children would be happier in school if they were confident that their differences would not cause them to be excluded, teased or judged as unworthy. Any hint that one way or rate of learning is superior to others will spoil the feeling that school is a great place for everyone, as commentaries in Honor Society assemblies often do. For example, "If you work as hard as these [winners] students, then you too can be in the Honor Society." This, like some of the other routines we don't think to question, could be the very ones that sabotage our goals for teaching every student. And it may not be so much what we do, but how we do it. Perhaps we should go through everything at schools, every word and act and place, to see how they could affect student achievement. Get rid of the ones that don't make sense anymore. Certainly get rid of the ones that compare children.

School defeats many children when we adults don't actively intervene in affective issues, and then we defeat ourselves as well. Children whose achievement is different from their classmates, or who are teased or bullied don't want to come to school and lose faith that they can belong. Their talents are lost to communities when they stop trying and stop believing in themselves. This is far from the ideal of universal education where everyone acquires critical academic and aesthetic skills, the ones that give them access to full participation in the world of thought of their time.

Chapter 5

"I Love This Book"

It's 6:30 Monday morning, cool and fresh, but on the horizon the sun looks huge and promises a sweltering day. In front of the school, which is heavily littered with trash, hangs a white plastic sign, "We're focusing on Literacy." It's suspended by one end from the second story, and can't be read. I drive around the corner, park in the teachers' lot and walk toward the back entrance of the school on a sidewalk bright with yellow and red leaves. Something hard crunches under my shoe—broken glass that needs to be swept away before the children arrive. I open the door and enter a silent hallway, the echo of my footsteps the only sound. It's still cool in here.

This old school was remodeled three years ago, and although the remodel didn't include air-conditioning for some steaming-hot days, it created an attractive, well-equipped library, updated the cafeteria and added a computer laboratory. I like it. I open the door to my classroom, grab my broom and dustpan, go out and sweep up the broken glass, along with some cigarette butts, candy wrappers and a paper cup.

I go back inside to prepare for the day. I could have done this last night, but I'm tired by the end of the day and want to go home. Coming in early is better; my mind is fresh and there aren't many distractions at this early hour. Because the needs of each group of children are different every year, and because I regularly have new ideas about teaching and strategies, I always have preparation to do.

I choose a read-aloud story, *Barefoot*, and write my questions for it. I print a poem on chart paper, go to the office and make copies of it for poetry notebooks. Luckily the copy machine isn't out of order this morning. By now the halls are beginning to fill with teachers greeting each other and the office staff is just arriving. I dash to the library to see if we have picture books about soil and rocks. I hurry back to the classroom, read the teacher's guide for the day's math exploration and prepare the materials for it. I check the reading conferences poster to see who I'll meet today: Abdulrahman, Abubakar, Ali, Derek and Brenda. The bell rings.

The children come in busy with their intentions and conversations. By now they've passed from "Good morning" to "Hi Ms. Stark!" A few of them stop to tell me something important that happened to them at home or at school. Abdulrahman walks in, looks at the conference appointments, walks over to me and says: "We have a conference today."

"I know. How do you think you're doing?"

"I think I'm ready for a new level."

"Well, we'll see, right?" He nods and moves away to the coatroom.

He and the others chatter while they put their backpacks away and return from the coatroom to sit on the carpet. Much like his classmates now except that he never chatters and rarely speaks, Mufdi comes in, puts his things away and sits down by Abdulrahman, who is happy to see him. Then they all look up at me standing in front of the calendar, and I ask them, "Who knows what day it is?" Stragglers continue to come in, put their things away and sit down.

We'll start and end the day with some kind of reading, but everything we do will have a subtext of learning to speak English. They'll learn English as they learn to read. I have promised myself that when they go to second grade they'll know how to decode words and how to find meaning in most kinds of texts. I've promised that they will do this as well as native English speakers. This is my challenge to myself and it motivates my every action at school. I will use the same foundational reading elements that other reading teachers use: phonemic awareness, basic phonics, vocabulary development, fluency, and comprehension strategies. The difference will be that I will have to use simpler language and constantly support language growth.

I have a political reason as well for teaching reading. My students must learn to read to survive in mainstream English classes or they'll fall academically behind other students, more often than not, forever. Statistics for ELL students' academic achievement are among the nation's lowest, and much of the failure is due to low English literacy. I believe that if I don't teach my students to read, I fail them.

The prospects for success look good so far. It's mid-October. They like the many books we have in the room, and they like learning to read them. They've enjoyed the early activities that lead to reading, especially the beanbag game.

By now, every child has memorized the letter sounds and most can read a few words by sight. I dropped the alphabet and letter-sounds centers two weeks ago and now use texts alone for reading instruction.

In the class this morning while the children read independently, I'll have my conferences with Abdulrahman, Abubakar, Ali, Brenda and Derek. Conference appointments are permanent: five children see me privately on their scheduled day, Monday through Friday. They like their conferences and are keenly aware of them. They remind me about them and are disappointed if anything interferes with them.

I like the conferences too. They involve one of my favorite kinds of teaching, the give and take of guiding one person's learning. I have to observe, think, listen to what the student says about his or her understanding and processes, and then synthesize what I see to pinpoint the child's learning needs. Then I have to find the words to address them. The children's limited language makes this more complicated than it sounds. I find similes, metaphors and make drawings to create understanding. I use my body, recruit other children for demonstrations—anything. The yearlong meetings help me to watch the development of understanding. Being a learning guide rarely involves a quick fix; it involves time, give and take with the student, trial and error, and reflection. It's a kind of research on a microlevel, and it's exactly why I like it.

The growing pleasures of reading, the admiration of parents, and participation in the literacy community of the classroom and the school inspire the children to improve: "Test me! Test me!" they plead at lunch and recess, begging for official proof of their reading progress. Admittedly, learning to read in our class has some playful aspects, or game-like components, but that's all right. The end result is liking to read. The children know that the conferences help them to improve.

When I meet the children during conferences, I informally appraise their reading. They read aloud and I make suggestions to help them. If they read nearly without errors and understand what they've read, I give them a formal evaluation, a kind of test. If they can fluently read and retell the unfamiliar text of the test book, I move them to the next stage, or level of difficulty, where they'll have new skills to learn. If they can't read the test book almost perfectly, I ask them to spend another week reading more books at the same skill level. I make note of the kinds of miscues they make for future attention.

If there's not enough time for a formal test during their conferences, I ask them if they'd like to come at recess for the evaluation. They can choose to wait until their next conference, but that never happens; they've always wanted to come at recess. It's the only extra time I can find, their recess and my lunchtime, but supporting their excitement about reading is worth grabbing a rushed bite to eat. When they think they're ready for more difficult books, they want confirmation right away, and so do I. That's the game part of our reading program, like moving ahead a few spaces on a board game.

Today after the children and I read a song and a poem together and complete calendar activities, I read them a short story. Then I give a brief phonics lesson to the whole group and send them on their way. They get their books, find a place to sit, and begin to read. After the initial burst of noise and movement, the room is calm and I look around for Abdulrahman. I find him sitting at a table waiting for me whereas he normally likes to sprawl on the carpet. He may have noticed that for our conferences the tables are a little more convenient for me. I sit down next to him.

He has taken to reading easily. He mastered the letter/sound relationships without a problem and concentrates on his work without reminders. He's mature and quickly learned the process and purpose of the conference—he can discuss what he's practicing and quickly apply new information. He has a complex sense of reality and enjoys stories.

He is tall for a first grader, a handsome and solid Somali boy. The conference I report here is based on my March observational notes but it's similar to most of the other conferences we had. I draw on it here because it illustrates how he used conference information to grow as a reader. By March he was comfortably speaking English.

I open my notebook to remind us what we thought he should practice during the week, and then I ask him to read from the little book he has brought. I'll see if he has corrected the mistake he was making last week, consistently misreading four-letter words that had a silent /e/ ending. For example, he pronounced *fin* for *fine*. To help with this reading snag I've asked him to notice how final /e/ affects the pronunciation of many words: the interior vowel sounds like its name. I gave him a list of words for practice: *win*, *wine*; *car*, *care*; *pet*, *Pete*; *hat*, *hate* ("How different they are," we said).

He reads his book fluently without stumbling over words ending in silent /e/, so I bring out a test booklet for his next level, level L, in second-grade books. It's called *The Person From Planet X*. He looks at the cover and a few pages, chuckles, and begins to read.

He reads fluently and expressively, and I feel proud of him. He's reading the words with a silent /e/ ending with such ease that no one would know he ever had a problem with them. Then he comes to a sentence, "The alien wanted to come back." He reads, "The alien wanted to comb back." He stops. He knows something is wrong.

"So, this says, 'The alien wanted to comb back.'" I said. "Hmmm. I wonder what that means!" He laughs. He had used final /e/ correctly, but forgot to check for sense.

"Can you say why you read it that way?"

"Because the e, on the end," he answers.

"What do you think would be a good word here?" He reads it again.

"Come."

"Okay. Will you read it aloud please?"

"The alien wanted to come back."

"Does that make sense?"

He nodded. I explain that English doesn't always seem to follow rules so he'll need to think about what else a sentence says for clues. The final /e/ clue is only one of several possible clues. He understands immediately and looks at me with a knowing smile, sharing with me the experience of an insider about this sometimes surprising language. He continues to read the test book perfectly with the concept of how final /e/ affects pronunciation understood. He's becoming an accomplished reader and the more familiar he becomes with oral English the easier it will be for him to recognize words without applying phonics rules and letter sounds. I don't anticipate more problems with final /e/ and note that he's ready to read the next set of books, level M. I tell him, and he smiles. I have never seen him display more emotion than a slight laugh or a frown.

But one day a few weeks later he gave me an unforgettable teaching memory. It was during the busy process of straightening up after reader's workshop. As we walked by each other I stopped for a second and asked: "How did your reading go today?" and he answered, "I love this book!" clutching it to his chest with fervor, a second-grade chapter book that challenges many native English speakers, *Boxcar Children*.

"Why?" I ask, overjoyed to see his pleasure and curious to know more about his experience. By now he knew how much I enjoyed seeing his progress, and knew that I expected a genuine reflection.

"Because they're kids, and they do things."

"Do you mean they do things without adults?"

His face brightened and he replied, "Yeah!"

With a loving family that carefully supervises him, Abdulrahman embraced this story of children surviving without parents. That they are children from a different culture seemed unimportant to him; their predicaments and solutions are the heart of the story and he found commonality with them. It's a chapter book without many pictures so he must have focused on the action and pictured the characters or imagined himself in a similar situation. The fact that he could read and understand this book represented enormous reading and language growth.

"Ms. Cudahy has more *Boxcar Children* books in the library...," I say.

"She does?" he says, eagerly.

"Yes. She told me yesterday. If you want to go up and ask for another one I'll write a note for you."

He had progressed to this level with normal instructional guidance and family support, making use of conferences and brief whole-class lessons on phonics for his improvement. His family helped by expressing their pride in him, and by valuing the "Hurray! You passed your level!" awards. The more he read, the better he read, and it seemed as if he had discovered enough life in books to sustain his growth independent of the external rewards that motivated him in the beginning. By the end of this his first-grade year, he would be close to reading third-grade level books.

Next on today's conference schedule is Abubakar, wiry, active and constantly moving, also from Somalia. Unlike Abdulrahman, he has been slow to discover a personal reason for reading. When the class began to read books for longer periods, he wasn't able to concentrate. I noticed that he could focus if he shared a book with a buddy or sat by a buddy, but otherwise he was constantly up and down looking for another book, talking and laughing with classmates on the way, and causing disorder and turmoil. With a partner though he had enthusiastic fun reading and talked and laughed while looking at the illustrations or reading nonsense rhymes. As long as he read at his level, his eyes focusing on words, I knew that his skills would grow, and that eventually not only would he be able to read by himself, he would find books he preferred to read alone.

This is in fact what happened. He ended his first-grade year reading books that were for beginning second graders. He enjoyed telling friends about books he read, fiction and nonfiction. I could see him, a book in hand, laughing at characters and talking excitedly about stories. Occasionally he would want to read an interesting passage to me. However, my challenge today in mid-October is to motivate and nudge him along to self-awareness as a learner. During my bookstore and library visits I look for books he might like. Today I have one I bought a few days ago and I'm almost sure he'll like it. I read it to the class yesterday.

He is sitting with Mufdi, each boy reading alone. Mufdi by now is a more advanced reader than Abubakar. Once he mastered the letter/sound association and learned enough English from our songs, poems and classroom activities, he began to learn to read with the same ease as Abdulrahman. He amazes me because even though he is beginning to read, he still seldom speaks. When I question him about meaning in his reading, he answers correctly and can even be insightful, laughing appropriately at characters, even noticing humor where other children might not, and showing signs that he has opinions. Where is the obvious link between oral language and reading? He probably is capable of saying more than he does. As he began to excel he was rarely without a book. I asked him one day, trying to understand his extraordinary progress, "Mufdi, do your parents read to you at home?" He said "Yes." I'm not sure what they read, or in what language, but it looked as if Mufdi had a head start with literacy. He was much respected by the other children for this. One day in February he came to school with a book from home and sitting on the carpet, conspicuously began to look at it while he waited for the others to be seated.

"Look! *Koran!* Mufdi has *Koran!*" exclaimed Abubakar, tugging at my arm excitedly.

"No, that's the *Bible*," I said. "Look. It says *'Bible,'* right Mufdi?" Mufdi looked up at me with a pleased, shy smile and nodded. That the book was not the *Koran* astonished Abubakar; he became silent, a rare look of reflection on his face. "Mufdi, can you read that?" I asked. He nodded. "Will you read to me a little?" He did; he was haltingly able to read in Arabic. "How did you learn that Mufdi," I said, amazed.

"My Mother," was all he answered, but he appeared proud of this book and wanted us to see it, and I think, that he could read it.

With his calm disposition and exemplary reading behavior Mufdi models what I hope Abubakar will learn a little—enthusiasm for reading and self-control. He's adorable as he is, but I think he'd get along in life more easily with a little moderation. I certainly wouldn't force him though. Sitting by Mufdi, Abubakar is reading quietly and concentrating, while Mufdi seems to enjoy his company and occasionally helps him with unknown words. I sit down by Abubakar.

"Hi Abubakar. How's your reading going today?"

With fun-filled eyes and a gigantic smile that freshly lacks an incisor, he looks up at me. I sit next to him.

"Look this book!" He shows me *Walk the Dog*, a page where dogs are sniffing various objects, including each other.

"I can read it! Look!"

He could read it. Conceptually it's a simple book, but most of the children enjoy it. The illustrations are funny because they capture the essence of dog behavior, behavior anyone recognizes if they've seen dogs, so it presents no background problem for my students. The text is repetitive so new readers can access it. A new word is introduced with each two-page spread and if children can apply letter sounds, they can say the word and infer its meaning from the illustrations. And it's a book that I've read to the class.

"Walk the dog. Walk the dog. Sniff! Sniff!" Abubakar reads. He looks at me and sniffs with a question on his face.

"That's right," I say. "Good for you. Sniff. Did you see the /s/ and the /n/ together?" He nods, to my delight.

"Let's go to the next page."

"Walk the dog. Walk the dog. Lick, Lick." He reads and laughs.

"What's that, Lick?" I ask. He licks the air. I can't help laughing at his enthusiasm and the absurdity of what we were doing, and he joins the laughter.

"Mm hum, that's it. Read this page again. See how smooth you can make it." This time he reads more fluently, as I hoped he would. I show him the book I brought for him to try after he finishes this one. *Walk the Dog* is easy to recite without paying attention to the printed words, and I wanted him to try one where he would need to practice looking at words in order to understand.

"Do you want to look at this with me to see if you like it?" We looked at it together, Yo! Yes? It was perfect I thought—funny, germane to childhood experience (making a friend and overcoming miscommunication) and near his level. I admired how the author and illustrator could create such a complex story with so few words. Abubakar's face brightened when he saw it. I pointed to "Yo."

"Can you read this to me?" He looked at it closely and tried.

"Y is for yo yo, y,y y... Yo," he chanted. This book would be good for him. He could practice a skill he needed, applying the /y/ sound at the beginning of a word until doing so became automatic. He would enjoy the story, and would be successful. At this point the most important goal was to find books he enjoyed so he'd want to continue.

"You'll be ready for another level soon if you keep this up. Who knows what you'll be reading pretty soon!"

"Who knows!" he repeated.

Like so many of the children, Abubakar's eventual attainment of grade-level reading was supported by his parents, especially his mother. Always dressed in a veil and long garments, her hair was covered but not her face. At first she came to conferences with an interpreter, concerned about Abubakar's school behavior reported to her in lavish detail by Khadija, his sister and my former student, one year older than he was.

She regularly came by to visit me and always asked conversationally how her brother was doing.

"He's doing fine, Khadija. Sometimes he plays when he should be working, but..." I paused to find the words I needed, "...not bad."

"I'll tell my mother." Then she became stern. "He shouldn't do that!"

"He's improving," I said.

No matter. She was going to tell her mother.

Sure enough, one morning Abubakar's mother came to school. A messenger came to the room to tell me that she was in the office requesting a conference, and asked me to come right away. I asked Mrs. Vega to watch the class for a few minutes and went to the office where Abubakar's mother and a Somali interpreter, a community activist I'd met before, were waiting for me in a small conference room.

After a warm, formal greeting they stated the purpose of their visit. Both women expressed concern that Abubakar's school behavior didn't reflect Somali values and behavior, the interpreter as concerned as Mrs. Sheik was. I described what he did in class and in troubled tones they apologized for him. I explained that he was improving every day and that I thought he was immature, not bad. They asked to have him brought into the conference room. When he came in he stood before the three of us, the two Somali women and me, looking ready to listen.

The visitors reminded him in very concerned and disappointed tones that his behavior was not that of a good Muslim man. They talked about his father's behavior and compared Abubakar's to his. Again and again they looked at me and said, "This is not how Somali people act. Somali people respect school. Somali people are polite." The interpreter added, "This is what is happening to our children. They are forgetting Somali ways."

Abubakar looked humble and ashamed. It was clear that he respected these two women, and he promised to improve. We had two conferences of this sort and he did improve, although with his irrepressible nature it was a bit like trying to harness the wind. What we focused on was respect for the instructional goals of the class and what he needed to do to uphold them. I'm sure that the support of his community and the emphasis on Somali values helped Abubakar. His school achievement was less important to his mother than his behavior at first, but once she understood the connection between class behavior and literacy, and once a relationship was established with me, she added the quality of his school work to her concerns.

For a parent conference in late January she came alone. She sat down and said to me, "I learn English to talk to my children's teachers."

Touched by her love and concern, and surprised by her independence and the language skills she had gained so quickly, I was happy to have good news to report. Abubakar generally was following school and class rules, and his concentration during reading and other learning periods was growing. He was beginning to take control of his own reading process and was doing quite well.

She probed, finding it difficult to believe but hoping it was true at the same time. It seemed she wanted to be sure that I, an American, had as high expectations for her son's behavior as she did, that my idea of "quite well" was the same as hers. Knowing her wishes did help me with my standards for him. I could picture the kind of man she hoped to see one day, a man like her husband, and I could refer to those values when I talked to him. They weren't far from what I wanted for my own children.

With Abubakar's reading conference finished for today, I move on to Ali, a slight but muscular Iraqi boy with shiny black hair and bright dark eyes. His reading is a puzzle to me and challenges my ability to solve learning problems. He knows the letter sounds—he learned them as quickly as most of the other students, but he hasn't learned to apply them for reading. In addition, he doesn't work well in school. He forever tries to interact with the other students when they're working. Does he want to be friends and not know how? This is one of my guesses. I also wonder if he ignores his work because he thinks he will fail at it, and I wonder if he has a learning disability. During the year I approached his reading with these and other possibilities in mind. I knew that it would take time, repetition and probably various approaches before I found the key that would help him.

Today the problem I'm considering for our conference is that he is still on the first book in the reading series and hasn't made any progress with it. Ali is the only child in the room who is not learning to read. He acts as if it's normal that he can't read, and further, that it doesn't matter. Does his lag have behavioral, psychological or physiological origins? Does he have a memory problem? My intuition after a month and a half of observations is that Ali doesn't see himself as a learner yet—a psychological and behavioral reason. When there is something to learn his attention is distracted, flitting from one attraction to another. Yet I've seen that when he's learning something he likes, like the beanbag game with its growing pile of beanbags, he's completely engaged, focused and learns quickly.

His English is not the problem; he was in sheltered English kindergarten all last year and speaks English more than most of the new children. I frequently heard about him last year at lunch. The teacher and the aide would shake their heads with shared frustration and regularly send Ali to the office when he misbehaved. Did the distracted and disruptive behavior in kindergarten lead to lack of success there, and then did he begin to think that he couldn't learn at all? I wanted to see how far he could grow with regular classroom instruction, and if that didn't work, then I would immediately try regular classroom interventions—extra time with me, and special sessions with Mrs. Vega.

My hypothesis about Ali is that he wants to learn to read but doesn't think he can. He pretends to read texts to friends and to me during conferences, fooling no one. I see his pretense as a way to save face. His initial behavior in the beanbag game illustrates how his attitude can affect his learning, and also, how capable he can be when he tries. If he had a memory problem or difficulty discriminating between sounds, how could he succeed at this game?

When I began the beanbag alphabet game with the class he wanted to make a joke of it, and to connect with the other children by making them laugh. I didn't allow him to disrupt the game or to fail this way. Most of the children listen carefully to each other and to what I say so they'll know the answer when it's their turn. Ali didn't do this at first. But when he joked and called out, I excluded him. I wanted him to think that playing was a privilege. This was an intervention specifically directed at his kind of trouble. With another child, another strategy would have been more suitable.

"I'm sorry Ali, but you're spoiling the game. Sit over there, and if you can play nicely, you can come back. Let me know when you're ready." I waited until he told me he would cooperate, which he did. After two days of such exclusion, he stopped disrupting the game. While he sat out he noticed how the other children enjoyed the game and how they accumulated mountains of beanbags. When he re-entered the game, he began to try answers, and to play seriously. To help him, I pointed out several times what the others did that led to their success: looking and listening to each other and me.

He understood and I began to see him paying attention. It wasn't long before he learned what he needed to know to get those beanbags. The first astonishing right answer cemented his confidence. He played just as well as all the other children—no difference. He looked so happy with his piles of beanbags! These were signs that regular classroom instruction had a chance of success with Ali. With every conference I try to direct that same learning ability to reading. How can I help him to see the connection between letter sounds and reading words? I thought that special attention to word families, which we regularly composed and worked on together as a class would help Ali. I suggested to Mrs. Vega that she work on one of our early lists with him: *an, man, can, pan, ban, fan*, etc. We had a few easy puzzles with these words, and she could use sentences and use flash cards as well, pointing out how each beginning letter changed the words. He enjoyed Mrs. Vega and the private attention could and did focus his attention.

Another factor that I'm sure contributed to his slow start in reading was his failure to do the homework. Homework involved repeated readings of an assigned storybook. I'd found a set of slightly worn paperback books once used to teach reading. They had attractive illustrations with simple, interesting enough stories. I arranged them according to difficulty, made a corresponding list, and because most of the parents didn't speak or read in English, I recorded each book. I put each book with its recording in a large plastic bag and Mrs. Vega distributed them every week, one to each child. We kept a list of who had read each book, and when. If a family didn't have a player, which was rare, I lent them one of several I had bought for this purpose. Parents liked this homework and usually found a way for their children to listen to the recordings.

I asked the children to listen to the recordings and to read the stories aloud every night for a week. I gave them a homework form that I asked parents to sign after each reading session at home. When the children could read the book fluently to me, they would get a more difficult book for the next week. That was the purpose of the re-readings: to promote fluency and familiarity with the vocabulary and syntax. The parents were aware of the list and so could encourage their children. While nearly all of the children did this homework, Ali never did.

His home life could have affected his school work as well. It sounded disruptive with stories of his father chasing "men" down the street in his car, "men" coming to the door and shouting at his father, his father fighting "men" in front of their house, and the police coming for his father who drove away from them "fast, fast!" with Ali in the car. Ali was excited to tell these stories. He said that his father could beat up anyone who bothered his family.

He and his father considered Ali's mother to be an "angel" and it seemed that with his father's perceived ability to protect the family and his mother's nurturing attitude, some important aspects of emotional security were present in Ali's life. But I wondered if they were enough to provide the easy physical security that would shelter him from trauma and worry. There were signs that something was troubling him.

At the beginning of the year I'd found him lying regularly about where he'd been while presumably going to the bathroom, the coatroom, or the office; about what he was doing in Jayson's backpack; and why class toys were in his pocket at the end of the day. He hit classmates for no perceivable reason, and he made vulgar comments to the girls.

I worked hard to help Ali, but it was the input of his father that ultimately brought success. Earning Mr. A.'s respect had been an effort, but worth the trouble since I wanted to help Ali. I first wanted his help with his son's behavior. The lying, stealing and disruptions were interfering with everyone's learning, including Ali's. The father seemed suspicious of me at first and defended his son's behavior, denying that what I said could be true. I focused on Ali's strengths in my talks, expressed my fondness for Ali, and my confidence that with his parents' help he could improve. It was fortunate that Mr. A. spoke English. It was basic but serviceable, and better than my nonexistent Arabic.

Mr. A. occasionally came after school to get Ali, watching the class from the doorway before the school day ended. I would quickly approach him to give him a report, not always requested. One day after I had become used to seeing him, I greeted him with *"Salaam-a-lekum."* What a surprising and beautiful smile those words prompted from him! *"A-lekum-salaam,"* he responded. Then he added, "That's a very nice thing you said." Now it was I who smiled with pleasure, so happy to see his face transformed and to have reached him. "You say *'A-lekum-salaam'* when someone say that," he informed me. I practiced it until he approved because I wasn't sure that I'd heard exactly what he said. After awhile it didn't seem foreign at all and I used it with other parents.

Then one day, I think because he saw how the children behaved independently in the class, he believed at last that I liked Ali, and had thought about the reports I gave him, and his attitude changed. He listened to me attentively and promised to help. I saw an opening with this promise and discussed some of the details about academic goals in our class. He remained after the final bell rang, and once I saw the children safely on their busses, I came back to the room where he waited. I showed him the range of leveled books that Ali needed to read before the end of first grade, and explained what Ali needed to do to improve. He was surprised. He thought that all Ali had to do was learn to decode and the reading goal was achieved.

He and his wife were both illiterate in Arabic as well as in English so they couldn't help with their son's reading, but they could and did enable me to teach him by giving their support of class expectations for behavior. Like Abubakar's mother, they wanted their son to behave according to the values of the *Koran*. It was interesting and heartwarming to me to see the kindness and love with which they treated him, even when he disappointed them. Always they explained and encouraged, while their eyes were full of affection. The challenge remained largely mine to motivate him to learn the specific skills he needed.

After several months of regular class discussions about honesty, friendship, and the importance of making a good world in our classroom, and with the support of his parents, Ali's dishonesty began to disappear. The class procedures for problem-solving also helped. Children with complaints about him regularly invited him to the class problem-solving circle. He began to understand the connection between behavior and consequences.

Kids wouldn't be his friends when he behaved selfishly or called names.

He would lose credibility if he stole or didn't share.

His family would be disappointed.

No one believed his lies.

In addition, I explicitly prohibited his vulgar comments to the girls and asked them to tell him how his comments made them feel. "Sad," was the word they chose—explanation enough.

I concluded that he probably didn't have a reading disability because of his normal ability to learn the letters and sounds, and his exuberant accuracy with rhymes. He had measurably improved with the regular classroom interventions. But what a struggle it was to get him on a learning path. And I questioned my conclusions the whole time, wondering: "Should I refer him for testing after all? Was I serving him as well as I could?" I rejected time and again the option to have him tested for learning disabilities. "No. I know he has the cognitive resources to read," I told myself. I watched his development, talked to his father about how he learned at home, and remained uncertain until I saw that he began to respond to our classroom instruction and intervention.

I think that when children are identified as having a learning disability they will have the expert help they need to learn, and I view this as very positive for struggling children. However, I only wanted to refer Ali if I was persuaded that he had a real disability, in which case I wouldn't have the knowledge to address it. If not, if there were psychological or behavioral reasons, I wanted to apply everything I knew to find them and to help him. He had markedly responded to this kind of intervention as well, and by the end of the year I was persuaded that with capable instruction, he would develop as a competent student.

So, back and forth, back and forth my thinking went. I worried over this referral because I had to be sure I was doing the right thing for Ali. First, the referrals were important and involved many school and district staff members, and the child's parents, who I knew would be worried, perhaps for nothing. Second, a diagnosis would follow him forever, a good thing if he needed special help, but bad if the diagnosis was wrong, affected by his lack of complete English and past feeble effort in school. His skills would be under grade-level expectations, but not for reasons of disability. Supporting my concern was the fact that recently reading disability experts had concluded that current IQ-type testing is too unreliable for capable decision-making, even for English speakers.

I decided not to recommend testing because of his easy familiarity with the sounds of language, and accurate knowledge of letter sounds. He probably wasn't dyslexic, and other diagnoses, Attention Deficit Disorder, for example, didn't seem appropriate either. Furthermore, the assessments were language-dependent; there was no one who could test him in Arabic, and the practice of waiting until an ELL student spoke passable English before administering a test would not have yielded an accurate assessment of what he knew. Passable English wasn't enough because he had knowledge in Arabic that wouldn't appear in English. It would be at least five to seven years before his English—like any ELL student's English—could be considered at near-native-speaker level. By that time, Ali's reading would be far behind what it should be. I had to help him myself. Still, the questions remained vigorously present in all my interactions with him: what's going on?

"Hi Ali. What are you reading?" I already knew the answer.

"This." He shows me *I Like to Jump*, the first and easiest book from the reading series. He's been reading this book for two weeks but still doesn't figure out any words from letter cues or sight recognition. He uses the illustrations as text—he looks at them and says what he thinks the words could say. He's another child who wants to be up and about, "Looking for a book to read," he says. He's supposed to have enough books in his book bin to last for three or more days, and shouldn't need to 'look for a book to read.' He sits a little longer now than he did at first, but he has a long way to go, and this was another concern. What was the cause of his lack of focus? Was it a way of avoiding work where he was unsuccessful, or was it an attention disorder?

"How about reading to me?" He begins to recite what he has memorized, and to tell about what he guesses from the illustrations, but there's still no correspondence to what's on the page. "Use your finger and follow the words.

That might help you." He is blocked. I pick a word and ask him what it is. He
has no idea.

"Look at this letter. What is it?"

"H."

"How does it sound?"

"Huh," he says, getting the aspirate of the H.

"Okay, let's try the next letter. What is it?"

"O."

"How does it sound?" He makes the sound for short "O."

"Good. Now, what's this letter?"

"P."

"And how does it sound?"

"Puh."

"Good. Now let's put them together. Follow my finger." He succeeds
but awkwardly and with complete dependence on my help. Still, the clumsy
success was promising enough to convince me once again that eventually he
would be able to read.

"Ali, you can do this. We'll keep on, and you'll see. You're going to read!"
He smiles, as if to show me that he cares or believes me, but it's a show only. If
only I could find a way to help him understand how to learn. If only he'd focus
on reading as I've seen him do for other kinds of learning; if only I could make
him believe that his effort would produce something of value. What will be his
key?

I kept on like this for months—encouraging him, showing him, trying different approaches. It was discouraging. Did he care? Nothing indicated that he
did. Classmates who had been with him in kindergarten at first laughed at his
'I can't do this because look, I'm funny and I'm not trying to do it,' stance. But
I took this away from him. I told the children several times in his presence that
we needed to encourage him to do good work and that we spoiled his chances
when we laughed at him. I explained that they could help him if they encouraged him. "We want Ali to know how to read. When it's playtime and he's
funny, that's a good time to laugh."

They began to say "You can do it, Ali." Hopeful signs began to appear
here and there. One day Ali recognized *the* as a sight word and remembered
it the following day, and then, *boy*. After about six months I noticed that he
was beginning to watch when we read poems and songs together, or when
I gave short lessons to teach helpful reading clues. He began to listen with
attention. My hopes had risen and fallen daily for six months, so I wasn't sure

this attention was going to last or produce any changes in knowledge.

Then one day in early May he began to read, to look at words and understand that the written letters revealed the word, that when a word wasn't immediately recognizable, studying its letter sounds could help to discover what it was. He hadn't read enough to know many words automatically, but he knew some and began to accumulate more. He began to get books, not to look at and approximately recite like a preschooler, but to study and read. Imagine.

He was so proud of himself. He would look up at me with an astonished expression when he used a few beginning letters and suddenly recognized an entire word, or when he read a whole page. He begged to read to me. He remained seated and worked at going through words he didn't automatically know. It was thrilling.

There were signs that he wanted to belong in the literacy club of our class. He joined conversations with classmates about what his next book would be and talked about books he was reading. He sounded affected at first, as if his reading was simply to be in the club, but I believed that this would lead him to genuine appreciation of reading and what it had to offer him. More and more words became automatic to him when he read.

His reading didn't soar to grade level in the brief time remaining of the school year, but in mid-May, May 11, he fluently and easily read and retold the test stories for two levels. It's unusual for someone to finish two levels at once. He moved from the first to the fourth. The entire class celebrated and his father's and mother's faces beamed with hope and pride when I told them. He was on the literacy path.

Now I look around and find Derek, the next on the list. He is noticeably wellgroomed; his wavy brown hair always trimmed and combed; his clothes immaculate and ironed. I've met his parents and know that they are concerned about his achievement and everything else that has to do with their Derek. They read to him at home and try to teach him his letters in Spanish. They haven't had much luck and are worried about him. I have questions too. He hasn't started to read.

He is an exceptional artist and especially loves to draw. Everyone admires his fanciful, unique, intricate drawings with stories so imaginative that I wonder how he thought of them. There are monsters and castles, magical clouds, odd princesses.... He gives me elaborate oral explanations about the action. He doesn't talk much otherwise, never volunteers an answer, and has been slow to learn English.

Like Ali, he learned the letter sounds quickly and normally. He hasn't made the connection between the isolated sounds and how they function in printed words, and I wonder if I need to think of a special approach that might involve drawing. So far, I haven't thought of another approach and still haven't given up on what I've been doing. When I sit down with him today, we labor over using letter sounds to uncover the words in *I Like to Jump*. Over and over again with my help he successfully finds the letter sounds in the words.

"What's this letter?"

"L."

"How does it sound?"

"LLLLLLLLLLLLL."

"Yes."

And so forth with nearly every word as he went through the motions of our conference. He went through the words with me, but couldn't do it alone. "Derek, let's look for some more books at this level, some books you might like." I knew he played with the miniature cars and trucks at recess, so we walked over to a bin labeled "trains, planes, and cars" and looked through them until we found one he liked and that was at his beginning level. Then we moved to a bin with simple animal stories, which he also liked. He chose one, we checked for how hard it would be for him and he put it in his book holder with the other one. "You can practice using the letter sounds with these words Derek. Go through each word just like we did together." I was finished with his conference today and moved on to the next child on the schedule.

Then one day in early December there was a breakthrough for Derek. For several weeks I'd seen him with *Walk the Dog*. During indoor recess one day as I walked by him, I noticed that he was reading *Walk the Dog* again, reciting it orally for no one's benefit but his own with the appearance of complete pleasure.

"Ah! *Walk the Dog!* Do you like it?" Surprised, he looked at me.

"I can read it!"

"You can?! Would you read it to me?" I said this to make him happy and to encourage him. I was busy and on my way to look at some papers I had to read, and knew I would hear his memory at work, not what is considered true reading, still. . . .

"Walk the dog. Walk the dog. . . ." He recited the text mechanically, which he remembered from when I had read this story to the class. He was proud of what he could do. Then he came to a place where he'd forgotten the words. He stopped his recitation, looking stumped and embarrassed. I never could have planned a better opportunity.

"Derek! That's why we use letter sounds, for when we forget a word! Look at the first letter. It gets you started. That's what readers do." I made my suggestion sound as if it was exciting to have this resource and as if he'd found a fabulous clue. Many, many times I had said the same thing to the class, and to Derek, but he never understood. Today, a look of realization suddenly flashed in his eyes, the sort of look that is intangible and useless as data, but that is solid information for a teacher. He looked at the word and the first letter.

"Bh." He paused. "Bark!" He looked as pleased and surprised as could be in his quiet way. He finished reading the book to me using his new tactic whenever he forgot a word. For Derek, it was January when he began to put all the components of reading together. He would continue to read this story for awhile, but now he would look at the words and would begin to remember them how they looked, or by sight.

He entered the path to reading proficiency just like the other children. By the end of the year he would be two levels away from completing first-grade district standards. At his request, I tested him on the last day of school and he capably read a difficult story, *Noise*, difficult because a more complex syntax made it harder for an ELL student to understand than earlier stories in the assessment series. On this last day of school he moved to a new and more difficult reading level. I knew that he was on his way in reading, and could be comfortable in second grade.

My final conference for the day is with Brenda. A smile creeps onto my face. Brenda is eager, wise, and insightful about people, sturdy, playful, fierce, loyal and kind. But not especially focused on learning to read. If learning to read had meant isolated, forced work, Brenda would not have been engaged. As it was, however, the option to make reading a social activity drew her into the process—that and perhaps wanting to be friends with me.

She didn't know much about books or letters when she came. She didn't know the alphabet in Spanish or English, didn't know how to hold a book, and had never been to school. She had to learn to manage herself independently and I had to make the work engaging to draw her into it. At the beginning of the year she and her buddies liked to chat about friends and families, about nail polish or about new bracelets—but not books and reading. One day, for example, Rosalinda brought blue nail polish to school and it appeared for inspection while the class prepared for independent reading.

The class's four girls had begun to gather at her table to see it, and I'm sure that without my intervention, to apply it. I moved over to the table to see what was going on and, seeing the polish, asked Rosalinda to put it away and not bring it to school again. I explained that nail polish wasn't something we had agreed to use during reading time—this made them laugh—and if an adult saw it around the playground, they would confiscate it. It wasn't allowed at school.

"Doesn't nail polish seem like a good thing to talk about at home?" I asked, as usual with gestures as well as words. "Then nobody would bother you, and you could put it on." They laughed again. I reiterated the task at hand and reviewed the reading rubric with them. I asked them what they were reading, and helped them find spots where they could read.

Their personal talk is important, an activity with educational value, but I want them to gain other important skills too. They will have to broaden their personal focus to include reading. I needed to help them view reading and discussions about reading as interesting, as interesting as nail polish and other topics they enjoyed discussing.

None of them, including Brenda, was consistently off-task. They're cooperative and enthusiastic girls who, like a number of the children at this early stage of self-management, need reminding. Often I look at them and find them doing just what they should be doing. It was more or less a month before the girls understood that the freedom to make choices during readers' workshop meant choices that lead to reading. A month is a very short time considering what a big cognitive step they were making. There were wonderful results.

One of my favorite memories of children's reading is of Brenda and Rosalinda sitting comfortably on pillows in the library corner, laughing over a book opened between them. I was delighted. I chuckled and asked, several yards from them, "What's funny?" Brenda looked up brightly but couldn't stop giggling enough to answer me, and she was prolonging the moment of shared laughter with Rosalinda. I waited, smiling. Finally, she said, "This story. It's funny. Dragon...." She couldn't finish and started laughing again; she and Rosalinda looked at each other and laughed even more. I walked over to them and they indicated the passage I should read. It was from Dav Pilkey's *Dragon's Fat Cat*. They paused in their laughing and eagerly watched to see my reaction. It was funny, even to me—a dragon innocently allows himself to be exploited by his new pet cat in absurd ways, but the humor is ironic and I was delighted that the girls had the literary sophistication to understand it. I laughed. Dav Pilkey is the author of the *Captain Underpants* series, and is an author who understands children's sense of humor and the ridiculous.

It was wonderful to see Brenda laughing over a book. She understood the subtle humor and I hoped she was learning that reading could be rewarding. *Dragon's Fat Cat* was an early chapter book and her ability to read it showed how her skills were growing. How gratifying it was, in view of the hard work it took to get her to this point. The early conferences were productive. What she needed was a reason to read more.

For Brenda's reading conference today I sit next to her on the carpet where she is reading a book from the leveled book series.

"Hi Brenda, how are you doing?" She brightens.

"Good," she says, sounding objective.

"Great. Let's see. Here's a good page. Will you read it please?" I chose a page I thought could have been hard for her, yet would indicate progress if she could read it fluently and explain the meaning of what she had read.

Today, with the regularity and nature of Brenda's miscues in reading, she knew before I said anything that she wasn't ready to move to another level.

"Brenda, have you read all the books on this level?" I ask.

"Yes."

"How do you think you did with this book?"

"Not so good."

"Do you think you're ready for the next level?"

"No," she answers. I'm not surprised.

"What do you think your problem was with this book?"

"This, and this, and this. . . ."

"Very good observation! I agree with you. You read very well except for those words."

"Let's think about what you can do to get better," I said. "How about this; do you know what this word is?"

"Slllll i p."

"Good. Put the sounds together. Watch my finger and say the sound where my finger is." I put my finger under the letters and tried to move her along. After several tries, she pronounced "slip." It sounded like a word.

"What does it mean?" I asked.

"I don't know." She had pronounced what was nonsense to her. I stood up and showed her what happens when someone slips. "Now, read the whole sentence." She read it fluently and had no trouble explaining what happened to the girl. Even so, I wrote a short list of words in her reading journal with today's date and said, "Try these words now," and I wrote *clip, clop, slap, stay, small, smell,* and *class.* I guided her through them, and with each word she became more confident.

"These were the kinds of words that were hard for you today, and they all were the kinds of words with two consonants together. I think that you need to practice these kinds of words, don't you?" She shook her head in agreement. "Great! Next week we'll see if we solved this problem with this work. I'm pretty sure you just need a little more practice in putting the letters together, these consonants."

In her reading notebook I added *play*, *clay*, *black* and *trip* to the list I had given her—words I was sure she could make out and whose meanings she knew. I helped her with them the same way I had with *slip*. Then I showed her a tub of books at her level that focused on blends and suggested that she read the ones she liked, but as many as possible.

"If you read these books I think you'll improve. You'll be a champion with words like these," I said, indicating the list I'd given her. "The next time we have a conference, we can see if they're easy for you. If you have a problem with them before then, be sure to tell me."

I would use *slip* with the whole class because if Brenda didn't know what it meant, then probably most of the others didn't either. It would be a useful word in the winter when it snowed, and to remind myself I noted it with my observations about Brenda's reading.

"There you are," I said, "Ready to learn something good, right?" She smiled, and I stood up to address the class: "Time for lunch. Clean up."

The conferences for today, five of them, are over. The kind of teaching that occurs in these conferences is a kind of research, the scientific part of teaching, but that requires empathy and intuition as well as the analysis of quantitative data. I can't simply count miscues. I need to assess comprehension, the most important part of all and much more complicated for my ELL students. I need to make the child comfortable enough to relax, and I need to interpret the reason for a mistake (miscue): is it a result of misunderstanding, or of reading too quickly? Once their reading strengths and weaknesses are located, the children need to be encouraged to go on, and I must find a way to help them understand their next step or a concept they haven't grasped. I have to make reading a pleasure.

The privacy of the conference means that the struggles of learning were for the child alone, to tell or not to tell anyone else. They help me too as I try to solve puzzles about each child's understanding—how s/he is understanding, what are the words, gestures and approaches that will lead to the "aha!" moment of it, and for me as well, there is increased understanding; sometimes a child has understood, but was unable to say so in a way that I would recognize. I had to remain as flexible as I could, which I needed to remind myself to do all the time. The plans decided in conferences with their measurable, achievable goals gave the children a quick reward for their efforts, inspiring them to master the next goal. Each small success stimulated them to try to learn something else, and convinced them that they could. The private conferences created a public space where the children worked cooperatively and independently. Each child knew exactly what to do, and how to do it. The intimate collaborations between the students and me, multiplied twenty-four times, drew us together and supported our group work throughout the year, as if we had developed a shared language. One child's privately achieved insights became part of what he or she brought to our group discussions and created more complexity in their thoughts.

The greatest advantage to having conferences is the opportunity to teach all the children according to their individual levels and to focus on one child at a time. Small-group teaching, where several children are called together if they have the same skill to learn, is a recommended and plausible strategy, and I use it sometimes, but somehow, at least in my experience, the children's needs are rarely if ever exactly the same, even when they are on the same reading level. It seems that even in the small groups everyone is a little different and needs a different approach. I still need to talk to each one separately and so can't focus enough on interpreting one child's processes, a difficulty perhaps unique to me. I prefer the individual conference above all other methods I've tried. Once they discovered how to read in their own way, they could work together on books for decoding and comprehension practice. That usually was more fun with a friend anyway.

Ali and Derek, for example, although they both needed to practice using letter sounds to help discover what a word was, were very different children. Ali wouldn't have focused with a joint conference, and Derek wouldn't have been comfortable enough to commit to a response. I could and did call them together to review applying letter sounds, but their struggling and puzzling was with me alone in a conference.

The children's achievement was never a function of just one element, like having the conferences. It was always a result of numerous factors, but parent's cooperation and our attention to the children's motivation, i.e. their happiness, comfort, sense of self-determination and fun, were among the most effective. They required as much attention and planning as any other aspect of the classroom functioning.

Children enjoy, love, learning to read, and this includes ELL students. I see no reason to withhold this pleasure from them. Since there were so many languages in the room, I couldn't teach the children in their first languages, but there are elements of reading in English that they could master while they learned the oral language, and the two aspects of literacy—oral and written—feed one another. They could work on vocabulary learning techniques, experience the feel of fluent reading and of comprehending a text, and could know how the language sounds and makes sense, and finally, they could learn to enjoy reading—all qualities that good readers need in any language. The children were proud of their ability to read, and so were their parents. I think of what I worked for and what the children achieved as learning to read, not learning to read English.

Figure 5.1: Abdulrahman and Elmer reading together

Chapter 6

Put Your Lives on the Paper

We begin writing workshops during the first week of school. "Bring some chairs here," I say one morning, beckoning them to imitate me as I bring a student chair up to the front of the room where there was a large screen.

The children gather on the squeezed-together chairs, looking curious. With a show of a mysterious something to come, I slowly pull out the overhead projector. They buzz with anticipation, and when I turn it on, there is an "Oooh!" of amazement. When I begin to draw pictures that evolve larger on the screen, the buzzing becomes exclamations and finally attentive silence as they watch what I begin to draw.

I'm illustrating a stay in Oaxaca, Mexico that I had in August with my husband. Drawing a series of pictures on the overhead transparency, I show our relationship with hearts and my rings, husband, and the sequence of our experiences with a drawing of the airplane, a few activities, and our return home, like a comic strip.

The drawings are simple, with a particularly poor airplane. As I draw, I relate what we did and add a few labels. They liked hearing that "We studied *español*," because at least half of them understand *español*. They laugh at some of the drawings, but their laughter is so contagious and good-natured that I laugh too and, in fact, I begin to encourage their humor. Maybe they'll believe that if I can tell drawn stories, they can too.

Shaping the daily events of their lives into narratives is the introduction to writing that has worked for me with my students, taking what seems ordinary and seeing the wonder of it. Ultimately I want to convince them that the writers' workshop period is a time of freedom and enjoyment and that their lives, dreams, frustrations and imaginations are valuable to everyone and can be communicated by writing. This is the only message I want them to remember from my teaching about writing. Especially I want to avoid facile clich in aphoristic form, like "show, don't tell," because I don't want to get in the way of what young writers might invent without these formulas, either now or as the adult writers I hope to nourish them into becoming. If I were a celebrated writer or highly trained writing instructor I might feel differently, but that's not the case.

If I succeed I will have a class that looks forward to writing and students who will want the skills to make their writing worth reading. I want the borders between work and play to blur as the pleasure of anticipated communication merges with the thinking, fretting and learning that are necessary to do it well. Perfection isn't the point, I want them to know, communicating ideas is the point. I give them the same message for oral language.

I pass out unlined paper next, and individually chat with the children about their drawings as they work. The pictures they produce today show that they understand the assignment somewhat, but this approach has its drawbacks as well. Many of the drawings are single pictures of their families smiling out from the page with no apparent narrative thread. For the next several days I repeat the modeling, illustrating personal stories with a few labels, encouraging narratives in their drawings.

"Your life is so interesting! Can I show the class?" I mime. When I read to them, I make connections whenever I can between the characters in the books and the characters who live in our classroom—the students and myself. I read simple memoirs and books to them written from the first person point of view. If we experience something unexpected or surprising at school, we write a group narrative about it. We start a class list of horrible, wonderful or mysterious events that we experience together. This was the beginning of a yearlong fondness for memoirs, and a habit of noticing details that could be eventful.

I Remember Somalia, and *My Life in the Mountains* were two memoirs that we read together later in the year. Without fail the children liked to see non-fiction books about their countries. They always had expressions of pride on their faces: they were the experts, and also, they revisited their pasts. Abubakar and Mohamed were proud to see the book about Somalia, to be the owners of the information.

"That's my Somalia!" exclaimed Mohamed possessively and proudly the day I introduced it.

"My Somalia too!" insisted Abubakar while Mohamed looked doubtful. I asked them if they could write about Somalia to let us know what it's like—

how it looks, where people live, what people do, etc. I suggest that they might like to work together and make a Somalia book for the class library. This was a fabulous writing and art project. They worked on it for three weeks and produced a book that told more about the spirit of Somalia than the book we had in class. It took some research because already some of their memories were growing dim. Abubakar had spent several years in a refugee camp in Kenya. Both Mohammed and Abubakar's parents were brought in as resources.

There are several reasons why I started writing instruction with narratives about families with my ELL students. One was that the vocabulary for family, *Mom, Dad, sister* and *brother*, was among the first the students learned every year, and so communication about the writing would be easier. Another was that all the children seemed to understand *mama* and *papa*.

"You can draw about your families. You can draw your mom, your dad, your sisters and your brothers...." *Mom* sounds a lot like *Mama* and *Ma* in many languages; *Papa* is a word I used to connect the concept of father since it's also common in several other languages. I thought the demands on their cognitive resources would be reduced by using these words. They would understand what I meant.

Another reason I encouraged them to write about themselves and their families was that at this age my students' world was still centered on family life. What their parents were doing was important. Finally, the family and what happened in the children's lives was an area where the children were the experts, and generally they had something they wanted to tell about it. This was their opportunity to share their lives and to reflect on them. As they focused on narrating their experiences, I thought they could be introduced to the challenges of written expression and might acquire the habit of looking around in their own environments for inspiration just as mature writers do, and as we modeled in class with our list and shared writings.

They enjoyed composing these picture narratives and gradually, as the early days of September were slipping into October, and as their English language and literacy grew, more words appeared on their pictures—some labeling and simple phrases. By October, they all knew the letter sounds and the letters in English. At first I nudged some of them during conferences.

"Who's this?" I asked Glenda.

"My brother."

"What's his name?"

"Ciro."

"Let's mark his name!"

"Okay!"

"How about 'My brother, Ciro. My mother, Anna, my father Carlos, my sister Laura?' "Okay!"

"Bdr." She wrote.

"Good. Listen. Br-o-ther. Do you hear anything else?"

"I hear uh."

"That's right! Put it in."

Brudr. She looked at me with a question on her face. She had started to read in Spanish before she came to the United States and had read in Spanish to me with good fluency. This would be a great help in her English literacy. I knew she suspected her spelling was wrong, and knew I'd better be honest with her.

"No, but it's close and anyone can tell what you mean. It does sound like /uh/," all this I communicated with a great number of hand and facial signs, nodding of my head, and so forth. Then I wrote "Brother" for her. She wrote "Ciro," and could spell all the names of her family members.

Once the children knew their letter sounds and understood basic English, I urged all of them toward more written language.

"You can make your illustrations after you have your story," I tried with Elmer one day, who had been spending entire periods on his drawings while many of his classmates at his level of literacy were writing little sentences and labeling.

"I make pictures first," Elmer explained without looking up, "then I write my story." Elmer had begun English last year for a few months.

"Well!" I said to myself. "Is he right? Should I leave him alone, encourage him to write? Inquire about when he thinks it will be time to write?"

I was pleased that he was taking control of his work and decided to follow the development of his method. He didn't know that he was ready to make pictures and stories with words, but I did, or I was almost sure. Better to leave room for doubt. I would keep an eye on him and keep encouraging him.

There were a few others who like Elmer preferred their elaborate drawings to writing, and as with Elmer, I was pretty sure they were ready to transition to written narratives. I nudged these children, as I had Glenda, to begin to add words. Most of them required only minimal encouragement to make the transition from drawing narratives to writing them, especially when their friends were beginning to read their written narratives to friends or to the entire class. This is what happened with Elmer.

Once they could put words on paper and understood what the words they wrote communicated, I began to help them progress from the writing they were producing to shaped narratives, from lists ("I love my mom. I love my baby. I love my daddy. I love my sister. I love my grandma," or, "I like Salam. I like Abubakar. I like Elmer. I like Abdulrahman. I like Etienne. I like Ivan," in some cases, day after day) to something that related an event or an idea.

At first they were delighted with their lists, proud of having produced text, regardless of its quality. Their pages looked like real writing, looked like the pages in their storybooks. Lists like these are commonly seen in children's early written work and are viewed as a developmental feature of their writing. Other students instead of lists wrote one or two sentences each with unrelated subjects.

Some, like Abubakar, for instance, wrote only letters. "I C 1 D." I saw one day on his paper. I was stumped. I asked him, trying to hide my puzzlement, "What is happening in your story?" He pointed to each letter and read: I C (see) 1 (one) D (dinosaur.)

"What an interesting story Abubakar!" I liked this very much, amazed at how much he could say with so few resources. He was enjoying the writing workshop and his enthusiasm wasn't dampened by his limitations.

On October 9 my conference notes show:

10-09: *He wrote "I C F I C 1 F"*

(I see fish. I see one fish.) Where and why did he get "fish?" Here my notes end, cryptic but helpful, at least to me. I was so curious about his unexpected vocabulary word that the next day I asked. To answer, he sang, "F is for fish, f, f, f." I thought I'd take an opportunity to nudge him a little further.

"Do you hear anything else in "fish." I emphasized the /i/ sound.

"I hear /i/ " he answered, and added it.

"I wish I knew more about that fish! Can you tell me more about it? How big is it? What color is it?"

"It big!" he said, ideas growing.

"Let's put it down! Do you want me to help you?"

Using the phonemic sounds again, with my prompting he wrote "its" (sic) and "big."

"This is so interesting Abubakar! You said so much! Are you going to make an illustration?"

He progressed steadily and enthusiastically. On October 17th I wrote in my notes about him:

10-17: *Writing numbers and ABCs. I explained that at writing time we write words, using imagination or writing about something real. I truly think he was figuring out what to do. Also may have wanted to see a lot of text on the page, or have been exploring what he knows.*

On November 6:

11-06: *Rather lost I think. We discussed 'What was your idea? Do you want me to help you?' 'Yes.'*

But, on November 20th I could write:

11-20: *Beginning to put sight words. Has ideas. We worked on putting more of them down, using sounds he knows.*

By February I wrote:

Beginning to write imaginative stories. Told me he was writing this one (My monkey) for publication.

The entry for March 19 says:

3-19: *Helping him give shape to a story, to plan it a bit and write from the heart; the truth.*

On April 2nd I wrote:

4-02: *Uses sounds, constructing a fiction story about his pets—2 monkeys and a cat and how he washed them.*

Perhaps he was inspired by *Mrs. Wishy Washy*.
And on April 30th:

4-30: *Has written a fine metaphor poem. Today he is recopying for publication.*

Looking back on my observations I recognize what a gradual process it was, the children's evolution from no writing to their final, fine ending point. It seemed rapid to me in the classroom, each child's new step a source of amazement.

As with all past classes, it was February before the majority of the children were able to speak with a conversational fluency that, although it included many errors, conveyed their ideas and flowed easily. In February as well, and no doubt related to their increasing language skills, their writing began to bloom. Like Abubakar, most of the children this year had a long way to go before they could become model narrative writers, much less invented-story writers, essay writers, math writers, and poetry writers, but the journey was exhilarating.

Although not easy. Perhaps at first the task of choosing their own subjects was too vague for six-year-olds—to locate out of the amorphous world of thought one thing to form into concrete habitation on a page. Certainly language had to be a factor: they had many experiences from which to draw, but they were experienced and remembered in other languages. Mixed with these hurdles was the fact that writing demands awareness of a reader and most of these young children were still developmentally egocentric.

In addition to their shared challenges were the children's individual personalities, backgrounds, degrees of family support, and experiences. They wouldn't all develop at the same rate or in the same way, and would be different kinds of writers. To accommodate their differences I had to teach them individually, some with their lists, others with one or two unrelated sentences, others without any idea whatsoever about what to write, and some who seemed born to write—all reasons why the individualized workshop approach was ideal.

Salam was one of those without an idea, so his conferences at first focused around finding one and later, developing it. The Iraqi son of two teachers, he could read and write in Arabic and was making rapid progress in English literacy. He understood the task for writing time, but couldn't find a topic that satisfied him. He had enjoyed making pictures of his family when school began, but now that more was expected, he was rarely satisfied. Perhaps I was asking him to transgress a cultural view of schooling by asking him to find his own idea, or a familial view, or perhaps it was his awareness of what adult writing is, and his inability to produce that level of perfection. I had to be sensitive with what I said as I tried to discover what he wanted to do and what he was thinking.

One day in early October he extended his hands into a gesture of puzzlement mixed with frustration. I knew that he demanded the best from himself and sympathized with him. I sat down and responded to his appeal with words and gestures, "How are you Salam?" He looked at me and told me what he was thinking with the frustration on his face. I patted his shoulder. He had one sentence on his paper, "I love my mom." I had met her. She was gracious and modern with a kind, intelligent face and deep concern for her children. He knew that we were talking about someone I could picture.

"Can you tell something more about your mom? Why do you love her?" This wasn't easy. Most children say 'She buys me things. She helps me.' Salam wasn't one for an easy answer, and although he was thinking, my question wasn't helping much. I tried something else.

"Can you tell us about what she likes to do? Is there something that makes her laugh?" He looked reflective and it seemed as if this idea might work.

I guessed that his cautious, rational nature impeded his early writing at least as much as any lack in skills and was revealed in his reluctance to stop worrying about making mistakes. Never did Salam disobey class or school rules, shout at anyone even under duress, behave selfishly or even childishly. He was exceptionally mature and wanted to know canonical standards and to conform to them. He was also an exceptionally capable student. With no one to tell him what to write or how to write it, there was no one to please but himself. Since his achievement in Arabic was advanced for his age, it must have been frustrating not to achieve the same quality in English.

He and I developed a list of topics together. This approach suited him. He used the list and alleviated his problem but didn't eliminate it. On October 13, one and one half months after his arrival in the United States, his portfolio writing sample was:

"I love my mom because she is make four me keic."

This brief sentence expressed a feeling and a true event, but he had spent thirty minutes on it, thinking about his topic, its spelling and how to write what he wanted in English. When I stopped by his desk to see how he was doing, he was experiencing neither fun nor pleasure, but frustration, puzzling over how to spell "cake" at this moment.

"If you put down the letters of how it sounds, we will know what you want to say. Isn't that the important thing? I have an idea. I can give you a list of words, and you can add words to it that you need or like. Then you'll know how to spell a lot of words." It was then that I was inspired to give everyone in the class the Dolch list of one hundred basic words for their writing folders.

He looked unsatisfied; he wanted "cake." I believed that if I gave him the spelling this time I would reinforce the idea of correctness over truthful content and so tried to avoid it. I helped him use the letter sounds to come close to his word, expressing sympathy for his feelings of frustration.

"Salam, mistakes are our friends; they help us learn. We want mistakes. Make a lot of them!"

I joked a bit but was utterly serious, and I knew he was familiar with the message since it was one I repeated all the time. Not surprisingly, it took more than one repetition for him to absorb it and to believe in it. In fact, it took months of repetitions, but eventually he understood and allowed himself to use best guesses on spelling and English.

"When you finish with your pieces and you want to publish one, you and I can fix the spelling together," I told him. "All writers need help with their writing."

This promise, given numerous times and modeled with other children, reassured him and finally bore fruit. Once he understood the editing and publishing processes, terms I used with the class, he gained confidence that I would indeed help him with the spelling and he began to write more fluently, but it was months later.

Even by February he wrote only this brief passage:

"I love my mom because she macke to me a cake and I ate the cake. Is good and my dad he came baq."

Not that he had been writing that same sentence for four months; he hadn't. But this sentence reappeared—a new cake? For Salam to write,

"... and my dad he came baq,"

was a victory, as was the elaboration about the cake. He told about something that had just happened in his life, and he had extended the cake story. But there was no connection to the sudden appearance of Dad in the story about the cake.

"Let me read this back to you Salam."

I read it, and without prompting, he recognized that the sentence about his dad seemed unrelated in the text.

"It makes me wonder; did your mom make a cake because your dad was coming back, or should you tell about your dad in another piece?"

"She make it because my dad came back. She make good food."

"You can add that. We don't know why your mom made the cake. What could you say?"

He mentioned several things and I read his text back to him incorporating his suggestions one after another. Then I left him to make his own writer's decisions.

On February 27 I wrote in my notes:

> 2-27: *Has understood the writing process! Wants to publish his story about playing with a dog. Needed an ending.*

However, he had many more fascinating stories to tell that were not appearing in his writing. By the end of the year he had made acceptable although measured progress, writing for his last portfolio offering:

> In Iraq there was no snow, only rain. When we came to America first it was spring. When December came I made a snowman and I slipped in the snow. I made a snow angel. Some time I don't like snow because is cold. Spring is better than snow and is fun to play.

I was satisfied with his progress. He had elaborated one subject and had expressed an emotional stance about his topic. His ending related to his beginning, and there was some nice complexity in his syntax. All elements were tied to one another. He may have been the kind of writer who would prefer expository writing as an adult. His written math explanations were nearly perfect—logical and clear. What I didn't see in his narrative writing, and what I had hoped to see, was pleasure.

Fortunately, there was other writing during the school day, especially math writing, that reinforced the lessons of writers' workshop and provided opportunities for children like Salam to write for additional, authentic purposes. The math program I used was a curriculum that focuses on understanding concepts through exploration, explicit teaching and student analysis. It hadn't been adopted by the school yet but would be. The students learned to write about what they did—how they found their answers, and what they found. They supported their answers. Because these explanations required a kind of narrative structure and the vocabulary of first, next and then, like their story narratives, my instructional work in math was a lot easier; the two writing forms fed each other. Guidance was required to make the connection.

"First we put the blocks together like...then we...." As Rosalinda spoke for her group, I wrote her oral narrative on a large sheet of blank paper, showing them how to transform the oral narrative of the day's math exploration into written form—early expository writing. Since these math explorations occurred daily, they provided more practice in writing for an audience; they had to share their results with other groups. Salam's writing in math was a model for the other students.

I arranged writers' workshop much like readers' workshop. The children had regularly scheduled conferences with me which took place after a short whole-class lesson about writing skills. For example, in a mini-lesson in late October I showed them how to add pronouns instead of repeating the same noun. On a large sheet of chart paper I wrote:

> "I love my mother. My mother is good. My mother helps me. My mother buys me toys."

I read it slightly exaggerating "My mother." A lot of you are writing these kinds of pieces. Does anyone notice anything?" I asked.

Jayson was the first to pinpoint what sounded odd.

"You say, 'My mother, my mother, my mother, all the time my mother."

"What else could we write?"

They looked as if they were thinking hard, but they couldn't find an answer.

"What do you think of this?" Finally I showed them,

> "I love my mother. She is good. She helps me. My mother buys me toys."

I asked Jayson to read it aloud to the others. He was quickly learning to read so I knew he would read these sentences well.

"How does it sound to you now?" They thought that it was better.

"Can anyone say what I did?" No one answered, but I resisted the temptation to tell them. I waited.

"You put 'she,' said Sara finally. I explained then about using pronouns for variety. They approved the change but I said, "I still don't like it." I frowned and read it aloud again, as if for myself.

"Can we keep thinking about this one for awhile? See if you find any ideas to make it better."

After this lesson I reminded the children who had writing conferences with me about replacing repetitive nouns with pronouns, and we looked at their writing to see if something they'd written would be improved with such a replacement. The short whole-class lessons rarely if ever were enough to make permanent changes in the children's writing. Their purpose was to establish concepts for future conversations and practice. Predictably, the use of pronouns appeared in only a few of their writings that day, but after several weeks of practice and coaching, with reinforcement in classroom situations, the use of pronouns became automatic for all of them.

We practiced the replacement of pronouns for repeated nouns several more days and then we returned to the first sample writing to re-examine it. The children didn't know how to improve it, but they did recognize that it could be better.

"Well, I thought of one thing that I wanted to show you. It's something that you could use in your writing. Watch." I wrote:

> I love my mother. She is good. She helps me and she buys me
> toys.

"Do you see what I did?" I asked them.

"You put 'helps me' and 'buys me toys' together," said Etienne.

I explained how I put two sentences together with and.

"You still have "she, she, she. Too many she," said Jayson.

"Does anyone agree with Jayson?" All hands went up.

"I agree too. Hmmm." I stopped to think. I didn't want to add another language element today... or should I, to credit their observations...?

"I know what to do. We'll leave these sentences up, we'll look at them again, and maybe we'll get some good ideas." I gave them an idea to ponder, "Sometimes writers change a whole sentence around or even all of the sentences in a paragraph...." I let my voice attenuate. We ended up with:

> "I love my mother. She is good. She helps me and buys me toys."

After several lessons on one aspect of writing I sometimes told them that I expected them to try this in their writing. "I think you can do this now, and I want you to try it," but usually I presented information and said, "You could do this in your writing."

I wanted to be cautious about corrections. I was afraid that I might cultivate away their voices or tighten the imaginations I wanted to loosen. I've realized that the ubiquity of Western culture's imprint on my life makes it impossible to recognize all its influences on me. Nor can I objectively identify all of my cultural assumptions. I keep uncovering new ones. I wanted my students to express freely what came from their lives and cultures, not mine. I believed that if I interfered too much, in spite of my best intentions, my culture, my point of view would be speaking as well.

Since I couldn't possibly know all about each culture represented in my classes, I've decided that the only way to avoid imposing my background is to locate and examine my assumptions, to suspend judgments as much as possible, and to learn about each child with every encounter. I try to keep unbalanced in a way, or to maintain disequilibrium, searching. I tried to learn about their intentions in their writing, what they wanted to do. It took me several years of concentrated effort to learn to listen so carefully.

The very act of my note-taking reminded me to remain alert to clues about the child's unique learning and helped me to contain my culturally based impulses. I carried a binder with a section established for each student. I could take notes during conferences and keep reminders there for the students and myself. The students participated in the note-taking as well, and had a folder where they could keep notes of their own. My notes were an excellent source for reflections and served as a record of students' progress over a year. It is heartening to see how they change from:

Learned to write from left to right.

to

Today Salam started a story about a castle. Found the idea without help.

After surveying several years of notes I've become more optimistic about outcomes—the children make surprising progress during a year often with unpromising beginnings. I began to have more faith in their possibilities for growth. It's never a fast process.

I often think that I never did find the limit of their capacity to learn in the first grade. So often when I thought something was too challenging for them, they learned it, as they did with metaphors for instance. I was able to teach metaphors and similes in late March because the children's language and reading abilities had advanced enough to grasp the ideas. Afterwards, they were able to recognize metaphors in literature and in a play they saw at school.

"A metaphor! He just said a metaphor!" Abubakar shook my arm excitedly. He was right, too. I was astonished that he was able to understand so much oral English, enough to notice a stylistic feature. The key to teaching a challenging concept was to find a way to present it that was accessible to them. And there are real limits, limits of time for practice, time to develop a topic deeply, and time to link a new concept to an old one. We began so humbly.

"Write it. Date it. Share it with a friend."

These three requirements comprised the first writing checklist. The requirement to "share it with a friend" helped them to understand the concept of audience and of making writing comprehensible. In addition, they learned the English words for *share, checklist, day, month, year,* and *date.* They learned from reading to a friend that they sometimes left out words they thought they had added, or transitional links that were necessary for meaning. Thanks to the habit of reading their work aloud, later in the year I could ask them to read it aloud to themselves alone to see if it made sense.

Sara was a child whose writing was probably influenced by earlier experiences. Her mother told me that she had had a miserable first year in another school in a mainstream English class. "The teacher didn't like her and always complained about her." Her English was at the most beginning level when she entered first grade in my class, despite her entire year in a mainstream English classroom, and she seemed afraid that I would criticize her for something—she was guarded about the most innocent activities, generally those she initiated without permission. It took months to persuade her that I wanted her to think for herself, to convince her that she was in charge of her behavior and its consequences, and that I liked her and had confidence in her.

Her writing mirrored her expectations about school: It was banal and unexpressive despite the imagination suggested by her inventive behavior with friends. Sara was always up to something and cautious to see if anyone (the teacher or a tattler) was looking. I wanted to see this dissident imagination on paper. The blank page, I hoped Sara would discover, was the very place where she could, should, test what her imagination invented or write her darkest thoughts. I wanted her to consider writing as an outlet for her spirit. Without trust in the classroom, Sara wouldn't learn to write at the expressive level I dreamed of for my students.

She began with the drawings of her family, smiling and holding hands day after day. Sometimes a friend would be among the family members, or a puppy. When she transitioned to writing her stories, at first they were the lists:

"I love my mom. I love my father. I love my brother."

I knew that Sara had a world of ideas to relate and needed to be nudged beyond her lists and repetitive texts.

"What a good family you have! You could tell more about one of them. What do you think? Could you pick one person in your family and tell us about that person—what they like, what they do, the funny things they say—would that be interesting to write?"

This suggestion worked for Sara. She wrote:

"I love my mom. She is good. We have a dog. The cat plays."

Very slowly, after weeks of writing about her family, slowly learning to eliminate irrelevant details, and add more about her topic, she began to broaden her choice of topics. She started to write about flowers, toys she liked, and about friends.

One day when the other girls in the class, all four of them, were shunning her for something she'd done, she wrote about it during writing workshop. Right or wrong from an educational viewpoint, I reacted to the content of what she'd written.

"They're doing this!" I said, troubled. "We need to talk to them, don't you think?"

Then I tied her writing to the fact that it was providing a format for our discussion about what she had done and what she could do to resolve her sad situation.

"You see Sara? You wrote the truth; you wrote something important and now we can talk about it." I called a lunch meeting with all the girls to discuss what was going on. It turned out that they were very upset; they could think of nothing else. I seized the opportunity.

"Why don't you write about this during writers' workshop? Then we can talk about it."

The next day's writers' workshop produced lively pieces about what had happened. We talked about them at lunch again, and I asked them if they'd like to write about solutions for the next workshop. This was a highly success-ful writing project for these girls. Quickly, with the requirement to solve the problem together, they, including Sara, forgot their resentment and gathered to-gether to discuss solutions. As long as they whispered the class agreed that the talking would be a good idea; they should talk before they wrote their ideas.

The kind of bullying girls do to one another is quiet and not physically dis-ruptive to the class. It's invisible because little girls will suffer in silence. They seem to feel that they've lost face when they're rejected. If I consider the sad-ness that girls' shunning causes, and how it interferes with a child's learning, feelings of self-worth and concentration, it's as disruptive as a physical fight for that child, and thus immensely important. I won't allow it in my classroom. I do want to handle it in a way that will teach the girls and not vilify them. The writing and talking were what this small group needed.

Mufdi's writing development presented another kind of challenge. Because he had never been to school, his writing was slower to blossom than many of the other children's, although once it did, he became an enthusiastic, ever more prolific writer who never lacked for topics. Guiding Mufdi's writing concerned tactics to get him started and to bolster his confidence so that he could accept guidance. He at first wanted to be perfect right away.

As I review his portfolio and my observational notes, I can see that once he grasped the concept of print and the functions of literacy, his progress was quite rapid. He began with little squiggles, then strings of random letters as he learned to write them, and then the first letters of words he knew. Finally he advanced to simple but imaginative narratives, often about animals.

His early drawings were fairly developed for a child who was unfamiliar with pencils and paper—adorable figures with hair, circle ears, noses, eyes, arms and legs, smiling mouths and even necks, some of these unusual features more consistent with his age than with his status as a literacy beginner. Given his early misery in school, I was grateful for those smiling faces.

My notes on Mufdi say:

> 11-09: *Mufdi is simply putting letters on his paper, many let-ters. I tried to communicate what we do in writers' workshop as writers—communicate our lives, our thoughts. We'll see!*

On 11-29 I wrote:

> 11-29: *Showed him spacing, idea of writing own ideas.*

> 12-07: *Using his own ideas. Reiterated inventive spelling and spacing.*

> 1-09: *Writer's block. I got him going. Spacing.*

> 2-14: *Writer's block again. We discussed whether he might need a quieter place to work. When he moved he began working imme-diately.*

By February 21 he wrote:

> I see cat. We like it too. [the "too" was correctly spelled and had a period after it] We see dog. I have 1 cat and I have 1 dog. Do you see the pig? We do have a pig. I found a pig. Cats and kittens and a pig! My mom says this pig is funny rascal."

"Rascal" was a word he had read and copied from the book where he read it, using the text as a resource. I attributed his growing skill in writing to his prodigious reading and attentive listening in class. The fact that he could mention the cat and then refer to it with the pronoun "it" showed impressive linguistic growth as well.

2-28: *I asked Mufdi to add more details and to read it to me.*

On May 4 he wrote:

> I love my monkey because he is funny monkey and I know his name. His name is Apera. He is saying "Ouaa." When he get up to the tree next he said "Ouaa."

This story is fiction, a fiction that evolved out of personal narrative writing. He is still the protagonist, but he has imagined himself in a situation he thought would be interesting. His final portfolio offering, was:

MY TREE
I like my tree. He gives me much treats and we got no apple, he got an apple to give us. Next day we found the tree knocked at the door and he give us an bubble gum. Then I go out and tell my tree: Are you going to buy the thing and he said yes.

It's hard to explain completely why I liked and still like this story so much. In part it was that I loved the way he personified his tree, the way he appreciated that apples are treats from a tree, and that his story has cohesive elements that reflect growing skill with the craft of writing. But it's greater than that, and I think it may be because it's so easy to imagine Mufdi in his story. It's so much Mufdi's spirit, which turned out to be drole, kind, sensitive, and full of understated humor. It was evidence that he had adapted to the class, seemed at ease, and was on the path to a literate life. He ended the school year as one of the top four readers in the class. With his love of any literacy act and his exceptional spirit, I wouldn't be surprised to learn that as an adult he had become a great leader, a wise man or a respected teacher at the highest level.

From one of his writings I learned how his family had fled to Egypt from Sudan. I encouraged him to take it home to show his family, not sure that the information on it was something his father would want to become public, but sure that he would be proud of his son's progress. That day he had so much to tell, about how his father:

> 'Put on his white clothes and went back to Sudan to be with his men.'

The words filled the page, ideas tumbling out one after the other, English syntax often so mixed that I couldn't be sure of what he meant, except that he had managed to tell his true story. I'm not sure he intended an audience for this—it was like writing to understand and remember, or to give form to something lurking in his memories. Although I coveted this piece for his portfolio, I sent it home to his parents. It belonged to his family's life.

Once the students were writing personal memoirs and understood the ideas of beginnings, linking ideas in a text, telling a story and having some sense of ending, they were ready, I thought, to be nudged toward another genre, writing from their imaginations, or fiction. Some of them—Jayson, Etienne, Derek had already taken this step. To my daily writing message to them: "You can write anything, whatever you think or dream. When you're angry, put it on the paper. When you're happy, write about it, I added, "Whatever you imagine."

As I read stories aloud the children reacted emotionally to them, laughing, crying, frowning and commenting. I tried to show them that they could write such stories, that writing is real communication and efforts to make it excellent bear desirable fruit: readers will like your stories. Although I hoped they would embrace fiction writing, I believed that the more important message in first grade was to think of their writing as their own project. I wanted them to be writers, people who wrote for their own purposes.

Some of the children were full of ideas for invented stories. For others, expository writing was the greater pleasure, making the writing efficiently communicate something. I needed to expose them to as many kinds of writing as possible so they would be aware of their choices and so they could find the genre that best suited their objectives.

"If you like dinosaurs, you could write a story about dinosaurs. Then we could read them." "How did Dav Pilkey make us laugh right here? What's funny about this?" I asked, or for an entire week's mini-lessons, "Let's look at how this author started her story. Look at this! She started with what someone said."

And day after day I linked what adult authors did to what the children could try in their writing. These authors were my guides to teaching writing and to accessing the children's latent potential as writers. They were models for imaginative writing that stepped away from memoirs. They were models for good writing.

The story of the class's writing growth through the year wouldn't be complete without descriptions of the two champions, Etienne and Jayson. They were such enthusiastic, accomplished writers that they inspired everyone else in the room. When the class heard Etienne's partners early in the year react-ing to his stories with laughter or exclamations, many wanted similar reactions. Although Jayson and Etienne seemed to write for different purposes, Etienne to amaze the readers, Jayson to tell the personal adventure of visiting his imagina-tion, they had several similarities as writers. Both were early and enthusiastic readers, both of them understood narratives almost immediately, and both of them had lovely illustrations, descriptive and fully realized.

Jayson's writing had a narrative thread from the first day. He created sev-eral drawings in a story which involved a creature that was, as he explained to me in Spanish, climbing a tree to get away from a dinosaur, a dinosaur with the sharp teeth of a carnivore. I wasn't sure what the animal was that was climbing the tree—it could have been a cat or a lizard, but he had an involved oral com-mentary about what was taking place. By October 30 he had begun to include simple labels on his drawings. By February his writing had matured to compli-cated narratives that had discernable shape and related important events in his life:

> When I was in Salvador I was walking home. I see my friends
> and I walked. Next my friends kicked me. And the next day my
> friends started kicked me again. And my mother tell them "Get
> out of here. Or I will tell your parents." The End.

He began to bring in narratives and stories in English or Spanish that he wrote at home.

> One day I go to my first day at school. I was don't know English.
> I count the number. Then I learn more English. Now I am a good
> reader. Then I had fun learning. Then I learn more English. I try
> until I learn more English. Then my teacher help me how to learn
> more english. Now I know how to speak English.

And on the 25th of April he wrote this poem which included a metaphor:

> The moon is a banana
> It makes me want to eat it
> But is too high and
> I can't get that far.

The poem with a metaphor was an assignment, one of few during the year, but the choice and quality of the metaphor and its extended image in the poem were Jayson's. The third line "But is too high and" reflects a Spanish construction, "*Pero es demasiado. . . .*"

As for Etienne, his writing was the enduring point of optimism in his school experience. No matter what else was happening in his day, writers' workshop was a time of satisfaction. Everyone wanted to see what he was writing, and when he eagerly and confidently sat in the reader's chair to present his pieces, everyone listened attentively, prepared to be entertained.

He had begun the literacy acquisition process a little ahead of the others; he knew the letters and sounds in French, and could form letters. His first offering was a picture of his family with his parents labeled—touchingly in view of the sad evolution his home situation would take—"*maman*" and "*papa*." With his rapid growth in English, his early start in French reading, and his perhaps innate linguistic talent, his development in writing was rapid. My work with him focused on discovering what he wanted to do and helping him with it, organizing his ideas and increasing the suspense he wanted in his stories. In March he wrote:

> I go to a beach and I see a monster kill my grandma and he kill my grandma. I cry because she's my grandma. She's kill. She's kill. And I called the police and he kill the brother. Was bad. The police took my grandma. My grandma is old beautiful bird. Didn't cry a good grandma. I didn't cry. Good.

This writing has numerous undeveloped ideas and surely was emotional for Etienne to write. It is heart-rending and true, and I did not ask him to edit it. Before some of the writings my students produced I was silenced by awe, and this was one of them. It illustrates the role that writing can play for a person in Etienne's circumstances. I think it is beautiful with its metaphor,

"My grandma is an old beautiful bird."

In late May he produced this story which he edited and published as an illustrated book in the classroom:

> One day when I was swimming in Haiti, I saw a mean shark. The mean shark had a baby shark. When the baby shark moved up to eat me, I kicked the baby shark in the water. Boom! Then I saw an old lady. "Don't eat me!" cried the old lady. But the mean shark was sad about his baby and he ate the old lady. "Help!" He ate some children in the city. But a man saw that the shark wanted to eat them. The man pulled the shark out of the water (His drawing

shows a man in a boat pulling the shark out of the water with a fishing line.) The mean shark was dead. Then the afternoon me and the man were eating the shark. It was delicious! For a long time the shark was not there to eat anybody in our city where the children live with the magic man. "Ya! Ho!" They call his name Magic Man. "Magic Man" said the people.

And in June, this suspenseful, unedited story that he did not have time to finish:

Once there was a little boy named Jack, but the people call him red sun boy. One afternoon he wake up. Why he wake up? Why he wake up because he was going for a walk. There was standing a gorilla! Then the little boy look up. He didn't see nothing at all, but the gorilla was disappeared. Behind him was standing the gorilla. When the little boy looked around he saw a gorilla! The gorilla jumped on him. After that he take the boy to his cave. Then he tied him up. The little boy was afraid of the gorilla. When the gorilla got to sleep the little boy got escape from him. In the morning the gorilla wake up. He wash his eye. Then when he saw the boy was gone, he shout: you can not hide from me, little boy!

There are many promising features in this piece that show just how much Etienne enjoyed writing and its purposes. He read them to the class in tones rich with mystery and excitement, and his classmates, like me, responded with delight.

I loved all the children's writings, including the math writing. To me they represented not only the birth of just what I hoped to see in my students' writing—imagination, celebration of vocabulary, and the world through the children's eyes—but they were also concrete evidence of the language they had learned during the year. Many of the words I barely dared to imagine could become parts of their language in the beginning of the year: *bleak, escape, glimmering, joyful, fragrant,* were solidly present and appeared in their writing with the increasingly English-sounding syntax.

Writing was interwoven with the other literacy activities we did in class; each one reinforcing the others. If I had taught writing without the shared reading of stories, songs and poems, without the alphabetic instruction, the oral language instruction, the read-alouds, the shared writing, the children wouldn't have been nearly as successful as they were with their writing. But together

these activities showed the children what writing is and does, and that it is radi-
antly attractive as a subject of study. Countless times during writers' workshop,
when it was time to clean up, there were groans from children who wanted to
continue and I had to apologize and remind them of their good fortune to have
writing again tomorrow. Sometimes they couldn't bear to stop and took their
writing to recess to work on one of their ideas.

An important element in developing this excitement was the prospect of
sharing their writing with a community—friends, teacher and parents. Without
an audience, they wouldn't have been so engaged. Knowing that they would
have weekly conferences with me, knowing then that their work would be seen
and discussed regularly was motivating. Since my reaction wasn't predictable,
there was an element of mild excitement for them. I would tell them that they
could do more, better, or had made a wonderful improvement. The shared
nature of our work, where I was the enabler of their intentions, was very satisfying to them and to me as well. They always looked forward to the writing
conferences as much as they did with the reading conferences, both geared to
each child's needs.

The fact that they had intentions at all was a consequence of encouragement, having an audience, and having decided themselves what they would
write. The writer's task of choosing a topic became a habit; they weren't waiting for me to tell them what to do. Once again, their self-determination brought
motivation and unexpected learning. At some point in their school careers they
would have writing assignments, but it was important to start them off as in-
ventors of their own work. They would discover that writing is useful for many
purposes—to inform, remember, amuse, tell and frighten their readers—and
that the act of writing is a source of pleasure. Once they enjoyed writing and
saw themselves as writers, assignments could be understood as a part of school,
but not necessarily what writing is.

Starting with picture stories was an accessible way for beginners to enter writing, and above all, it helped nonEnglish-speaking, nonliterate children
learn about narrative structure right away, and to learn the purposes of writing: to communicate. They also started to understand the needs of readers, a
big step for many young children. As their speaking and reading grew, so did
their written expression. To help them glide into ever more complex writing; I
showed them how to put what they knew into written form.

ELL children are capable of learning many if not all of the broad concepts
in writing that native speakers learn, and they can do it well before they are
able to produce error-free English. Their thinking is more complex than their

language levels, and they are cognitively able to grasp substantial ideas, able and generally eager. By no means should teachers be defeated by the lack of language fluency or feel unable to teach them before their English is communicative. I'm not saying that form should be neglected; I believe in teaching grammar. I simply question how helpful it is to the student's writing growth if they think the teacher cares more about the correctness of the writing than the content.

Some of the world's most esteemed writers, like Nabakov, Kafka, Conrad and others, wrote in second languages. The very fact of their outsider status in the language, their slightly nonstandard rhythm, syntax and word choices may have been among the very elements that made their writing so fresh. It seems wrong-headed to insist on form over content in writing when the writing of nonnative speakers can add so much to the language and its literature. They bring a new sense of the language, a fusion perhaps between English and their heritage languages. English thrives on such contributions.

Chapter 7

More Words

The activities of the first two months at school gave the children a good start in basic English. Our early literacy activities—the songs and poems, the repetitive stories, the predictable class routines with their predictable phrases—made a core of basic syntax and vocabulary understandable and available to the children for asking simple questions and communicating simple needs. My talk to them so far had been short, grammatical, and usually about concrete, present-time topics in sentences where the subject and verb have an unmistakable relationship to one another. I emphasized the content words.

"Me..." asked Ivan, looking toward the door trying to think of a word, Ivan a child with a wry sense of humor under the surface of his quiet demeanor:

"Yes. You may go to the bathroom," I answered. He smiled, recognizing the humor of not having said much, but of having communicated everything. That it was about going to the bathroom added an edge to this first-grade experience. Soon he, like most of the other new students asked, "Me, bathroom?" and then, "Me go...bathroom?" and finally, after several days of whole-class coaching, "May I go to the bathroom?" one of only two sentences I coached. Language that communicated was the goal, not correct grammar and syntax, not yet, and not for oral language in first-grade ELL. However, I made an exception with this sentence since I thought they could use it as a template to ask other need-oriented questions. This minor explicit instruction was part of the shared experience of language exploration. It seemed motivating for them, as if they thought, "Oh. I can do this," and they used it for all sorts of requests.

The functional words like *the, in, a, without* were largely missing from their speech and would be for a long time. So were the lower-frequency words of mature language users like *merchant, perform* and *fortunate*, and the many uses of the basic words they soon knew from their frequent use, like *give* or *go*. The less frequently used words were the ones they would need for future academic success—reading comprehension especially. They were the kinds of words I needed to introduce into our talk after this beginning stage. At first we would focus on the content words—verbs and nouns. Nouns were the easiest since most of them were tangible and could be explained with objects and pictures.

Compare my first-grade ELL students' vocabularies to those of heritage English speakers. My students knew from 0-60 words, with the majority of them at no more than 10. English speakers enter first grade with vocabularies that range from 2,500 to 5,000 words, and every year add about 3,000 more. To reach native-like proficiency this is how many words my first-grade ELL children students needed to learn, as well as the extra 3,000 per year so they could do well in their classes. I wanted my students to become competent users of English before they left first grade, with the ability to write clearly although imperfectly about a variety of topics, to read in English at grade level with comprehension, and to speak English so that anyone could understand them without too much strain on either the child or the listener. Then, I thought, they'd have a foundation for future learning at their grade level. Continued focus on vocabulary acquisition throughout their school years would be critical for their academic success.

They couldn't learn as many words as they needed in one year, but I intended to take them as far as they could go with words while I was responsible for their learning. The goals I had for them all required vocabulary enrichment. Beyond native-like proficiency in English-language use, large and varied vocabularies have been found to have a strong causal relationship with reading comprehension and, by extension, academic achievement. These were compelling reasons for paying attention to my students' vocabulary growth.

If I hoped to see them achieve a solid level of language proficiency, we would have to work hard this year, possibly more than some other students and teachers in mainstream classes. The key would be to have a classroom where talk was valued and encouraged—spontaneous, meaningful and urgent talk where words were needed. If I hoped to move their vocabularies to more advanced levels I'd have to set up these conditions.

In my experience, active learning lasts longer than strictly book learning. I mean that with active learning, and in my classroom that means projects that extend over several days or weeks, there are ample opportunities to reinforce concepts and language. Over and over the language and concepts are used for genuine purposes. An advantage for ELL students is that when words are used in context for genuine conversations, the children also develop a feel for the rhythm, and idiom of the words, difficult if not impossible to teach when the words are divorced from communication needs. With the repetition, concepts and language, especially vocabulary, have a better chance to enter long-term memory. I didn't want my students to learn something for a test and then forget it. That would have been a waste of time, which we couldn't afford.

With no time to waste, we would need to use the time we had with focused, intensive work, but that would only be possible if the children were engaged and motivated to learn. My students wouldn't learn through grinding out work given to meet my goals for them; I knew that. They would learn by being captivated by something, by wanting to discover more about it, or by wanting to master it. The "work" would seem like play and they would seek and retain knowledge because they needed it for their own purposes. Then the spontaneous talk would emerge from necessity. Then they would be focused and engaged, acquiring knowledge they wanted along with language. We couldn't have a classroom where I decided who would talk and when; as much as possible it would have to be the children who would decide that, talking as they needed and wanted for their own purposes. Those purposes would be to do their school work, if the work engaged them.

I had to pay close attention to their talk and recess choices to discover their interests. Then I had to figure out how to take those interests and weave them into activities that developed what they needed to know while making the classroom activities seem like their play—or even better. If things turned out as I hoped, they would be working hard, the work would be fun, they would understand and they would talk for important purposes. And their vocabularies would grow.

For example, I noticed that after rains they were fascinated by the worms that came out on the sidewalk leading from the playground. In science we were supposed to study landforms, erosion, and the creation of soil. Worms would fit into a study of soil, and I was pretty sure that an earthworm project would be exciting. Besides, worms are slow and controllable, and I had an educationally sound resource for information and activities. The chances were strong that the children would be motivated to talk to one another and to me. Explorations are hands-on, playful activities, and so is learning something surprising and unexpected. The work with worms could have the intensity we needed but with a sense of play, not drive or drudgery, and it had the potential to produce a lot of talk.

In addition, vocabulary instruction for such a study would seem natural because the new words would be needed and so repeated in varied situations for genuine communication. If they were inspired to talk about worms together for example, they would need the worm vocabulary. The repetition of words and expressions wouldn't be forced or out of context. That doesn't mean that all word learning would happen automatically. I would have to mine any project for the new words it would allow me to teach and use. I would need to continue the strategies of vocabulary building that I began at first, drawing the children's attention to new words and encouraging them to remember and value them.

These steps were very important. I was persuaded by what the research says about the importance of explicit instruction in vocabulary development, that it is particularly helpful for struggling readers and children who come to school with low vocabularies—surely my students, because they were learning in a new language.

"*Hoist* is a great word that you can use," I would say one day during an American History project. "It means to lift something up. Hoist the mainsail." Or, "Sail is what you do when you go in a ship that has sails. You sail. We will sail across the Atlantic Ocean, and we will use our sails." I ask the children to repeat the words, to feel them in their mouths when the words first appear, to count and note the syllables and spelling, and to enter them into their vocabulary notebooks while I or one of them puts the word on the board. Then when they talk about building a ship, with my model, they will talk about hoisting sails.

What's more, the science and social studies projects, because of their complexity, involved categories of words and their kinds, the words that are often not a part of ELL vocabularies, or that can be different among languages. The one word *dom* in Russian and Polish translates as both house and building, but in English these words belong in different categories and stimulate different mental images. Chicken isn't classified as meat in all cultures. These kinds of differences can cause lack of thorough comprehension in the oral and written language of new language learners. Science and social studies curriculums naturally elaborate such classifications.

There is some urgency for paying attention to this element of language when teaching ELL students because knowing categories affects thinking and how people are able to talk about their thinking. The category words and their subordinate parts thus affect students' academic possibilities. It's easy to forget that they could know *bird*, but not *sparrows*, *pigeons*, *crows*, etc., words and concepts they could know in their first language because of home experiences.

My answer was to pay attention to my students' speech, and if they consistently used a general term when a more specific one existed, I took it as an opportunity for introducing new vocabulary. The opposite occurred too; they could call any bird of prey an eagle, or a tent a house, using one specific word they knew to cover an entire category.

A useful strategy we had for elaborating knowledge of classifications in vocabulary study was to keep the new and interesting words together on the board in their categories as signs of learning. When useful new words appeared in a book or conversation, up they went, frequently at a child's suggestion.

"Is this an autumn word or a dwelling word?" It was challenging sometimes to make such distinctions, but I saw them pondering over the questions and was pleased to find one more area where critical thinking could be encouraged. In addition, the more we discussed a word, the more it was repeated for an authentic reason, in a memory-jogging context, and the more likely it was to enter into long-term memory. The more we discussed it, the more likely it was that the word's use in their oral and written language would have the rhythm and idiom of English.

One of the arguments for focusing on content-laden words like *hovel* and *scurry* to language learners before worrying about the functional words is that since they are already likely to know or have been exposed to the concepts in their heritage languages they can attach a new word to this already-familiar concept. The work of vocabulary building is a little easier with most nouns and verbs. They can see a picture or physical enactment of an action or thing and understand what it means more readily and in greater depth. Many times I heard an excited, "I know!" when someone grasped what I meant as I tried to demonstrate a word meaning. They knew because the concept was familiar, not the English word for it. These nouns and verbs are the words that convey meaning in statements and so will provide learners with broader prospects for comprehension and communication.

Other words, functional words like *the, however* or *since* are much harder to understand and their meaning is hard to communicate. They can't be explained physically with pictures and movement. They have to be heard often, and I think it is easier to memorize them in context. That's why I like to have the children memorize poems, songs and lines in plays. These kinds of words finally register in correct syntactical position. Abundant talk using new words accomplishes or reinforces the same thing and is one of the purposes for teaching science and social studies curriculum as a means for language building.

The children's curiosity about holidays presented a ready-made opportunity to exploit their interests to advance their education. I learned quickly that the hubbub in school that surrounded every holiday puzzled my students and made them feel left out of the school community, so I began to invent projects to teach them about these holidays, except for Christmas. The children's backgrounds were too diverse, the nature of the Christmas holiday too religious and commercial for me to figure out how to tell them about it, so I pretty much left it alone. It became a celebration of winter.

This wasn't always the case. Most schools avoid religious explanations of Christmas because of religious differences among students. I used to tell them about the secular Christmas—Santa Claus and the night before Christmas, a small tree, little gifts... leaving anything religious up to the families. Then one year, when the holiday break was over, a little Vietnamese girl, Trang, looked up at me from the carpet during the morning calendar activities and said with a mixture of disappointment and curiosity in her voice, "Santa didn't come to my house." Trang was short and sturdy with a round face and an open expression, a child who wanted to know everything we taught at school. She liked to talk to me and trusted me. Her eyes looked directly into mine, sure that I would have an explanation for her. I was seized by remorse and shame and couldn't speak for a few seconds, desperately searching my mind for something to say. What I found was far from adequate.

"I'm sorry Trang. I don't know what happened." I paused and asked "Did this happen to anyone else?" and two more hands went up. I talked to them until I felt they were all right, but that was the last year that I did anything about Christmas. I remain ashamed that I was so insensitive, that it didn't even occur to me that Santa might not come to everyone's house, but of course he wouldn't. The next year, it was winter that we celebrated, with snowflakes, decorated trees, and stories about snow.

"Who is Santa Claus?" someone asked.

"Some people believe that a man comes into their house one night and leaves toys for children. The parents make sure he comes." I repeated, "It's what some people believe, but not everyone. Do your families believe that?" Then I had some really interesting and valuable conversations, much better.

Halloween was another holiday that we began to ignore in school. I agreed, although I know that with its mystery and excitement it's one of children's favorite times of the year. The way our school had celebrated Halloween, with parties that involved eating too much junk food and a schoolwide costume parade that took hours and embarrassed a lot of children who didn't have costumes was unsatisfactory, at least to me and several of my collegues. I was always making up masks and makeshift costumes for our class. I couldn't justify the time spent at school, and started feeling frustrated by it.

Reflecting about it now, I believe that I probably could have invented some kind of project about costumes or, better, masks. The children could have made masks and paraded with them. Mask-making is global, or nearly. We could have explored the uses cultures make of them, the materials they used.... Too late now. At least the little readers' theater play we produced, the one about pumpkins, was a good use of school time given the language growth it produced.

After the apple project and the Halloween pumpkin play, the next project was about Thanksgiving. The project began when all around the school, including the cafeteria, commercial pictures of turkeys and pilgrims began to appear on the walls. In art, they were going to draw turkeys. In music class they were learning a Thanksgiving song.

"Why they put those pictures?" asked Derek, looking at displays in the hall, who noticed everything visual. I could see him struggling with vocabulary here, because his face showed the struggle before he gave up and said "pictures," instead of what was on the pictures. I could have answered, "It's for a holiday," but he wouldn't have had the answer to his question. Once he asked the question, other children in the class also wanted an answer. I began to plan a project.

The Thanksgiving project would be more advanced than the earlier ones because by the time we began it the children's language was more sophisticated and they were able to talk about ideas and nonpresent topics. Thanksgiving was full of opportunities to explore important and difficult social studies themes, cultures and their differences, as well as the more concrete academic subjects. Planning the project was greatly complicated by the actions of the pilgrims toward the indigenous Americans. It's a challenge to explain abstract concepts like dissimilar views of property ownership, justice and injustice to young children who are new language speakers as well, but I believe that Thanksgiving can't be taught without some recognition of these important aspects of history, and this was a history study.

So several weeks before Thanksgiving I made the children pilgrim hats—tall black hats for the boys and little white bonnets for the girls. I assigned each child the name of an original English immigrant, printed them on strips of paper and hung them around each child's neck with blue yarn laced through holes.

I asked them to pretend that they were pilgrims, and that they were in their own church in England. I asked them to pretend to pray the way that the English religious rebels prayed in those former times. When they didn't know what a church was, I drew one, and put my hands together. "I know!" Etienne cried out, pleased.

"I know!" exclaimed the Spanish speakers. Mohammed, Abubakar, Tamathor and Abdulrahman, all Muslims, also knew and were ready to play. They sat in a section of the room labeled "church" with their hands together to indicate praying. There they were, quietly and obediently showing Puritan prayer. Then I, with my crown and label "King" roared at them.

"Why are you praying here and not in the Church of England? You may not pray that way! We don't do that in England!" I was stern and spoke in an authoritarian tone. The children stared at me in stunned silence, not sure whether they should laugh or feel guilty, and cautiously they looked at one another.

"I am the KING," I said loudly and firmly, "...and I will not let you do that." I wanted them to have an idea of what a king is, and the kind of power that the position confers. I wore a crown. "We only let our religion be here!"

"You are going to prison!" When they continued to look at me, I ordered. "Go on! Get in that prison!" I had a sign, PRISON, hanging from the ceiling in the library. (Thank goodness they didn't connect library with prison.) Now some of them began to hurry to prison, ready to play, and the others quickly followed. Several tentatively dared to giggle. When I remained serious, they stopped. In prison they were silent, and looked up at me. I almost felt sorry for them.

Now I changed characters and became Ms. Stark for a moment.

"What are you going to do?" I asked them. The king won't let you pray the way you want to. You don't want to be in prison...."

"We will fight him!" suggested Ali.

"He has a big army, many fighting men, and he will win."

"We can go to his church?" asked Sara.

"But you don't like that church. You don't want to pray that way. You think it's bad. You like your way." My language was simple for their comprehension, and there were difficult concepts to communicate, concepts that I really wanted them to consider.

"We can build another church," said Jayson.

"The king won't let you. He doesn't want that church in England." The children are thinking, and I've led them a bit by saying "...in England."

"We'll go some other place!" said Etienne.

"Yes! We'll go somewhere else."

"Okay. Where will you go?"

"To Mexico!" Said Hector. "Mexico!"

"We could go to Mexico," said a few others, looking at me.

"Hmm. Yes you could. Some people did, people who spoke Spanish, but not these people. Look. Right here, on this continent, some English-speaking people already went there."

"To Vietnam" said Hung.

"To America!" cried Jayson. He had connected the school's holiday posters and today's lesson with the United States, which is what he meant by 'America.' He and Etienne were usually the first to make such connections.

"Ah!" I said. "That's what they finally thought too, because of the English people who were already there. Everyone was talking about it in England—'a new beautiful place' they said, but a scary and hard trip. But how will you go?" I paused to let them think.

"Look," and I showed them the globe again. "Look at all that water on the Atlantic Ocean. This means they have to go far, many, many kilometers on the ocean." I stretched my arms out as far as they could go, to show far. "How will they do that?" Now they were stumped again, but not for long. The connection of distance with the globe and the idea of scale may have been vague, they would study that later, but they seemed clear that it was far.

"We can get a boat," said Etienne. The other children looked at me with questions on their faces. They seemed to think that the boat was a good idea, judging from their expressions, but they wanted my opinion.

"It will take more than 60 days for this trip. What do you think?" I asked them. "Does anyone think that a boat would be a good idea?" They all agreed that it would.

"Well, you'll have to build a boat then, pilgrims." They looked at me. "Go ahead. Make a boat." They remained seated, looking at me, and I repeated, "Make a boat." As I said this, I spread my arms around to indicate the room.

"Make a boat?" asked Jayson.

"Yes, make a boat."

Etienne's eyes lit up.

"Make a boat? Come on! Make a boat!" he cried. He began to push tables. With eager cries the children joined him. He organized everything and everyone, assigning tasks. Jayson resisted his authority quietly, trying to follow his own ideas, but soon he recognized Etienne's command of this activity and followed along. They joined in the make-believe with no hesitation. There was an educational objective for this; it was good for them to solve problems they would have to define themselves.

"How will the boat move on the ocean?" I asked, looking at their ship. I let them think for awhile, but finally I showed them a picture from a picture book we had about the European migration to the Americas, and pointed out the sails on the ships of that time.

"These are sails, and the wind blows them. Then the ships move." I showed them this with a piece of paper I taped to a pencil and stuck into a small eraser, repeating the words as I worked. They talked among themselves about using paper, but rejected it because of how small the pieces of paper were that we had in class. Over and over they correctly used the words ship, sails, wind and others, in true English syntax and rhythm.

"Where's the big paper?" asked Jayson.

"Butcher paper?" I asked. The children nodded enthusiastically.

"I'll get you some. That sounds like a good idea. How will you get it up?" They didn't know, and neither did I, but I suggested the broom handle which was removable. I unscrewed it and gave it to Etienne. Cheers went up. I went to the coatroom storage area and found an old piece of yellow butcher paper I was saving—just what they needed.

Etienne, Ivan and Abubakar eagerly took the broom handle and hurried to the boat to fit it with a sail. They taped the paper to the broom handle using large gobs of tape everywhere and then with the help of nearly everyone, under Etienne's direction, they mounted the sail, plunging part of the broom handle between two tables that formed the front of the boat, adding more masking tape to hold it in place. The paper sail still wasn't standing opened out and they looked at it, dissatisfied. So did I.

"Hmm," I said. Suddenly I had an inspiration.

"How about a meter ruler; will that work?" I hurried to get two of them to show what I meant. Immediately Etienne seized them and gave one to Jayson. Ingrid and Sara were paying close attention to all of this and helped to tape the rulers to the top and bottom of the paper sail. At last they were ready to go across the imaginary Atlantic Ocean in our room. They had supplies and a fine ship.

I joined the passengers on the boat so I could help them imagine the voyage with whales, hunger, huge waves, a sick little child who might die on the trip, the diminishing food supplies often full of insects, the friends and families we were leaving behind, and our mixed sorrow, fear and hope....

"There are worms in my biscuits! Ewww!" or, "I'm sad," I said. "My mother and father are saying 'good bye.' " I waved at my imaginary mother and father. I looked around. "Is anyone else sad?"

"I'm sad!" said Ingrid.

I said. "Look! Whales! Here they come! Hold on to the sides of the ship!" It was a great pleasure to have a make-believe trip like this with the children. They entered into the game completely, leaving behind their 21st century selves, and I know from comments that they made to other staff at lunchtime that they learned even more than I had hoped from the day's adventure. One friend reported to me that she asked Jayson what he had done in class today. He answered, "We went to our church and the king came and put us in prison!" She said he spoke seriously, with an astonished expression.

"Then what did you do?"

"We make a boat and go away."

After this session, and each one, we had group discussions to give shape to the experiences and to find meaning in them.

"Did any of you leave friends when you came to the United States?" I asked. All hands went up and some children talked about some of the friends in their countries of origin. "How about families? Did any of you leave grandmothers and grandfathers when you came?" Again, hands were up all around. "Were you sad?"

"I was sad, and I was crying," said Rosemary.

"Was anyone else sad?" I asked. Again, hands were up all around.

"Maybe the pilgrims were sad and excited at the same time, and scared too," I said, to prompt some thinking.

Once in the new world, our pilgrims found no roads or electricity, no ovens, no cars, nothing to eat. . . .

"What will you do for food?"

"Aren't you cold?"

"What is the most important thing to do first?" They decided that they needed to build houses just as they had built a boat, shoving chairs and tables around to form them.

"What do you think you would use if you were really pilgrims in this place?" I asked, showing them prints of early paintings that depicted the American wilderness. The children concluded that they would have to use the materials in the environment, the trees and stones, and there was another opportunity to help them understand why homes look different around the globe. It was another opportunity to discuss the reasons for differences in peoples' customs.

I pointed out with pretend wonder some people in the forest who had a different way of living and who already were using this land.

"They keep looking at us." I showed prints of the first American residents as they had been drawn during the colonial period. "Look at our clothes and look at theirs. And our hair." I stopped to let them absorb the differences.

"We want to look at them too, don't we?"

"Do you think this land belongs to them? Can we build our houses here?"

"But can you build a house when some people are here?"

"Okay. We have guns, but will everyone live together and be happy if we use guns to get what we want? Won't someone stay angry?"

We explored many questions this way, difficult questions with the simplest language and conceptual frameworks. During the make-believe I brought up questions. After, when as a group we wrote a shared journal, we discussed them. I tried to communicate to the children that I didn't know every answer either. For example, I know that in human history, migration and land appropriation are usually violent and unfair, and I told them so, but I didn't think I wanted to promote these actions as acceptable, or to censure them either. I didn't and still don't know enough. I said, "Just because we always have done it, should we continue? I don't know. Maybe that's just how humans do things. What do you think?" I asked. Then I asked, "Can we change what we have done for so long?" These young children absolutely loved conversations about these important questions. All children I ever taught reacted the same way— intense interest and eager participation. I think it was because they felt their ideas were being heard, and they knew that these were important adult themes.

I regret that I can't quote all their responses, but I have a clear picture of them sitting on the carpet with me in serious discussions, and I remember the high quality of these discussions despite the early level of the children's English.

"I think..."

"Yes, but..."

"We're having a feast, but I'm thinking about my little daughter who died, and I'm sad. I'm happy and sad."

It was an obvious step to tie this project to the earlier apple orchard project of October. The children had already learned the vocabulary for planting and harvesting, autumn and other topics from studying how apples are grown. They knew that when seeds are planted, the harvest comes later. Thus they had the vocabulary and concepts to understand that if the pilgrims planted seeds, they might not have a lot of food to eat until their first crop was harvested. They figured out that the pilgrims might have to hunt, and would lack fruits and vegetables. When the crops were harvested the children held a small celebration in class.

The final product for this weeks-long project was a large chart-sized album with photographs of the children engaged in all the activities. In the album were typed copies of the class journal describing the experiences and what it was like to participate in them, including some of the ideas from the discussions. All of the Thanksgiving vocabulary was listed too, copied from the board: *fruit, vegetable, album, ship, sails, shore, plant, hunt*, etc, and under the category PLACES OF WORSHIP, we listed *mosques, temples, forest*, and others. Derek and Ingrid drew and colored a cover for it.

The project had included geography, reading, history, writing and reading and vocabulary development. Originally there was no math involved, but I had an inspiration to ask them one day when we talked about how the English arrived in the new world, how their own families had arrived—what means of transportation, for what reasons, how many were in their families, etc. I said, "Let's make a graph!" and we made a large, impromptu class graph of this information.

Another fruitful project, fruitful and fun, was the study of snails which we began in early spring. Who would think that anyone could become attached to these slimy creatures as if they were mammalian pets? That's what happened though. Each child had a snail. After measuring them ("Here, put the tail at zero, not one"), conducting experiments with hypotheses to see which foods snails preferred, staging timed races to see which snail was fastest, almost all of the children became fond of their pets. At recess they made them playgrounds, racetracks and block castles and then put the snails in them to see what they would do. During class they made them homes in jars after reading what snail qualities to consider for making a proper snail environment. The children made informational booklets about their snails, which included the drawn snail and its name, with labeled parts, food preferences, speed of movement, habitat description, measurements, and more. They named them and wrote stories about them, all of which they attached to their snails' abodes. Sometimes a few children would take their snails to sit with them while they read, for companionship.

Then they took them home.

"What did your moms say about the snails?" I asked them the next day at calendar time.

"My mom throw it away!" said, Ingrid, who had been particularly attached to her pet. "She say is yucky; not good for the house."

"My mom too," said Ali.

"Did everyone's mom throw out the snails?"

"My mom say my snail is good," said Jayson.

"My mom say is good, but for garden."

Sad to say, many of the snails weren't appreciated. The same was true of the earthworms.

Before introducing the children to the worms, I took them outside to a concealed area of the school yard and asked them to scoop up a half cup of soil. Inside again, I gave them handheld magnifying lenses and asked them to write down, with a partner, what they saw, and to put the objects in small waxed paper baggies, labeled and taped to a piece of butcher paper. They were supposed to find out what soil is, what its component parts are, and they found results that surprised them. They thought they knew already—dirt is dirt. Instead of "dirt" they found parts of leaves, insect wings or dead insects, small pieces of wood, pebbles, sand, trash, etc. They went around the room to see one another's discoveries and the room became lively with their talk—which included *soil*, *baggy* and other new words. Afterward we made a composite chart of what they'd found and discussed what soil is, noting the results on a large piece of chart paper.

With the project on soil, studying earthworms was an obvious and lively connection, a chance to connect biology with physical science. The students had brought in a satisfactory collection of large glass jars and the night after the soil investigation, I bought thirty fat earthworms from one of the local bait stores. "The fatter, the better," I told the owner. I brought in a large package of sand, a large package of potting soil, and a small, mysterious carton.

"I have a surprise for you today," I said, with a significant smile to give them a clue that the surprise might be something unusual. I brought out the bag that contained the carton of earthworms. Immediately they became animated and wanted me to tell them what was in it. I went to where Ivan was seated first, only because he was closest. The children were silent and watched, fascinated. Slowly, I reached my hand into the carton of worms and brought out one.

"Ewww!!" they cried with delighted revulsion. I put the worm on Ivan's paper towel. He sat back and looked at it, not sure what he wanted to do, although a little smile played on his lips. I went to his neighbor, Derek, who tentatively smiled a little as well, but didn't touch the worm either, and then finally controlled it carefully with a pencil. Next was Etienne who boldly held his worm in his hands and examined it with a handheld lens, showing off his fearlessness by talking loudly about what he saw. Ingrid seemed genuinely repulsed. Sara was too, or copied the friend she admired. When the worms were distributed and the children had had a few minutes to examine them with handheld lenses, I asked Glenda to pass out rulers and said, "Let's measure them."

Most of the children didn't want to touch them at first. "Ewww," was the reaction all around, while they physically recoiled. I helped a few of the children and it wasn't long before all of them were busy measuring. With the earthworms there were amazing discoveries to be had, even for me. I had a resource book to help with the exploration since I didn't know much about worms, and I had found a few nonfiction books for the children to study and read.

"Shhh. Listen to the worms. See what happens when they move." I put my head down to listen. "Wow!" I said. It was an astonishing discovery. I didn't know myself what they would hear, or if they would hear anything at all. The guide said they should, but my science results don't always coincide with what resource books say will happen. The children put their heads down to listen carefully. Scritch, Scritch, Scritch. The worms' feet made surprisingly loud scratchy noises on the pieces of paper. I was astounded along with the children that these feet that couldn't be seen with our eyes could make audible sounds. They seem so smooth.

"I hear it! I hear my worm!" cried an amazed Abdulrahman. All around there were similar expressions of amazement.

"If you hold your earthworm in your hands and stroke the belly like this," and I demonstrated, "my book says you should feel the *setae*, some little hairs." I brought out a large picture of an earthworm and showed the children the many tiny hairs that earthworms have and asked them to look for them with their lenses. They were also going to count the worm's segments and notice the clitellum. After examining their worms and watching their movements, they would draw and label them. Finally, they would see what earthworms do in soil. I explained that the material left behind the worms was called *castings* and was considered good for the soil.

The next day I passed out the large jars they had brought in and showed them how to make layers of sand and dirt. On top of the final layer, we put lettuce leaves and then placed the worms on top with the mix. We covered the top with aluminum foil and the children poked some holes in it for air. During this process they heard and used *layer, soil, sand, earthworm, sound, observe, jar* and other words many times, words that became part of their active vocabularies.

I put a list of 'earthworm' words on the chalkboard. I knew that the children wouldn't remember many of the most technical words, but they would know that animal parts could be named and studied, and they would have heard and used the scientific vocabulary of experimentation: *examine, determine, observe, conclude, hypothesis, observations*, and others.

As with the snails, they made informational booklets about the earthworms and wrote stories. They made graphs that illustrated the worms' preferred foods, which they discovered in one of their explorations. Would they eat peanut butter, or bread? Did they like bananas or spinach? They made hypotheses and tested them. The fascinating pathways the worms had made in the sand and soil-filled jars explained very vividly what earthworms do to our soil. By the time the project ended, the sand and soil were mixed, and the worms had eaten the lettuce leaves.

I sent the worms home. It sounded as if they horrified many of the parents, and they suffered the same fatal ending as the snails: found guilty of being disgusting and condemned to the backyard or the garbage. The children reported these results to me with airs of incomprehension and, once or twice, hurt.

Education based on projects needed to be explained to some of the parents, whose ideas about education were based on their own early experiences. They thought all school learning should come from papers and books, and that scores of completed and graded papers should come home every week. Our classroom, with its workshop approach to reading and writing, and the active learning with projects just didn't produce that kind of evidence.

That's why when the children worked on projects, I thought a product needed to be created—something that would reassure the parents and show them that their child was learning. The administration needed this reassurance as well. The worm and snail informational booklets were important as evidence, and also could serve as artifacts of the children's childhood if the parents wanted to keep them. Nearly all of the parents said something like what Ingrid's mother said, "I wish school was like that when I went."

Of the learning projects, theatrical productions were especially rich with the kind of learning opportunities the children needed. The plays were appealing because they combined art, music and fantasy; they appealed to our senses and our spirits as no other subjects in school did.

Other projects, although they could require one or the other, didn't combine them in this playful way, and other projects lacked the excitement and danger that plays had: they were performed for an audience. The plays were especially alive with opportunities for language expansion since repeating lines over and over again in a meaningful context created automatic language for later use.

"Tikki Tikki Tembo No Sa Rembo Ikka Na Noo Na Kanna Ron Tombo." I still remember that boy's name, and I imagine the children do too. *Tikki Tikki Tembo* is the name of a musical play for primary grades. I copied all the lyrics onto big charts before I gave them smaller copies for their poetry notebooks. Sitting together on the carpet, with their lyrics in hand and the charts before them, they wriggled with anticipation as they heard the recorded songs and learned that they would be performing this musical. Mrs. Vega and I were eager too, but with a few qualifications. Unlike the children, we knew how much work would be involved, but we also knew that the "work" would be a pleasure for us, and that the results with the children's learning would be worth our effort.

It is the end of April, and the children know enough English to tackle a piece like this—a major production and the last theatrical presentation we'll do. It is rich with opportunities for reading and vocabulary growth. Producing it will be a way to celebrate the end of a wonderful year, and share evidence of successful learning with parents. If we are going to put on a show we'll be proud of, we'll need to take some time, beginning rehearsals now and staging the production in late May.

The educational publisher Milliken in St. Louis, Missouri produces six of these musicals and I have three: *Three Piggy Opera, Three Nanny Goats Gruff*, and *Tikki Tikki Tembo*. I've used all of them, but I'm beginning to prefer *Tikki Tikki Tembo* over the others because its Chinese setting offers a chance to expose my students to a culture, time and place they generally don't know. By using it I can teach reading, social studies, geography, art, drama and music in an interesting and motivating framework. The children learn letter-writing formats when they write individual invitations for their families.

The play is based on a folktale about how Chinese mothers changed the tradition of honoring a first son with a long important name while giving the younger siblings short ones, to honoring all of their children equally, giving each a short name. As women still do in many countries, including some of my students' countries of origin, the mother in the story washes clothes in a stream, and the family gets its water from a well. These are valuable customs to explore, comparing and contrasting them with one another's experiences, along with the problematic nature of change.

In addition to the interesting cultural aspects of *Tikki Tikki Tembo*, the songs are completely enchanting, with tunes and lyrics that can be serious or funny, depending on the situation, and quite lovely. The theater package comes with a cassette and a resource guide with easy directions for costumes and scenery. It includes instructions for having a small band where some of the children play simple instruments usually made by the performers.

One by one we work through these songs, learning words and what they mean. The vocabulary and syntax are a step or two above what the children know, so I expect that work on this play will nudge them to a higher level of language proficiency. The melodies are so musical that learning the songs is easy once the words are learned. That's their secret; these tunes are slightly more sophisticated and lyrical than many songs for children. The only challenge is to help them learn to sing some of the notes beyond five tone intervals. It's good for them, and an important learning experience for careful listening and music appreciation.

The art teacher, Mr. Almon, is supervising the scenery construction during the children's weekly art lesson, and has even made the well. No one in the class knew the word for "well" before we worked on the play, but the marvelous one Mr. Almon made us was realistic looking and sturdy enough to survive numerous practices with multiple falls and rescues, so many that the word *well* was soon a part of their active vocabularies. During the children's art class he helped them make the background, using a picture from the teacher's guide.

"It says here that they lived in a mountain village with a stream, so we need mountains and a stream. Who wants to draw the mountain and who wants to make the stream?" he asked, showing the guide illustration one day as I stopped to see how things were going. He had repeated mountains and stream three times and would repeat it many more as they were being drawn. To communicate with him, the children were obligated to learn the words. I'm fairly sure that Mr. Almon didn't know how important his repetitions were, but since the situation required using the words many times, they happened naturally.

Our sets are extraordinary this year thanks to his direction and the children's inspired work. The costumes, for which Milliken provided illustrated instructions, were simple and easy to make, so easy that Mrs. Vega, the children and I made them.

We practice the songs during literacy period. Since learning the songs and lyrics involves reading, I substitute them for the poems and songs we usually read together before independent reading and conferences. Milliken suggests not over-rehearsing and I knew from experience that this was right—too many rehearsals and the fun is gone. We will have no more than three whole-group stage rehearsals, but many more individual scene studies that involve two or three people. This is necessary if we are going to have a high-quality show because like everything else the children do, in order to accomplish anything, they have much more to learn than native English speakers.

It is May 27, the day of the performance. Early in the morning, before anyone else is at school I go to the auditorium to make sure the set is ready. It looks marvelous and all the more beautiful for being an obviously school-made project. Mr. Almon set up the well several days ago so Jayson and Etienne could practice falling into it, and last night Mrs. Vega and I got a ladder from the custodian and pinned the background to the backstage curtains. The river is a long stretch of blue crepe paper strips that run from the butcher-paper background to the front of the stage. Mother will do the wash here and sing her lovely solo. We also have a big freestanding tree made by Mr. Almon because Abubakar, the old man, has to lie under a tree with his strange cotton beard (we cut out a beard shape and glued cotton balls to it, with strings for tying it around his head) and snore while someone tries desperately to wake him. The chorus in the meantime is singing the snoring song, one of their favorites— "Snore, this" (chorus snores loudly) "Snore that" (chorus snores loudly again). Although I'm not performing, I'm beginning to feel queasy and excited.

The children come to class this morning barely able to do anything but talk about the performance, their hair and faces shining for the important day. A month ahead of time they wrote letters inviting their parents, many of whom are coming; they need to know at least a month in advance if they are going to come. After the performance there will be a reception for the actors with homemade cookies and sparkling apple juice that we'll set up after lunch. The children will learn the word *reception*, and will experience what it is.

I go to the cafeteria early to bring them up from lunch. They expect me, and when I arrive at the cafeteria door, their anticipating eyes are already looking in my direction. They cry, "Mrs. Stark! Mrs. Stark!" and are all ready to leave. Somehow, in spite of their excitement, I get them through the halls to our room in relative quiet. In the classroom they're a little noisy and focused on the party and their parents' predicted arrivals, but with my reminder they put on their costumes and help me set up tables for refreshments.

Meanwhile, Mrs. Vega goes to the auditorium to reserve the first two rows of seats for parents by putting up a sign "PARENTS." At 1:30 I steal away for a quick look and see that in noisy irregular lines classes are beginning to enter and sit down. My students' parents, mixed with the school population are hurrying in, many carrying babies and holding the hands of preschoolers. They stand out in that rush of young students in the halls, but like their children they look eager and dressed up for the occasion. Some of them recognize each other by now and I can see them greeting one another. There is a loud, animated buzz in the large auditorium space. The principal steps up to the microphone and prepares to settle the students and remind them why they are here.

The children line up at our door in correct order for the performance and out we go, to the auditorium and through the stage entrance behind drawn curtains. I walk down to the proscenium to direct the music. When everyone takes their places, trying hard to be quiet, Mrs. Vega pulls the heavy chord to open the curtains and the show begins with a choral song. The children look at me full of excited anticipation and I raise my hand. In perfect, poignant unison, they sing.

The performance is a huge success—sensational I think, and so do Mrs. Vega and the children. Parents, friends and relatives came and so did most of the classes at school. Abubakar was hilarious as the Old Man with a beard who finally wakes up and hobbles to the well to rescue the two brothers, and Sara a triumph in the role of the mother with a long aria to sing. Getting rambunctious Abubakar to slow down and hobble was a real victory. *Hobble* was another word that became very familiar by the end of this production.

"No, No Abubakar! Too fast! You're an old man. Your bones hurt. Ow! Ow! You *hobble*. You're slow. Oh, it hurts to walk." He can't resist clowning, and has an irrepressible sense of humor, so rehearsals were times of constant high spirits and laughter. The audience loved him today.

Etienne and Jayson handled falling into the well with aplomb. Although we practiced a lot on this part of the play, the moves never did become completely reliable. There was too much involved and there were too many possibilities for mishaps. The boys had to step onto a chair hidden behind the well, and then step onto a chair in the well, on cue, to stumble and fall realistically while in perfect control, and finally to crouch down, hidden for several minutes.

"Etienne! We can see your head!"

"We can still see it!"

"We can still see it!"

"Stay down Jayson! You're in a well."

"But I can't see the play."

"Okay. Watch this time, but tomorrow you'll have to stay down."

"We need two people to hold the well or it will keep moving."

Because we know these two boys and what they had undergone and said during rehearsals, for the other students, Mrs. Vega and me, their performance was a triumph. When the big day came, despite all the potential for disaster, they were solid performers. They overcame a moving well, a chair that was turned around and someone who altered a line. They were so flexible about adjusting to unexpected snags that for the audience, the boys fell into the well without a problem.

At the reception hugs and kisses and happy faces were everywhere, and the children were rightly proud of their work. They performed beautifully—watched my signals for group singing, bowed together, remembered their lines, and helped each other when something went awry—and I was proud of them. Abubakar's mother and her friend kissed him and laughed and laughed with him as he provided insider details about his performance. They were happy with him.

Only a few of the children's parents didn't come. As always, their children's faces showed combined disappointment and their attempt to act as if it didn't matter. I wonder sometimes if parents know how important they are to their children, or the importance their attendance at events like this has for them. Not everyone can take time from work or bring a newborn to a school play, we adults know, but when so many friends' parents and family members do manage to come, very special explanations are needed for children when someone can't.

However, they seemed to recover from their disappointment and were soon busy with friends. The school day was almost over and when parents began to leave, some of them taking their children with them, I gathered the remaining children together with me on the carpet. We talked for a little about the fun and how the audience had loved them, and then I pulled out a book to read to them before they left, *Tikki Tikki Tembo*. There was no problem with understanding this story, that's certain.

At the end of a year like this, it was easy to teach and talk to my students. They could understand nearly everything I said without the gyrations and extraordinary measures I needed nearly all the time in the beginning. It was still important to check for understanding when I read stories or talked about an unfamiliar subject, but for general conversations, communication had become easy. As I had hoped in the beginning, there was no undo strain on most speakers or on the children as they tried to speak to each other in English.

I had focused on vocabulary growth in teaching English, vocabulary growth supported with nearly constant opportunities for the children to talk for real purposes, not in contrived discussions about food, clothing, occupations, etc. The vocabulary for these traditional language-teaching areas had evolved with normal classroom talk, but was included by design in the day's seemingly casual conversations. "I like your skirt Rosalinda."

The comprehensive projects in science and social studies, the plays and readers' theater, combined with the weekly poems and songs had had a perceptible impact on the children's reading and oral language fluency and understanding; they used the expressions and syntax from the learned texts in their oral conversations and writing. Once they knew new words, they plugged them into the syntax of memorized phrases and used them to put English to work for them. Extraordinary, useful and odd words had surfaced, and accompanied by common words, they would help the children understand the increasingly complex texts they would read in upper grades.

To encourage vocabulary, language and subject learning all at once, the use of many-faceted projects was a treasure in the strategy coffer, a way to extend the focus on language and literacy throughout the day while assuring that the children could still learn the important concepts of the sciences and humanities. The hard part of this process was to develop projects broad enough to include several disciplines at once and to teach complex subjects to children who spoke so little English. Since so much had to be learned, a lot had to be included to make the most of precious time.

The solution was to emphasize main ideas and, although including them, not to worry too much about the details. It took research and study of the district's new curriculum guides, distillation of the overall objectives for mainstream first graders, and research into the subjects themselves. Even though increased work was involved, I found it made my job more interesting. I had to think about how to bring subjects to my students, but also thought more deeply about the subjects themselves. I rethought the settling of the Americas, the formation of the Earth's surface, and the connectedness of living things on the planet. These explorations were thought-provoking, and my deepened knowledge made the teaching easier and perhaps more interesting to the children. I could answer more of their questions.

Words not fancy, but not plain either, words like *merchant, escape* and *encounter*, are keys to a life that goes beyond survival to participation and contribution. With them people can appreciate what they read and hear, and can describe their experience of life so that others understand. Exposing children to a wealth of words is in part an effort to give all children a chance to do this when they become adults. If they choose.

Chapter 8

Etienne: Our Lives in Stories

"Rat had a best friend named Possum. Rat and Possum did everything together..." I read. The illustration showed Rat and Possum looking serenely happy together in a junkyard—I had explained junkyard before starting—and from the minute I began reading the children's eyes were riveted on me and on the exposed pages of the book. I read further. Possum had to move to a new junkyard and Rat's life sadly changed.

"This reminds me of my own life!" I said to them. "When I moved to Kansas City, I had to leave all my friends and it was hard for me. Was it hard for you when you came here? Did you miss your friends too?"

I invited the children, seated on the carpet, to turn to their nearest classmate and talk about how they thought Rat felt, and why. These smaller conversations would lead afterwards to a whole-class discussion about how they felt when they moved to the United States. This was one of four daily read-alouds, one of which was always like this, a read-aloud whose primary purpose was to stimulate thoughtful conversations about literature. Stories, the children's true stories and the authors' invented ones, would be the foundation and cement of classroom life this year.

At the beginning of the year when I read I rephrased passages whose syntax and/or vocabulary were beyond the children's language level. Although it's possible to find storybooks with elementary language and complex topics, they're rare. Rather than settling for mediocre literature that they would easily understand, I preferred to make a great yet linguistically complex story accessible to my students by simplifying the language as I read. It wouldn't be too long before they could understand without so much paraphrasing, and some stories were just too fine for them to miss before then. Besides, a great conversation requires a subject complex enough to sustain exploration.

There were many reasons why this was one of my favorite parts of the day. Literature discussions could foster the children's critical thinking and reading comprehension, encourage their enjoyment of reading, and show them how to plumb the depths of a piece for meaning; I could literally see their skill as thinkers grow, and this is deeply satisfying. The authors of these stories were excellent writers who also served as models for the children's writing, another advantage for the literacy focus. I tried to choose stories that would lead to discussions about tough or fascinating topics, topics that sometimes mirror the children's own life situations. Etienne, one of our most gifted writers, would soon present us one example of this, of life and fiction coinciding. Well-written children's literature was critical to this complex process.

It was late October, and after nearly two months of school the children were speaking English well enough to communicate their needs and thoughts at a basic level. They were creative with the words and phrases they knew and uninhibited about using them. To promote their language development, I planned situations in our class life to encourage intercultural friendships; they would need to use English to make friends.

With their growing friendships grew curiosity about different ways of living. Abubakar's sister's veil, Vinh's desperate kowtows, Rosalinda's pink and lavender clothes—these differences originally caused a reaction of wariness and rejection, but now that they had experienced such differences as interesting to explore, they were fascinated when a new cultural element appeared in the class or in a story. Once they understood, they paid little or no further attention to them, focusing instead on what seemed more important, making a friend. Story time was perfectly designed for promoting language in addition to its academic goals, cultural understanding and friendships.

The story of Rat's loneliness and need to make a friend echoed the children's circumstances as new immigrants. When his best friend moved from the junkyard, Rat withdrew from its other residents, responding to their invitations with insults until their attempts to include him ended. He was making himself unhappier by the moment until a new resident, Dog, moved in. Dog was as lonely and defended as Rat was—hiding his feelings by acting gruff and independent. This story was bursting with topics of deep interest to the children, and they were eager to talk about them.

As I read, I tried to ask questions that were open, and that wouldn't lead the students inevitably to my personal conclusions. Part of the approach was to speak aloud all the processes of my thinking as I read so they would learn the thinking processes of a master reader. By this time in my teaching career my tendency to manipulate answers was so ingrained that to avoid the habit I began to preplan my questions. If I carefully crafted them beforehand, I could avoid wording that revealed my opinions and I produced more thoughtful questions. Since I liked to limit my questions to five or less to maintain the flow of the story, the questions needed to be pithy.

"Why does Rat want to be alone?" I read from my post-it reminder on the page, looking genuinely puzzled. Or, later, "Rat looks miserable, doesn't he?" or, "Oh! Rat is moving closer to Dog! What is going on?" I asked myself aloud, as if I were alone. I stopped to think silently about this question. "I think I didn't understand something there." I turned to the children. "Did this part make sense to you?" None of them raised a hand. The passage, syntactically complex and beyond their level of English comprehension, was one I had marked for examination. I suspected beforehand that they wouldn't understand it.

"Let's go back and reread what happened before this. Maybe that will help us." I reread and then read the difficult passage phrase by phrase.

"I know! Let's close our eyes and imagine it! Each time I read a part, we'll see it in our minds and add it to what we already saw in our minds."

"Did you see dog?" I asked. "How did he look?"

"His head was down," said Brenda.

"He did this," added her buddy Rosalinda. She mimed shivering.

"He was shivering?" I gave the word for it. She nodded.

"I'm not sure I agree with this illustration for these words, do you?" I reread the words to them to let them consider how they would have drawn it. I could have stopped here to let them illustrate the passage—maybe later. I didn't want to interrupt the engaged listening this story had inspired. As I read and talked aloud, I turned to them with a question on my face.

"Do we really need friends?" "What do you think?"

Up went two hands, then one more. I enjoyed having them examine standard assumptions like this one about needing friends. Even if they agreed with it in the end, at least they would have looked at it and learned that such assumptions could be questioned.

All serious responses would be considered. They had to understand that their ideas were important if they were to be confident about offering them. I promoted the idea that book talks were a gathering and consideration of various ideas, that together we sought an understanding—either we could form a consensus or agree that we would have different interpretations. A small idea could grow into a fabulous insight with tweaking in a discussion.

"We're workin' hard!" says Jayson enthusiastically.

I wanted them to understand that for some problems our group brain could be larger and more creative than our individual ones working alone, and I wanted them to be familiar with the labor and satisfaction that collaboration could produce. Also, the questions the children and I asked in the group were the kinds of questions I hoped the children would learn to ask themselves when they read alone. Nothing could have explained the process as vividly as Jayson's observation and the pleasure with which he made it.

I repeated Sara's question. "Did you hear what Sara said? She said...." Repeating a question in words that the children could understand and hear was a technique that I often needed to use to guarantee everyone's participation.

"Does anyone want to add to what she said? Do you agree with her?" Once they understood that collaboration was a tool for finding answers to difficult questions, they stopped feeling diminished when someone had a different idea from theirs.

At first the process depended very much on my facial expressions, on what I said, and how. Even one slip and we could lose a child's responses for several weeks. Later in the year when the children assumed responsibility for most of the discussions, the process depended more on how the children reacted, but by that time they had been trained to have civil discussions and I never heard them belittle anyone's contribution.

It took me some years to find and develop a read-aloud approach in harmony with the way I thought children should be educated. I wanted their minds to remain opened to possibilities, not deadened by constant direction. Above all I wanted them to think originally.

In my early days of teaching I asked questions to promote the children's thinking with the answer I hoped to hear already in mind. I was acting as the supporter of their searching—for my answer. And when I questioned them then, I tried to ask thoughtful questions that led to analysis, synthesis and application to other situations, but I didn't model critical reading and self-talk, and I wasn't genuinely seeking their views. It was the questioning of an expert to lesser thinkers.

By doing that, I lost an opportunity to appraise the children's understanding, to help them develop as thinkers, to make a thinking community, and to develop the habit of seeking meaning. Guessing the teacher's idea is far different from individually interpreting a story.

I had at least learned that my young students could have startling insights and I began to listen to them with closer attention, but I was still the person in charge instead of a fellow thinker and explorer of books. I could do better, I thought, but how? I tried different questioning techniques—students acting as a teacher and questioning the class, facilitating brainstorming sessions and recording the ideas.... They weren't completely satisfactory for book talks because they took us too far away from the enjoyment and experience of the books and weren't elastic enough to permit the exploration of tangential subject matter. I continued to search.

Then at last I had an opportunity to watch a skilled teacher in New York City lead first graders in book talks. I knew that she had found what I wanted. What I most admired was how she asked questions without seeming to expect a predetermined answer, and how she had the students turn around to talk to one another in pairs. It wasn't her invention; it had been developed and refined by a number of educators, but she had been trained to apply it, and it was helpful to see it in action. It was simple, but inspired, I thought, and I recognized that with her work she was preparing her students for the kind of lives that I wanted for my students, lives where thinking and considering various points of view would be common practice.

Even though she had done it with native English speakers, I knew that my students could have such talks if I could show them how. I would need to learn the language for thoughtful discussions before I could be effective, and then teach it to my students by using it and explicitly promoting it. This would be in addition to the kinds of thinking and reading habits I hoped to promote with the book discussions. I had no trouble finding expressions to use for discussions. I made a list of them for my desk as a reminder to use them regularly when I talked to the students. This was the only way the terms would become theirs, by regularly hearing and using them.

As I worked my way to being the master practitioner I saw in my mind's eye, I improved. I wanted to be an experienced reader who modeled the way that expert readers read, subtly guiding novice readers to do the same. However, I don't think I'll ever be as expert as I once hoped. The masterful practice I had in mind when I began keeps changing with the insights I have about its use. I have realized that true mastery in teaching real children in an ever-changing world means remaining open to new methods and new situations. Mastery cannot be "achieved," it is a process.

In addition to preparing children for thoughtful discussions and pleasure in literature, the book talks turned out to be windows into the children's lives, windows I never planned or wanted to look into, but that sometimes demanded recognition from me as a respected adult in their lives. If a conflict arose between family privacy and the need to talk, I chose privacy and directed the conversation away from the personal topic. I could talk to the child alone if necessary.

Their remarks during discussions often gave me helpful knowledge about their comprehension but also about what they were enduring as children in changed, sometimes confusing circumstances. I could try, with their classmates, to help them untangle situations or events that bothered them, brought to light by related events in books or by classmates' comments.

Amazing discussions about difficult subjects arose, discussions that were literally breathtaking to manage—parental preferences; stereotyping of different groups; unreasonable school rules; slum landlords who ignored cockroaches, rats, or broken heaters; people who fired guns in their neighborhoods; parents who couldn't find jobs.... We discussed them all, the children's faces looking up to mine for answers. There are no easy answers for these problems. How could I let little children know that human social life is sometimes grossly unfair?

Sometimes I did; I couldn't credibly deny what was obvious. Sometimes I could only say, "I hope that you will be the ones to change these things. That's why you need to learn as much as you can." Because we rarely found definitive answers to these hard questions, they learned to say, "Sometimes there's more than one answer." Or, "We don't know the answer yet." "Maybe they're both right!" This went beyond learning to tolerate ambiguity; it was learning to live reasonably in an imperfect social world.

"I wonder how Dog feels since he's new in this junkyard," I asked as if talking to myself. "Why did Rat and Dog act like that?" "Are they really happy alone?" "Why does he say 'Don't need friends; don't like 'em'?" Then I turned to the children.

"Would you be happy without friends?" They were quiet, but they were thinking. "This might be a good time to turn and talk to your neighbor," I said.

Sitting on the carpet in a circle, the children scooted around to face a partner and discuss how they would feel in Rat and Dog's new living situations. Rosalinda looked at me in frustration.

"Mufdi won't talk!" she said loudly without any sense of indiscretion. Instantly Mufdi ducked his head down. I went over and sat with them.

"Rosalinda, tell your ideas to Mufdi; maybe he'll have something to say then." She looked dubiously at me; hadn't she already tried? I repeated the question I had asked earlier: "How does Rat feel? How would you feel if your best friend moved and you didn't have any friends?" "What do you think, Rosalinda?" She studied me carefully and suddenly she understood. She perked up, looked at him and began to talk—she had been in the United States six months longer than he had, and had attended a few months of English kindergarten last year, so she was more advanced than he was in English speaking.

"I think they want friends," she said.

I tried to help: "What do you think Mufdi?" He looked at me, but didn't respond.

I asked another pair to join him and Rosalinda; Rosalinda needed the talking and the thinking. Mufdi would profit from hearing the conversation. Patting Mufdi's hand, giving Rosalinda a look of understanding, and thanking the new members of the small group, I moved on. The children had long ago decided that sometimes they wanted to talk in groups of four and even six, so this reorganization wasn't exceptional. Although he didn't offer any responses, I believed Mufdi understood everything that had occurred. He no longer cried as often as he had earlier and participated in class activities, but he still didn't talk spontaneously and still didn't respond to questions unless he could shake his head yes or no.

It would be Rosalinda who in early April would announce in the same uninhibited way, but this time in a tone mixed with amazement and delight, "Mufdi talked!" The whole class with a spontaneous turn of heads would look at Rosalinda and her partner, whose face by now held an amused smile, with the same amazement and delight.

"Hurray Mufdi!" Etienne would say, and the whole class would cheer.

"Good Mufdi!" several others would encourage, imitating as they often did one of Etienne's good ideas. The attention inhibited Mufdi's further participation in that day's conversation, but it made him happy. The next day his talk returned and remained everyday thereafter, although always reserved.

Etienne was on the opposite end of the oral communication spectrum, talking with such satisfaction that "Etienne keeps talking!" became a predictable complaint. If Etienne had the floor in a conversation, I'm convinced that he could have talked for the entire period, never giving his partners a chance to participate if anyone was present to listen. His voice would assume a musical rhythm and flow that his body would join as if the very rhythm and flow of language were the reason for talk and the cause of its existence.

The seating for stories depended on where the children happened to sit each time, and so Etienne's partners varied in assertiveness. Jayson, quick and sturdy, was a great partner for him, as was Salam, calm, alert and rational.

These two could talk to Etienne if he would listen, but even they would eventually look to me in frustration. I once watched Jayson look up, roll his eyes and say to no one in particular, "Oh brother!"

Less assertive children like Mufdi or Tamathor sat quietly and listened but said nothing themselves; the purposes of the book talk defeated.

I moved to sit with Etienne and Salam. On and on talked Etienne, basically recapitulating the events of the story as Salam grew increasingly frustrated. We didn't need to retell the story, we wanted to probe deeply into it and find answers to questions about motivation, consequences, connections to our own lives or other books we had read. We wanted to find out what everyone in the class thought. I took advantage of a pause in Etienne's talking to ask, "Salam, what do you think about what Etienne said? Do you agree with him? Do you think Rat was mean?" "Etienne, open your ears and listen carefully. See what you think about what he says." I stayed with them, pointedly looking at Salam and listening. I responded to his communication with, "Interesting, Salam! Is that what you thought Etienne?" Then, "Salam, listen carefully to Etienne."

Of course mature Salam was already listening, but I wanted to reassure Etienne that everyone was expected to do what I had asked him to do. As I watched, Etienne paid close attention to what Salam said and gave him a fine response.

"You did a good job listening, my friend." I said, patting his hand.

When they seemed for the moment to have the idea of listening to each other I moved on.

To discuss and question they needed to know how to listen, to reflect, to present arguments and to support them—skills that would need plenty of practice and guidance to develop. They seem like big goals, but they are attainable for children, including children learning to speak in a foreign language. These discussions were valid opportunities for employing the vocabulary of the stories I read to them, and for learning important thinking habits. That's why it was so important for the others to speak up, and for Etienne not to be silent, but to continue to talk and to listen to what the others had to say.

With the children I guided the creation of a list of statements and questions they could use for discussions. It was a gathering of expressions I had found for discussions of any kind in my quest to improve as a literacy teacher. This list would help not only their thinking and reading skills, but their English language knowledge as well: each opportunity to speak and use words in a new way would deepen their vocabularies—they would know numerous ways that words could be used. In addition, these phrases could be transferred to other kinds of discussions in social studies, science, interpersonal relations, public negotiations, and others.

The first part of the list took several days to make, and of course I had to explain certain expressions like *support* and *except for*. They had already mastered other expressions, like "I agree," that they had learned in the context of earlier book talks as I repeatedly used them. We added to it throughout the year as the children's conversational sophistication grew, and as new kinds of conversations demanded:

SOME THINGS WE CAN SAY IN BOOK DISCUSSIONS

- I agree with _____ because
- I want to add to what _____ said.
- I disagree with you because. . .
- Where does it say that in the text?
- Can you support what you said?
- I think that _____ because _____.
- I agree with you except for _____.
- But why. . . ? But when. . . ? But how. . . ? But who. . . ?
- Can we look back in the text?
- I used to think _____ but now I think _____.
- That reminds me of my own life when. . .
- This story reminds me of _____ story we read.
- I don't understand what you mean.
- That's a great idea!
- I notice. . .
- I remember. . .
- I wonder. . .
- If I were. . .
- I've changed my mind because. . .

"In a discussion everyone talks. We need everyone's ideas. You look at the other person, you open your ears and you think about what they're saying. You think, 'What does my partner mean?' 'Do I agree with this?' You can ask them to support what they say from the text." To assure that these concepts were remembered and valued, we made a class rubric to define not only what good listening looked like, but also what the interior state would be during good listening. I drew ears so that the meaning was clearer.

HOW TO LISTEN IN A CONVERSATION

Great listening	So-so listening	Poor listening
Ears are listening.	Ears listen to partner, but also listen to other conversations.	Doesn't listen at all.
Looks when someone talks. Eyes look at person's face or eyes. Ears are open.	Sometimes looks when someone talks.	Doesn't look when people talk. Eyes not looking at person.
Hands are still.	Sometimes plays.	Plays with hands and toys.
Thinks about what the person says.	Sometimes thinks about what person says, sometimes doesn't.	Thinks about own ideas. Doesn't pay attention. Waits for own turn.
Asks questions to understand.	Sometimes asks questions.	Never asks questions because not listening. Doesn't care!
Takes turns in conversation.	Interrupts, sometimes listens.	Does all the talking or doesn't talk at all.

I knew from past experience that these skills would develop and would help to support learning in every aspect of the curriculum. Once the concepts were established I could refer to them regularly.

"Are you listening? Are your ears open? Is your brain thinking about what _____ is saying?"

These class discussions were exciting and eventually helped to show Etienne the value of listening to what his companions said. He was a good thinker and loved a mental challenge. To participate in the fun of persuading, detecting faulty arguments, admitting a change in thinking, agreeing with others and adding to their arguments, he needed to pay close attention. The playful aspect of discussions—the way that logic and emotion can be manipulated—was the element that hooked him.

"I agree with you because…," "I disagree with you because…."

"You can't support it!" he liked to challenge with glee.

He had been the quickest to begin speaking to communicate—he tried almost right away, with only several words at his command. In these early months of school he dominated the other children with his strong will and imaginative ideas for play. He needed language for these purposes and acquired it eagerly. After hearing a useful term he repeated it, pondering it and savoring it in his mouth.

" 'Shake your brains; figure it out,' Ha, Ha!" I heard one day as he sat alone and practiced a song lyric without the music. His laughter had the color of fun; his eyes were fixed away as if privately considering the uses or wonders of this phrase. And he did use it—again and again. The new songs the students learned each week were an especially rich resource for his language requirements, like "Shake Your Brains," from the CD Teaching Peace whose songs are variously so lyrical or funny that the children begged to learn nearly all of them, even the mushy ones.

Etienne was also the first to master the letters and sounds. He had a head start with literacy from beginning under a French system in Haiti, and was advancing rapidly through first-grade English-reading levels. Like the others, he began with the first book in the first grade series, *I Like to Jump*.

When I sat down with him early in the year, he decoded: "I like to jump. Do you like to jump?" a rabbit asks an elephant who responds, "No. I like to walk." Since he looked unsure of the meaning, I drew my face into an exaggerated grin and jumped. Then I pointed to him and asked, "Do you like to [I jump and put on a big fake smile] jump?" His face beamed with quick understanding and humor. Over and over he read from the repetitive text, "...like to jump." By the end of the conference, the expression sat easily on his tongue. He grew to love reading and in the crowded bookshelves sought both fiction and nonfiction books to read for pleasure, prizing nearly any knowledge. His quick grasp of the reading process was a model for the others, who wanted to follow his success. Elmer told me that he intended to pass Etienne.

"Why, Elmer?"

"I just want to pass him."

"You don't know why?" He looked ahead and didn't respond.

"Well, Elmer, I don't know. Etienne's really good. You'll have to work really hard!"

"I'm going to do it!"

Etienne's voice and expression contained resolution with no doubt whatso-ever about the outcome and arrested my skepticism on the spot. "Who knows?" I thought. Etienne at this point had many more reading skills than he did, but Elmer's determination at his age was extraordinary in my experience, especially determination directed toward a reading objective.

I wanted learning to read to be fun, and I wanted students to proceed at their own rates, to be excited with their own growth, not competing with classmates. But here was Elmer, with his private intentions whatever they were: To be the best? To surpass Etienne whether he was the best or not? I noted his goal in my observation notebook, not quite sure what more to say or do at the moment.

Etienne's abundant reading was reflected in his writing; it was prolific and imaginative, and right away had a recognizable voice, usually alive with adventure and menace. He read his stories to other children whose excited reactions spurred him on to further development of these exciting themes, with story time as his source of literary devices, as "Suddenly...!" or even foreshadowing: "The boy look around but he couldn't see the monster nowhere. The monster was disappeared behind him. He was walking along and didn't see nothing. THEN...." The large print and exclamation marks were devices he adopted immediately.

He amazed me. Because he had the capacity to listen to observations and defend his choices or adapt them for sense and style, I looked forward to writing conferences with him. Our exchanges were thoughtful and mutually respectful. I enjoyed trying to understand what he intended and his effort to create excitement. He was full of ideas and planned to manipulate readers' reactions, aiming to delight and surprise them. He used me as a resource for doing this.

Early in the school year, September through February, he was an admired leader at recess, bright with ideas and energy for play. He knew how to mobilize friends for an activity, as he had in class during the role-play study of Thanksgiving. He eagerly led the group in constructing the ship to cross the Atlantic Ocean, sails and all. He loved challenges that required imagination and initiative, as they all did.

"Let's get some big paper!" was his suggestion when they were wondering how to make sails.

"We can put chairs here and make a church!" when they decided to build a church in the New World. The children had just learned *church* for this project. Every suggestion was an exciting possibility, and his classmates eagerly followed along.

However, the nature of his leadership changed as the year progressed. It evolved from suggestions to bossiness and even intimidation—a kind of tyranny. At recess near the end of the school year he began to take balls from classmates, or to try to exclude certain children from play because they didn't forcibly "know how to play the game."

When the other children, who had become increasing comfortable and expressive as the year progressed, began to offer ideas of their own, he didn't adapt. He began to appear in the problem-solving circle where earlier there had never been a complaint against him. He particularly tormented Abubakar who, although afraid, would stand up to him. There was an increasingly desperate nature about Etienne's behavior which I've come to associate with emotional distress in children.

His aggression spread to others. He liked to excel at everything, and when Salam in his cooperative math group proved the more successful at finding and writing up solutions to math problems, he made disparaging comments and once in a fit of jealousy scribbled ferociously over Salam's beautiful, logical proof. By the end of the year he had alienated nearly all of his classmates, while in other classes—the library, art, music, P.E.—I increasingly had teacher reports of his uncooperative and bad-tempered behavior.

The school had procedures to correct antisocial behavior with punishment that included after-school detention, seeing the principal, time out from recess, and others, but punishment was not what he needed; it increased his alienation. I talked to the school counselor who did not have time to counsel Etienne privately, and suggested the behavior modification formulas that I had already tried.

The family could not be considered a resource. His father, whom I met at the first parent conference meeting in November, was about 5′9″ lean, tense and well-dressed. His excellent French, the language of our one meeting, suggested that he had reached a fairly high educational level. This first conference of the year was interrupted every few minutes by phone calls to which he responded with intensely whispered words as he hurried into the hall for privacy. He would not allow Etienne's name or picture to appear in any school or class publicity intended for public use. I had clues that he punished Etienne severely with a result that seemed to be Etienne's greater unhappiness, fear and desperation.

One morning I was surprised to see Monsieur M. in the bustling hall with his children, surprising because he was never at school. His children's expressions looked highly anxious and I watched with a sense of alarm while all the teachers and students hurried to class. He spoke to his children in terse, quiet words while he gripped his daughter Matilde's arm. Her quick wince indicated the character of that grip, his face the character of the words he was saying.

I once had reported to Matilde, in French, that I needed Mr. M.'s help with Etienne: "My father say he send me to Haiti," Etienne said through uncontrollable sobs the next day. His sister chillingly added that their father had beaten and kicked Etienne the night before. "I don't like Haiti. Haiti bad," he said as he bitterly cried.

Mr. M. didn't send Etienne away, but the threat was there, repeated several times and reported to me by Etienne and his sister. With these threats in the way, I eliminated Mr. M. as a resource. The mere mention of talking to his father drove Etienne into a panic that I wouldn't provoke again.

It was a read-aloud, *Hansel and Gretel*, which precipitated further revelations about his home life and suggested some of the reasons for his aggressive, desperate-seeming behavior. The stepmother in the story is fairytale's archetypically cruel and unloving stepparent. After I read about her plot to leave the loving children in the forest, up went Etienne's hand.

"My stepmother say she hate me. She say she want me to go back to Haiti." How quickly he had adopted the word *stepmother*.

The room lost every sound but his voice. He looked at me silently, a look of expectation in his eyes. The other students looked silently at one another, at Etienne and at me.

"I...," I paused. I wanted to think of something wise and helpful, but I couldn't.

"Oh Etienne!" I blurted. "How do you feel when she says that?" With all the class as an audience his personal revelation was extremely sensitive. There was a need, or I felt one, to respect his and his family's privacy.

"I feel sad," is what he answered.

I recognized that a spirited, active and bright child like Etienne could be difficult for some adults to understand. He wasn't obedient, but he was rational and would listen. Anyone who wanted unquestioning obedience, especially for illogical or unfair demands, would not be happy with him. His experience as a capable problem-solver might have led him to think he was probably going to be right about most things, and in this childish confidence he believed he knew more than he did. The combined realities of his intelligence, his young age and his experience, advanced in some areas and limited in others, made a delicate combination to navigate.

He grew to hate his stepmother, and said so. There was no sign of this in the beginning of the year when he first came to the United States, but the longer he stayed with this person, the more their animosity grew and the more he talked of her with anger and resentment in his voice. He was constantly afraid of being returned to Haiti, his father's threat. At his young age, signs of cynicism were beginning to appear.

I felt at a loss. No formulas could help me with this, and I felt without resources in this school, in this school district, and in the community. There were no organizations to help a child like Etienne whose parents belonged to an isolated minority—at the time in Kansas City there were few Haitians—a family that appeared to want confidentiality for political reasons, and that didn't speak English.

The children were quiet, all now looking at me as expectantly as Etienne had. To preserve his and his family's privacy I diverted the conversation away from Etienne after several minutes by generalizing the topic.

"What can children do when adults seem unfair or really are unfair?" I asked. "Should we look at what we do too?" "Can we talk to them?" "When they seem unfair, what do we do?"

No need to say that Etienne's story was a lot like Hansel and Gretel's; the children were automatically making the link between life and literature. The connection was clear and the story was serving literature's frequent role: helping people to understand life. The children had many ideas for Etienne, not adequate for his situation, but it was an important topic for them that they were eager to discuss. Etienne listened, but heard nothing that he believed would help him. He shook his head at many of the ideas and finally became silent again, his eyes fixed toward the carpet in an expression of someone experiencing an inner world far different from the one around him, a world that seemed troubling.

Not much later I learned through his writing that Etienne had seen his grandmother violently killed in Haiti, and that he had lived in the streets, his mother, his sister and himself fed by neighbors. During a writing conference about a violent story he was writing, in which a grandmother, like "a beautiful bird," is killed, I asked him about his story, where it occurred and who his characters were. I thought the action of the story was too precise to be entirely the product of a young imagination, and fearing it could have been one of his personal experiences, I asked, "Did this happen to someone you know?"

He said, "This a true story. My grandma, she killed."

"Where did you live in Haiti Etienne?" I thought that he may have lived with his grandmother in Haiti.

"With my grandma. But she killed."

"Then where did you live?"

"All places."

"What do you mean?"

"I live in all places."

I was not communicating. "Did you have a house?"

"No house. I live in all places; every day a different place."

I finally had learned in pieces the sources for the violence of his stories and for the bullying behavior that at the end of the year became increasingly a problem for everyone, Etienne most of all. By June he would have lost his authority as a leader and even much of his desirability as a playmate.

Over and over again, crisis after crisis, I explained, talked, intervened, urged, recognized his positive qualities, diverted his attention, gave him time-out—anything I knew to put him on a safe path. At the same time I needed to protect the other children from his bullying. He was like Rat and Dog: he acted gruff and indifferent, unable to express his true feelings and unable to break through the wall he constructed around himself before our eyes, a wall thicker and higher every day.

His development remains a source of disappointment for me; I relive his days at school and wonder what I could have done differently. Generally I expect that children can be happy at school even if their home life is hard, but by the end of the school year I didn't see Etienne as a happy child. Surely good days at school can only compensate so much for an unhappy home. Even though he liked school ("I like school," and "I don't like home. I wish I always have school."), needed ongoing emotional support to have a productive, safe life, and this support wasn't available in our school's neighborhood.

Etienne's focus at reading time diminished in proportion to his increasing desperation. Elmer's unflagging effort in reading on the other hand enabled him to surpass Etienne's achievement just as he had said he would, due at least in part to Etienne's reduced focus. Luckily by that time Elmer didn't care about Etienne's reading or anyone else's; he had learned to read well enough to enjoy nearly any book that interested him and only wanted to find a good one to read. Thus he didn't notice what Etienne was reading, or innocently say anything that could affect him in any way.

Despite his trouble, Etienne remained one of the outstanding students in the class. My disappointment was that he didn't achieve what his potential indicated he could. I don't know where he is now, and I don't know what became of him. His wonderful mind is an asset that could save him someday, and he already possessed the asset of literacy by the end of first grade, but what kind of person would he become without love?

The read-aloud about Rat and Dog ended with a group discussion about what they had done to become friends, then about what we could do to make friends, which we noted on a list to keep as a reminder:

HOW TO BE A GOOD FRIEND

"You have to be nice." Rosalinda
"You have to share." Abubakar
"You help your friends." Jayson
"You can't be a bully." Abdulrahman
"When they're sad you talk to them about it." Ingrid
"You listen to them." Elmer
"You can give them things." Ali

We posted these ideas in the room.

Figure 8.1: Jayson and Abdulrahman solving tomorrow's problems?

Chapter 9

The Uses of Freedom

It was time for recess, time for the children to see their friends and relatives from other classes, time for fun and time for freedom from adult schedules. The pleasure of being together and the circumstances of broad possibility made recess one of the most exciting parts of the day.

To my students recess was especially marvelous. For many of them the kind of knowledge they could draw from recess included the very idea of the freedom to play. For some of them, early childhood had been spent avoiding danger and helping their parents obtain food and housing. By age six these children had little experience with play of any kind. Mufdi's early childhood was truncated this way, and so were Hong's, Etienne's, Glenda's, Ali's and Salam's. Most of my students also had limited or no acquaintance with toys so that when the doors opened to the outdoors for the first several times, they were carried forward with the rush of children only to stand and stare at the blacktop without a word, but not for long.

Recess was a period ignored by educational planners in the district and at this school, not planned except for passive teacher supervision, and not viewed as a time that needed to be formally "educationalized." What a blessing that was for the children. Because we didn't have organized games they could, in fact had to, choose what they wanted to do within the limit of a few rules: they couldn't go into the kindergartners' sandbox, they couldn't leave the fenced area and they couldn't fight. They were free to invent games, explore, and interact with each other however they wanted, as long as they appeared safe. A drawback was the bare blacktop that lacked play equipment, water fountains, shade, benches, and softer areas for play. Nor did the children have outdoor playthings.

In the past when my students had freedom from adult-organized play, I saw a noticeable increase in their ability to solve problems, to invent, to explore and to consider information before making choices. They treasured these free times, and I think the reason was the feeling of autonomy they had when making their own choices and discoveries, a freedom not present during the school day.

It was this sense of urgency that I thought would bring more joy and motivation into the class day and the children's work, the ability to choose and discover. This was not a new thought but I had never been satisfied with how much of it I'd been able to integrate into my class schedules. I wanted it to be more important, a major characteristic of the class.

Then one especially hot day in September this year a partial answer came with a decision about where to play when normally recess would have been outside. That day rather than deciding myself whether or not to play indoors, I offered the decision to the children, and when they couldn't agree about where to play, I introduced the procedure of voting to solve the day's indecision. The experience was so powerful for them that after that day voting was the children's first suggestion for making class decisions when there were conflicting choices.

"Would you like to play inside today? It's so hot. . . ," I asked the group that day, indicating inside by pointing to the floor, and indicating hot by wiping my brow and making a wretched-feeling face. It was undeniably a miserably hot day, and the children were already sweating. With no shade or water outside I could predict their discomfort better than they could; I had experience.

"Yes!" shouted a few children.

"No!" cried a few others.

"I know! Let's vote!" I said. "If you want to go outside raise your hand." I thought that this was a chance to introduce another small area where they could have choices. Little did I know how important it would be to our class. I pointed to the playground through the window. When they understood one or two words like this, go and outside, in the context of the situation, they could understand the meaning of the words. I raised my hand with questioning expression on my face to show them what I meant by voting for "Go outside." Several hands went up, which I counted aloud and noted on the board.

"If you want to stay inside, raise your hand," emphasizing the word inside while I indicated inside with my arms, again raising my hand to show a vote. Up went more hands. A number of children didn't vote.

"Everyone has to vote," I said, "That's how voting is. We'll vote again. If you want to play outside, raise your hand." I pointed outside again, raised my hand, counted the votes, wrote "outside" on the board, and wrote the number on the board. "If you want to play inside, raise your hand." I wrote the word and the number of votes on the board.

"Which number is the greatest?" I asked, finding an unexpected opportunity to bring in a math concept as I spread my arms open as far as I could. "Which number is least, I asked, indicating something small with my forefinger and thumb, then pointing to the numbers. Outdoor recess had the most votes and those who voted for indoor recess groaned. But the anticipation of play quickly triumphed over their disappointment. They accepted the voting results and prepared to go outside.

It proved to be a mistake for them; they were indeed hot and thirsty, and their energy was sapped by the heat. Nevertheless, it was their mistake and the consequences were theirs. The mistake gave them added information for future decisions, both about how weather would affect them, and about reflecting on arguments both pro and con.

Everyday after this they begged to vote about where to play. They quickly learned the usefulness of a model Etienne originated—persuading the others to join in their vote by explaining the reasons why one choice would be preferable to the other. Their arguments in favor of certain votes grew in complexity and persuasiveness as their language expertise grew, so much that often I could be swayed by their logic.

"We should play outside because then we can play Spider Man!" Etienne said one day in his most enthusiastic voice, emphasizing his point with exaggerated gestures and bright eyes as the class prepared to vote. His companions looked at one another considering what he had said and whether they really wanted to continue playing Spider Man, the game they had been developing the past few days. While the Spider Man players hesitated, a few nonplayers added their points of view.

"We don't like to play Spider Man," said Rosalinda matter-of-factly.

"No! We don't like to play Spider Man," reiterated Sara.

"Inside we can play with blocks!" added Elmer, eager to work through a garage-building project.

"Let's vote and see what happens," I said. They looked ready, so I called out the options and marked them on the chalkboard. The vote for outdoor recess was highest. Etienne celebrated, and I looked at the indoor voters. "What will you do outside?" I asked them as the class prepared to leave. They answered all at the same time with different plans and obviously had enough ideas to feel all right about today's recess decision.

Once in awhile I intervened in voting results, generally with an additional argument, but I always explained why I was going to override a vote. If I thought they'd been indoors too much, for example, I told them so. If a minority voted unsuccessfully for several days to play outside, I talked to the others about consideration, fairness and the health value of vigorous activity. Only once or twice did I have to say, "I'm sorry, but we will have to...."

I was so delighted with their developing conversations and arguments that I found more and more decisions they could make and took advantage of any opportunity: I hold up two books.

"Shall we read this book, or this book? This one is about friends, and this one is humorous (humor was one of our book genres) about how a hen takes a walk."

"Would you like to sit on the carpet, or in chairs?"

"Shall we sit in a circle, or do you want to come up close together?"

"Shall we have refreshments for your parents when they come? Do we really need refreshments?" There were even times when I honestly couldn't make up my mind about something and needed their help. We decided to have refreshments for the parents.

As much as possible we began to discuss the pros and cons of other, more important decisions. "Let's vote!" someone would inevitably suggest. This was an opportunity to promote discussions and to show them that some decisions required more thinking and consideration than choosing with a "yes" or "no" vote where to play at recess. Once they saw, with my guidance—I had to point them out explicitly—the many and diverse ideas that came from book talks, for example, they understood that, unlike where to play for recess, discussions about character motivation or about the main idea in a story were complex topics that couldn't be reduced to two definitive choices. Sometimes they couldn't be decided at all and the children had to agree that they had different views, providing another opportunity to point out that individuals are different in many ways, and disagreements didn't need to be causes of anger and shunning. Sometimes we listed various options and postponed decisions for a few hours until we could think further. "Inside or outside?" was easy compared with some of the decisions we considered. Sometimes when there were many views I made a quick list on the board with each child's initials and wrote abbreviated statements of what their opinions were.

In addition to wanting them to realize the complexity of some questions, I wanted them to know that voting didn't always need to be a zero-sum proposition. I hoped to teach them how to reach a consensus and to consider the well-being of all members of the class—the teacher and teaching assistant included. With my guidance during their discussions, and through experience with the voting process, they learned that they couldn't always have their way and occasionally would need to concede to others; there were times when their preferences were in the minority. That's why persuasion grew in importance. The children weren't entirely satisfied with their majority vote when some classmates were obviously disappointed. Often children wanting to console friends would put their arms around their shoulders and say, "Tomorrow we'll play outside, okay?"

At the same time that I taught them about consensus and voting, I encouraged them to say what they thought if a decision everyone had agreed upon seemed wrong to them. They learned that the majority and a consensus weren't always right and could be questioned, as they noticed in a study of the life of Harriet Tubman. "Most people said slavery was fine, but not Harriet. Who do you think was right?" "It's important to put your ideas out so others can think about them. It's all right if no one agrees with your idea. Maybe they will later, especially if you support your idea with excellent reasons." All these ideas and vocabulary were familiar by then because they were also reinforced in reading discussions. Luckily for us the consequences of votes in first grade weren't matters of life or death, because such subtleties would take time, practice and guidance to absorb thoroughly—years.

Voting, majority rule and minority concession to it, consideration of the minority, and discussion of decisions were the fundamental concepts they learned about democratic government through their voting. They weren't outcomes I planned, but when the possibilities occurred to me, I quickly exploited them because I saw how the effects transferred to their other learning, especially to reading comprehension and social studies. Even for finding group math solutions these processes helped since the children had learned to discuss and consider alternate solutions. These kinds of mental reflections and group deliberations were among the primary goals of my teaching and sowed the grains of an intellectual rigor that spread to all areas of the curriculum—support your statement. They were learning to ask "Why?" to seek justification for an idea, and to make responsible decisions. I was captivated as I watched them talk. There is something inspiring for an educator to see young children use what are normally considered mature thinking processes. These children, ELL students, were learning to question and to think critically.

One day in early October according to their vote, the children were going outside for recess. For this the school staff had developed a protocol: after lunch was over the children in the cafeteria formed class lines and were led outside by the teachers who had yard duty, today, Mrs. Price and I. The children boisterously, joyfully climbed the set of stairs that led from the cafeteria and basement and exploded onto the playground for half an hour's playtime.

Before them was a broad expanse of blacktop surrounded by a tall chain-link fence. But it was hot today, and there was no shelter from the sun, no water to drink, and no play equipment. Unlike the process for leaving the cafeteria, there was no plan for the time spent outside; students had free play on the blacktop. But without toys or play equipment they often invented games that teachers thought were dangerous or too rowdy or else they were bored and stood alone or in groups talking.

If recess were to achieve its full potential as a learning opportunity, on a bare blacktop crowded with children, some playthings would need to be present even if they were from the environment, like twigs, leaves, and little stones. Enough adults would need to be available to help children learn to resolve conflicts and to answer questions. These two conditions were missing at this school.

The reasons reduced to the same ones always at play in public education: there was no money for additional staff to supervise the children outside, and no money for outdoor playthings unless teachers sacrificed some money for in-structional supplies to purchase them. The bare blacktop eliminated the found playthings. Struggling to parse available funds for basic staff and supplies to implement the focus on literacy, the administration and teaching staff didn't consider playground equipment a priority.

To complicate the matter further, many teachers resented recess duty. They wanted a break during the day and looked forward to days when they didn't have duty so they could relax from a state of constant alertness, talking and problem-solving. Some liked to use the time to gather resources and make preparations for afternoon activities.

Making the best of an undesirable situation today, Ms. Price and some of her friends had brought out chairs and were beginning to chat. These colleagues, like Ms. Price, had taught at this school for years, long before the arrival of an immigrant population. When one of them had yard duty the others came out as well to keep her company. They could help with emergencies, but their availability for answering questions or solving problems of unfairness was very limited.

Because my students had so much to learn about recess and about social life in the United States, and because I was convinced of the learning value of free play, I wanted to circulate on the playground, not to tell them what to do, but to intervene in disputes and to get to know them in a relaxed setting; I was never without something to do at recess. The children had some playthings I bought with my own money—balls, sidewalk chalk and jump ropes.

Today, as I turned one end of a long rope and sang a new jump-rope rhyme, students in a wobbly line eagerly waited for their turns, which came fast. No one in my class was very good, at least not this early in the year, since all of them were new to this activity. "One mistake and you're out" kept the line moving and the play lively. My students were visibly happy when English-speaking children from other classes also learned and recited their jump-rope rhyme, and when they all joined in the jump-rope line.

Monitoring the school yard as I turned, it wasn't long before I saw Ms. Price with Abubakar and three boys from mainstream classes, the boys gesticulating intensely and Ms. Price looking frustrated.

"Glenda, will you turn this?" I asked quickly. "I have to go and see about Abubakar." She agreed, and I rushed across the school yard.

As I approached the group I heard: "He took our ball!" Ms. Price was looking accusingly at Abubakar: "Why did you take their ball?" His face a blank, he looked back at her, at which point I arrived. Ms. Price turned to me, knowing a first-grade ELL student would be mine. "He took their ball."

I paused a minute. The ball was one I had bought. "That's the ball he brought out for recess. The boys have his ball," I said. "Let me have the ball for a minute," I said to Abubakar, holding out my hands.

This request elicited loud cries of protest from at least ten other boys who had also been playing with the ball.

"I'm afraid that you haven't learned to share," I said, "and I don't want you to hurt each other over the ball."

"But we were playing with it!" All the boys shouted at me, trying to make me understand, and I did. "He take ball," put in Abubakar, a little bewildered but ready to stand up for himself. I looked at Ms. Price who remained silent, and then I turned to the boys.

In situations like this the kids are predictable, passionate, utterly sincere, and only barely able to take another's point of view. Because it's important that they learn to share and negotiate disagreements by themselves, such incidents offer an opportunity to intervene at just the time when they are intensely concerned in the outcome of a discussion. With this motivation in play, they can be nudged toward cooperative behavior, careful listening and the art of finding a solution that satisfies everyone—the art of compromise. With teacher-organized play, opportunities like this wouldn't occur. And the difficulty of children's circumstances on this playground needed to be acknowledged by adults: it was hot, and they needed some playthings.

"This is Abubakar." I put my hand on his shoulder, which immediately relaxed, and he moved his body slightly toward mine. "He's really a nice friend if you know him, but he doesn't speak much English. He doesn't understand what you're doing. This is his ball today because he brought it out. Can you guys play with him? Abubakar, can you play with them? Can they play with you? Share?"

With gestures and emphasis on the words he knew, I tried to show Abubakar what I meant and he seemed to understand. His expression brightened with understanding and he said "Okay," although it was clear to me that his understanding didn't extend to entire satisfaction with the solution.

"Boys, you have to share the ball. It's his ball and he should play too, right?"

"Okay Ms. Stark!" they agreed, with predictable readiness. They all knew my name somehow.

I returned the ball to Abubakar to emphasize that he controlled it. This made him happier. "Share," I said and gestured between him and the boys to indicate sharing. The problems weren't over I suspected. Learning to negotiate requires experience and guidance and takes a lot of practice, so I added, "If you have problems again, find me again and we'll try to work it out." I looked at Ms. Price for agreement. She nodded but she didn't look happy about the results of the exchange. She silently had watched as I talked, but her expression said a million words. The four boys bounded off exchanging looks of potential friendship between them.

"He wouldn't listen," said Ms. Price.

"I'm sorry," I said. "He doesn't know English yet, and he's never been in school before." I gave her a you-understand look, but she rolled her eyes. She believed in a strict teacher-controlled relationship with children and said so many times. She blamed children's misbehavior on lack of control over them by teachers and parents. I believed, based on my experience, that most of the time what adults called misbehavior actually resulted from lack of experience, misunderstanding, developmental level, and failure on our part to explain ahead of time what behavior would be appropriate—adult leadership and mentoring. When I had the foresight to explain in detail what behavior was required by the circumstances, my students' cooperation was nearly perfect.

I looked around to see if I was needed at jump rope. The rope-jumping was fine and the ball boys seemed to be cooperating, but my eyes caught Mufdi standing alone. After two weeks at school he still did not speak and cried easily and often. I crouched in front of him at eye level, "Do you want to walk with me?" I said, taking a few steps to model walking and giving a "Come on" gesture with my hand. Silently he came with me.

We started to walk around the yard. Tamathor, beautiful Tamathor bounded up, sweaty, her cheeks rosy and her eyes shining.

"What's wrong with Mufdi?"

"Nothing. We're going for a walk."

"Can I come?"

"Of course. Okay Mufdi?" He nodded, his head shyly lowered, his eyes quickly looking away.

Tamathor joined the rhythm of our walk and began to chat. From Iraq, she had spent a few months in American kindergarten the preceding year and could communicate in rudimentary English. The boys in the class liked to play with her because she could outrun most of them and could think of exciting games to play. Unlike the other Muslim girls at school she did not wear a veil or long clothing; her thick dark hair was braided and she wore pants and running shoes. And unlike many of the girls, she did not like to stand and chat with friends at recess; she preferred to move, always with joyful exuberance.

As we walked and talked I addressed my responses to both children to encourage their language and sense of belonging. Although recess was disorganized, it provided a setting for these relaxed conversations, priceless because they were difficult to have at any other time, and because they added so much to our enjoyment of one another's company. They became part of the intangible ties that eventually formed our class into a kind of family.

Suddenly Tamathor grabbed my arm, "Look Abubakar!" She pointed. There was Abubakar fearlessly butting up against one of the boys with whom he had had the misunderstanding earlier, both of their postures set to fight. "Oh no!" I cried. I raced over. Abubakar's body relaxed slightly and he seemed relieved to see me, although he didn't back down. Behind the other boy stood his friends, who had also been playing with the ball. Everyone was shouting at me about the ball and who should have it.

I listened for a few seconds to the surrounding boys to get a sense of what was going on and then turned from the desperate, frustrated boys for whom this ball possession was a life-and-death matter to Abubakar and the other boy who, their confrontation in tense limbo since my arrival, still maintained the challenging close contact I saw at first, each unwilling to back down before the other did. "We'll share!" said numerous voices in near unison. "We'll share. We promise!" But all evidence suggested the contrary. Interesting. They knew what the problem was, and probably what I would say.

"Wait a minute! Wait a minute!" I said. "Abubakar! Stop! Boys! Stop!" I finally had their full attention. "Look, I'm going to keep the ball." I looked from one to the other. "Remember how you said you would share? This doesn't look like good sharing to me. Tomorrow I'll bring out two balls for you to play with. Right now you'll have to find something else to do."

"We'll share! Pleeease Mrs. Stark!" they begged. Now their attention was completely on the ball.

"Ah, I'm sorry, but this isn't working out. The fighting is a big problem, and you keep getting mad at each other. What's your name?" I asked the boy who wasn't in my class.

"James."

"James and Abubakar, I want you to stand together and talk about what you could do to solve this ball problem. I'll be back in five minutes to see what you think." Although I knew that they were too inexperienced to solve such problems alone, I wanted them to understand that I believed that they could find some solution other than fighting.

This school was exceptionally calm compared with the other schools in the area, where fighting and disrespect were so widespread that substitute teachers refused assignments to go to them. Here fighting was extremely rare and was punished any time it occurred. Everyone wanted the school to remain a good place to be. I felt obligated to give the boys some time-out, even though only for a few minutes. The point about talking and not fighting had to be made, and I thought, needed visual reinforcement for all the children to see.

Mufdi and Tamathor, who had watched the scene, were waiting for me. I rejoined them to resume our walk. "Fighting is bad," said Tamathor earnestly. Before I could respond she cried, "Bye Ms. Stark!" and dashed off to play. "Bad, huh Mufdi?" I made a face and pointed to the site of the near fight. He nodded and quickly lowered his eyes.

We walked over to the two energetic would-be fighters and I said, "Have you boys thought of another solution?"

"Yes," said James. I looked at Abubakar, pointed to my head in a gesture he had seen many times in class to symbolize thinking and asked, "Did you think Abubakar?" "Yes. I think."

"What's your idea?"

"Don't fight," said James.

"But that's hard sometimes, really hard. What do you do so you don't fight? This is a really big problem to think about!"

I wanted to see some sign of social growth from this. They looked at each other, but without another idea. "Look. I have an idea that might help you. Here's the ball Abubakar. You see James and he wants to play. What do you do?" I emphasized the words he knew, but used natural syntax hoping that eventually he would be familiar with it.

"He can play."

"James, what do you do?"

"I share and act nice."

"Good ideas. Let's practice a little. Abubakar, play with the ball. James, you want to play. What do you do?"

"I say, 'can I play?' " His voice ended in a question.

"Sure! That's what people do. If you grab the ball, they get mad. If you ask and you share, they might be your friend. Let's see you try it." He asked, "Can I play?" and Abubakar responded, "Yes."

That was about all I could expect it seemed, and at least they knew what they should do and how it looked.

"James and Abubakar, can you be friends?"

"Yes Ms. Stark."

"Great! Can you shake hands?" With the prospect of an extra ball tomorrow and the resolution of this drama, the boys were willing to shake hands.

"Good," I said. "You boys can go now. Next time there's a problem find me and I'll help you."

"Can we have the ball?" Like the promise they had made earlier, this pleading was predictable.

"You know, you did a great job figuring out how to share the ball, and I think your ideas are just right. I'm just worried because you almost had a fight!" For Abubakar, I point to myself and exaggeratedly make a worried expression. "I have a problem: 'Should I give them the ball? Should I keep the ball? How can I help James and Abubakar learn?' Do you understand how I'm feeling about it?" I used gestures to illustrate my deliberations for Abubakar. Interestingly, James understood what I was doing.

They nodded. I think that what Abubakar understood was that I was considering what to do, and James understood the words. It amounted to the same thing.

"I'm feeling and thinking that tomorrow will be better, and I've decided that I should keep the ball just for today. And tomorrow I'll bring another ball." Tonight I'd have to be sure to buy that extra ball for them. They listened to my thinking with curiosity.

"Okay Ms. Stark," they chimed. They bounded off to their play in different directions, James to his group of classmates and Abubakar to play with Jayson, Etienne and Ali. With the provocative ball in my hands the chances for lasting calm were fairly certain. There were over eight months left in the school year during which they could develop the social expertise they needed for playing with balls on the playground—among them consideration of nearby children and teachers, and sharing. I didn't feel that taking the ball was excessively heartless; more balls would also be available tomorrow, and besides, my taking the ball might make the lesson memorable.

Recess was nearly over but there was time enough to talk to Glenda, who now was standing alone. She had come to the class late, two weeks ago, and knew no English. She was mature for her age, tall, studious, alert, quiet and unusually reasonable, a true pleasure to have in class. She had been living with her grandparents in Morelia, Mexico, and although I admired her exceptional maturity, I was concerned that so far I had never seen her play—no make-believe, no running, and no wild curiosity that could profit from free time to explore. I hoped that one day she would feel confident enough in class to express curiosity and ask questions about the social and material world, habits of mind that unorganized recess play could promote.

Although I spoke only English in class, I did sometimes speak Spanish at recess. The children enjoyed this opportunity to talk and be understood by the teacher, and to see me make mistakes in Spanish as they did in English.

"*¿Como estás?*" I asked. I patted her shoulder.

"*Bien,*" she answered automatically, but I was sure that the new school and new classmates presented a difficult adjustment for her.

"*¿Quieres caminar con nosotros?*"

"*Sí.*" She joined Mufdi and me, but Mufdi was ready to wander off on his own and did, to stand alone and watch the children at play. I gave a quick look to where Abubakar and friends were playing, and saw that they were having fun and were safe, then turned back to Glenda.

"*¿Quires jugar conmigo?*" I asked, holding out the ball. She agreed, surely to please me, but said that she didn't know how. I pointed out four squares painted on the blacktop and show her that she should stand in one square and I would stand in another; we would try the game two square. I tapped the large

ball over to her and she completely missed it. After she retrieved it, I tapped
it to her again and this time she awkwardly caught it. I showed her that she
should tap it back over to me, not catch it. Slowly she began to smile with
enjoyment, succeeding occasionally with a proper hit. Brenda and Rosalinda
walked over.

"Can we play?" asked Rosalinda. I looked at Glenda and explained in
English with gestures what the girls wanted. She agreed with an open smile.
Neither Brenda nor Rosalinda knew how to play either, so we spent time practicing ball handling. They were wildly inaccurate with every aspect—catching,
throwing and tapping the ball.

"Keep your eyes on the ball," I said, "then give it a good tap. It has to
hit in this square." Up went their arms with the uncontrolled ball flying in all
possible directions. Brenda and Rosalinda responded with irresistible hilarity
which Glenda soon joined. "Use your hands. Keep your eyes on the ball...."
Occasional successes were greeted with amazed cries of delight.

It was good to see Glenda interacting with the girls in this relaxed way
and in circumstances that wouldn't offend her sense of propriety. She actually
laughed a few times. Although the girls were now inept at ball handling, they
were learning other important skills—spatial relationships, cooperation (whose
turn it was to chase missed balls), geometry, turn taking, the fun of active play,
and because I was there, English vocabulary. The girls still had choices here;
they could have left at any time to play something else.

The bell finally rang and the children began wandering into their class lines.
No one ever considered that no lines at all could be a possibility. Getting the
students into lines was one of those school customs that we all followed for
the presumed safety of the children and for efficiency. It took too long because
some students didn't stop their games, some ignored the bell altogether....
This was another instance where training ahead or rethinking our procedure
would have prevented undesirable behavior. An extended recess caused by
inefficient lining up would mean that story time would be shortened—the read-
aloud time that they enjoyed so much and that was so valuable to their learning.

When the class finally was more or less together in line, I automatically
turned around to check before leaving and saw Mufdi crying, silently and
deeply. I walked over to him and asked, "What happened, Mufdi?" He kept his
head lowered and did not answer. I turned to the class.

"What happened to Mufdi?" I asked, but the children only looked up at me
silently. "What happened?" I insisted, now convinced by their silence that they
had something to tell.

Sara piped up, "Ali cut him." She looked at Ali with a satisfied expression. Ali regularly bothered her by saying "Hey, baby," an expression he defended by saying that his father used it all the time. "Mrs. Stark, Ali said 'Hey baby'," the girls would report with a mixture of fascination and revulsion. This was her opportunity to make him pay, or that's how it seemed to me.

I looked at Ali who shook his head slightly and lowered his eyes, a sign that he probably had cut in front of Mufdi. When he believes he is innocent, he defends himself loudly and passionately. I bent down so that I was at eye level with Mufdi and asked him, clarifying my question with gestures, "Did Ali get in front of you?" Looking at him so he'd know I wanted to communicate, I cut in front of him to demonstrate.

He continued to cry, his shoulders heaving, his nose running and his eyes flowing with tears. He kept his head down. I looked at Ali who, instead of protesting as he normally would have, simply waited as he looked at Mufdi and looked frankly sorry. These lines. Without them, we wouldn't have had this problem. There would have been a different one though, I'm sure. The basic problem was the children's need to learn to treat each other with kindness and respect.

"You have to go to the end of the line," I said firmly, intuiting his guilt. 'If you cut you have to go to the end of the line,' was a rule the class had made, and he knew it. He looked at Mufdi with concern as he turned to go. Mufdi's crying slowed, but once again his face was streaked with tears and his upper lip was covered with clear-flowing mucous.

I needed to protect Mufdi at this point. He was withdrawn and without the emotional resources he needed to address anything beyond survival. That's how I interpreted what I saw in any case, an impression reinforced by what I read about the experiences of the Sudanese who fled to Egypt—children left alone in dark filthy quarters all day while their parents went out to find food or some kind of work; abuse based on race; physical and emotional cruelty; abandonment—it was only the lucky few who could make it out to safer countries, a process that sometimes took years.

With Mufdi in our classroom I would have to rely on the help of the children to make him welcome. I would need to guide them to understand and empathize with the experiences of others. If I could do that, many of the kinds of difficulties that appeared at recess could be avoided and the children would take one more step to creating the kind of classroom environment that was necessary for a good society and for learning.

As I led the class back inside, I made a mental change in the afternoon's plan. If the children were going to have freedom at recess and I hoped in an increased number of class activities, they would have to learn to anticipate the consequences of their actions. What I was going to show them would encourage this. It would also teach them how to listen to each other and empathize with their classmates' feelings.

I asked the children to remain in a line as they entered the room, and to walk around into a circle. When the circle was formed, I asked them to sit down. I was going to introduce them to the problem-solving circle, a lesson I had originally planned for two days from now. It was a strategy that had been marvelously effective with previous classes. I would exchange a social studies project for today with the later problem-solving lesson I had planned. Besides I thought, it was also a social studies lesson, although not explicitly in the district's curriculum guide.

Children at school always needed some way to resolve their distress for the slights, hurts, and unfairness they experienced; fairness was an especially important concept for them. Those who had learned not to fight to solve problems knew no alternative means for resolving these critically important matters. Without the sense that there was some way to achieve justice without telling on a classmate, they became disgruntled and unable to focus on their work. I encouraged them to tell me if someone hurt them in some way so that I could help them, but still some children were reluctant to say anything. Sometimes they didn't recognize that a certain offense was truly something wrong and deserved attention; they just felt unhappy, as if they deserved to be treated badly, or as if it were normal.

Almost always these incidents occurred at recess. The problem-solving circle would offer an ideal solution for mediating the tension between free choice and responsibility. In addition to learning a way to solve problems, foresee consequences and develop empathy, they would be introduced to another use of language; they would learn the value of expressing what they thought and felt and they would begin to learn that they could affect the quality of their own lives and those of their companions with their choices. The expansion of how much freedom they could manage depended on the development of their empathy and awareness of consequences that I wanted them to develop. If they wanted to make a given choice, they would need to consider the positive or negative consequences of that choice before making it: Will my friends be mad at me? What is the best way to help someone? Will anyone be hurt? Do I care? What might the negative consequences be, and am I willing to live with them?

The barrier in general was that the children didn't know how to talk to each other beyond the most simple requests and observations. They didn't understand that problems could be solved with words and didn't know the words and structure they would need if they were to begin. They needed to learn to listen to friends, to process what they were saying, and they needed to develop the particular vocabulary and protocol of discussion.

These skills once learned would reinforce the same skills that I was encouraging through book talks and other areas of the curriculum as I sought to broaden their ability to comprehend and discuss ideas. The offenses at recess were great opportunities to do this because they were personal and added a vivid emotional element that I don't think would have appeared, at least to the same degree, in a perfectly controlled or structured environment, especially in academic areas like book talks. Because of this emotional factor the motivation was heightened: the children were eager to discover a successful way to solve their problems. Once they were introduced I could connect the skills they learned for this to the more traditional academic arenas. The problem-solving circle was a prime strategy for guiding the children as they learned such concepts. Without the freedom to make choices few of these kinds of social problems would surface, and the children wouldn't need to learn how to solve them alone; they would have me to prevent them.

"Did anyone have a problem at recess that they want to talk to someone about?" I asked.

Brenda's hand went up.

"Okay Brenda. Walk over to the person who needs to solve a problem with you." She went to stand in front of Rosalinda.

"Now say, 'I need to talk to you,' and walk to the center of the circle. You both sit on the floor, cross your legs so your knees touch, and then you look at each other's faces." They did. "Now Brenda, you tell Rosalinda what she did that you didn't like. Rosalinda, you keep looking at Brenda." These two made the perfect pair for an introductory lesson. They liked to talk, knew more English than most of the children, and were eager to be friends. They needed reminders to look at each other's faces, as Rosalinda wanted to turn away when she was accused. Nearly all of the children had a similar reaction.

"You made me fall."

"What do you say, Rosalinda?"

"I don't know," she said.

"How about 'I'm sorry?' "

"But it was an accident!"

"Well, you still say 'I'm sorry.' That's what you say when there's an accident. Maybe we're sorry because we caused the accident. Does that seem right?" She listened carefully and smiled.

"I'm sorry."

"Is that all right with you Brenda?"

"Yes."

"What can you say to her to let her know?"

"I don't know."

"How about 'That's okay.' Or, 'I accept your apology.' That means, you know she was wrong, but you're not mad anymore."

"That's okay," Brenda said.

"Can you shake hands and be friends?" They were happy to shake hands.

The process was an important one for our class and we kept it all year. By the middle of the school year during recess an occasional pair of children began to take the seating posture somewhere in the room without any prompting from me to solve problems—exactly the kind of transfer of control I hoped to see. Not surprisingly, the first to start this was Brenda. One day during recess, seated in front of Ingrid, she looked over at me with a cheerful expression and said, "We're solving a problem." Both girls looked as pleased as could be with what they were doing. No doubt the problem wasn't very serious.

Another child to begin independent problem-solving with classmates this way was Ali, who quickly learned not to make suggestive comments to the girls through the problem-solving circle, and who grew to like it as a way to solve problems. He also grew tired of the daily complaints against him from both boys and girls, fairly quickly learned to say "sorry," and to avoid provocative name-calling and teasing.

He appeared able to interact with his classmates more intimately in the circle than he could otherwise, and sought reasons to talk to them there, possibly because there was a protocol to follow and ready permission to expose feelings. Where earlier he had sought attention through inappropriate clowning in class, he now began to listen and respond to classmates' comments, eventually extending his new abilities to unsupervised classroom interactions. Eventually, his class work improved and showed the effects of his listening and ability to participate cooperatively in group work; they improved as his social confidence improved. He began to lose the need for attention at any cost, even though it might be negative, and consequently his focus at school changed from being one grand opportunity to get attention to working at the subject at hand, which was education. There would be especially fortunate benefits on his reading.

The fact that so many problems occurred during recess underlines the importance of allowing children freedom to make mistakes and to have some time together away from adult-organized activities. If I had tried to prevent children's mistakes through strict organization, I would have eliminated the chances for a lot of learning. Many of the problems that occurred were not the kind where a teacher ordinarily would have intervened, but rather were about perceived slights or insults where no one was physically in danger or in obvious psychological distress. They were, however, the kinds of problems that make the difference between happiness and unhappiness at school, and that could escalate into future fighting.

The children still needed help to work out new situations, but they knew a process and a philosophy. Surely that was as important as many of the academic skills they learned, and because there were so many opportunities to link the problem-solving skills with the curriculum, the time invested could be justified as an addition to the academic schedule.

It took months for Mufdi to initiate a talk, but in March he walked across the circle to Abubakar and told him that he needed to talk to him. Abubakar looked surprised but followed Mufdi to the center of the circle. They sat down and looked at each other, Mufdi looking directly into Abubakar's eyes.

"You pushed me," he said matter-of-factly.

"I didn't push you!"

"Yes you did," Mufdi insisted, once again calmly.

Abubakar looked at me for help. "I didn't push him."

"Yes you did," said Mufdi.

"Abubakar, sometimes we do things and we don't even know we did them. Then we just say, 'I'm sorry. I didn't know I pushed you.' "

He repeated these words to Mufdi, who was satisfied. I didn't need to interpret the lesson to the others because they were all listening, fascinated. To see Mufdi speak and participate enchanted us all. It looked as if he was becoming someone who could take care of himself.

The broad physical problems of pushing and bumping usually occurred outside, but there were days when we had recess indoors. Indoor recess play created different kinds of encounters and the need for different although related social skills, as valuable as those for outdoors, but for different circumstances. In the classroom there were no strangers to encounter. The children's mishaps were more exposed here because I supervised them alone, not seventy-five other children, and the behavior for the classroom eliminated certain kinds of disputes—for example, there was no running inside—so they wouldn't be bumping into one another. In addition, the same possibilities that unstructured play offered at outdoor recess with its opportunities for choices, creativity and mistakes were also present for indoor recess, but with a few differences that the changed circumstances created.

In this school, when snow or rain prevented us from going outside for recess, the students had to sit on the bare hallway floor by grade levels, always in forced silence, crowded together with legs crossed to watch movies, usually any movie that was available in someone's classroom. This system counteracted everything I wanted my students to experience at school, and I couldn't ethically participate except when I was obligated by recess duty. But when I didn't have duty my students always voted to return to the classroom instead of watching the movies. In the class there were special playthings ready for such times, and they had already developed patterns for the kind of play that they enjoyed.

The children seemed to relish playing together inside. I never could have thought of the many situations they developed if I wanted to create them for language instruction. Here at recess because of the freedom they had, they created them for me and I provided the vocabulary they needed and wanted, even more than I could for outdoor recess.

Watching them play so productively and with such pleasure inspired me to look for more playthings, the kind that left room for invention but were not appropriate for outdoor recess. "I have a surprise for you today," caused an intense level of glee and anticipation. The new toys, which I wrapped in colorful paper to enhance the excitement, were in the highest demand—for a day or two.

The large block set was among the favorites of the playthings I had collected for indoor play. They used it every time they played indoors. In groups or pairs and trios they created block castles and roadways, precarious towers, extensive marble mazes and innumerable other structures, role-plays and games. The fabulous towers were created by teams with intricate cooperation and thought. The roadways and towns appeared with the attributes they thought a town needed, which was one of our social studies objectives. Castles emerged with moats, towers, bridges and hallways where pretend battles were fought or pet snails from a science project precariously "raced."

Other favorites were miniature cars to race or compare, puzzles often assembled cooperatively, alphabet and word games where someone had to be the teacher, card games, a tea set where home situations were imitated, several marble mazes that also required cooperation and group thinking to create, a wide variety of papers, pens, colored pencils and water colors, hand puppets, a large collection of dominoes to create systems of chain reactions, and a set of children's floor-cleaning tools for play and actual clean-up. With these things their inventions seemed limitless, and their ability to collaborate on projects grew. All the while I was present with vocabulary contributions.

The physically subdued play and broad choice of playthings created different choices, but with those choices came the same need for responsibility. More delicate perceptions were required to notice when classmates wanted the same spaces or games that they did. They needed to talk more and with a slightly different vocabulary than they used for outdoor play or academic work because indoor make-believe games involved more conversation than outdoor running games, no matter how creative. There was always the same, very difficult need for learning to share. Because I could hear and see nearly everything that happened, the intimacy of the setting provided an opportunity for me to help the children with language, to support their problem-finding, to help extend their world knowledge, and to expand their ability to work cooperatively.

I could have organized games for indoor recess, as I had when I began teaching, but just as unstructured play outside promoted unexpected learning of many kinds and structured play didn't, structured and unstructured play inside had the same comparative advantages and disadvantages. They either promoted or prevented the mistakes and creative thinking that foster learning, and produced situations and kinds of learning that curriculum writers and I hadn't and maybe couldn't have imagined. With unstructured indoor play the children's freedom consisted in making choices about what and with whom to play, and even where in the classroom to set up games. I let them do almost anything they wanted if it was safe and could be cleaned up fairly promptly. I was busy with the children the entire time.

"Elmer won't share!" complains Jayson.

"But I need these blocks (Elmer holds up a column-shaped block) to make my garage."

"Do you need all the columns to build your garage?" I ask. He stops to think, and says nothing. His face says, "I'll listen, but I still want all these columns." "Can we figure out how many columns you need, and then maybe you can spare some for Jayson? Jayson, maybe Elmer will need all of these columns. Let's see." As always, I accompanied my words with gestures, although they needed less and less of them as the year went on.

Elmer agreed while Jayson stood by and watched hopefully as I sat down on the carpet with Elmer to work out his garage. We collaborated as he explained what he wanted, and we worked out a garage that needed fewer columns and even pleased him more. It was fun. "So then, is it all right if Jayson has these four columns?" I asked. He nodded. When he saw that his garage could be finished with fewer columns than he expected, Elmer forgot the disagreement with Jayson altogether and concentrated on his work, seeming taken with the demands of the new structure we'd built. Jayson happily went to work on his own idea.

My unscheduled time at recess was viewed as an asset by the children, just as I viewed their free time as an asset for me. They knew that they could call on me to help them and that they would have me to themselves. Many of them liked to expand on math and science explorations, and on writing or social studies projects beyond what we did together in class, generally wanting my input when they did. Jayson and Etienne wanted to see how different objects reacted in water—sink or float; Hong wanted to try a larger branch on the roof of the pilgrim's house and needed help; Rosalinda wanted to write a birthday message for her mother, and Brenda thought that although it wasn't her mother's birthday, she would like a card too. "How do you spell 'birthday'?" And everyone wanted to read to me.

The very elements that make freedom wonderful for adults, that liberate their creativity and motivation to live fully, apply to children as well. When they're free to make decisions about their day at school they assume ownership of it and do the kind of thinking that ownership brings: interest in the quality of their work and how it will be received, reflection about alternative courses of action, forethought about consequences, creativity, and others. The decision to yield as much control to the children as I could led to their learning about voting, problem-solving, and conflict resolution, and each of these led to heightened abilities in all sorts of unexpected areas.

Because children are inexperienced with freedom, they are expected to make mistakes. Undesired consequences and useful discoveries come from their trials and errors. With guidance, they learn from the consequences of their choices to be self-directed and to behave responsibly toward one another and anyone they meet. When the boys appropriated Abubakar's ball, they learned that they would have a better chance to play if they asked, and that they should share. Abubakar seemed to have learned that it might be wiser not to share his ball with such a large group of boys in the future. If he did, he now had a good sense of how the play would go. In teacher-organized play, sharing the ball would have been part of the enforced structure and the children wouldn't have learned the kinds of negotiation and thinking about social life that they learned when they played independently with guidance.

Elmer, with his block columns, learned that he could adjust his work in order to share, and with my intervention learned that he could consider alternatives, and that he should try to share classroom materials. I didn't make him share, that was his choice, but I showed him that it was a value, that if he could create an alternative plan, he could help Jayson. When he didn't need the columns, he willingly shared them. Jayson in that situation had a new awareness of other children's rights, discovering that maybe Elmer would need all the columns, and that he would have to respect Elmer's interest in working out his project.

The freedom of the group to make certain choices required cooperation and a means of resolving group disagreements, voting in our case. Voting and the discussions it produced did much to expand the children's ability to support arguments and weigh outcomes. They began to understand that making decisions in a group was a complex process. Voting and discussions also increased the children's ability to consider what other people think and feel, and showed them that discussions are useful in navigating social situations. How amazing a discovery it was that if a few classmates didn't want to go outside, they could be persuaded to change their minds with a few strong arguments, or a few well-chosen words. Even more amazing to learn was that one child could change the minds of everyone in the class with reason and language.

To resolve disagreements between individuals, disagreements often caused by poor choices, the problem-solving circle was equally helpful and instructive. The careful listening that it encouraged, the acceptance of responsibility, the awakened empathy and the belief in the right for redress of personal offenses, all acted to create a peaceful classroom and encouraged the growth of numerous social skills which transferred to other situations during the day. These were skills that made freedom in the classroom possible.

Added to the cognitive and affective advantages that freedom brought the children, there was always language use, the spontaneous bursts of unplanned, purposeful talk for the children's own motives, a broader, more varied language than I would have thought to teach them in a completely teacher-driven day. My only requirement was that they try to speak English in class. Most of their language use then was language they wanted and could use repeatedly, generated from the knowledge of their present and past lives—pre-existing awareness grown in their heritage languages to be translated through English to new circumstances.

In my experience, when adults decide everything for children, when they structure every minute to avoid disorder, children's cognitive, affective and social development aren't as great as they would be otherwise. Nor is their language growth as complex. Rather than thinking and planning, children wait for instructions about everything—what they will write, read, or play, what they can say and when.... Children's motivation increases and their achievement is greater when they have a feeling of agency.

Finally, I should point out that what the children experienced in class was guided freedom, or maybe pre-freedom. I helped them learn how to be free with responsibility. They understood from the beginning that certain behavior would not be allowed, or would not occur without consequences of some sort, not unfair and excessive consequences, but unwanted just the same. That knowledge seemed enough to keep their choices within a reasonable range. If they enjoyed their school days, the idea of being excluded for awhile was a strong motivation to cooperate; they were having time-out from their own purposes.

Choices add excitement to a day, and in a school environment where learning is the purpose, choice means possibility for exploration and discovery. I believe in the value of choice as a promoter of curiosity; it makes curiosity flourish. Human curiosity about how and why things are as they are has led to all knowledge we have, even the accidental discoveries. Curiosity even drives the search for wisdom in human life. That's the sort of place school could be, the place where curiosity flourishes, and discovery and exploration are possible. Schools at all levels should be community centers for the growth of human wisdom and knowledge.

Adding elements of choice into a classroom changes the nature of instruction and the character of the classroom. Choice starts leaking into all subject matter. The teacher becomes a guide and not an autocratic ruler. It is a pleasure to be a mature practitioner of something learners want to do or know, a guide and enabler of their explorations, or a fellow learner whose contribution is the expertise of knowing how to learn. It's a role I like, it creates the environment I want for my students, and it's a way to make education valuable to the children themselves. Perhaps if they think of school as valuable, as the place where they gain skills they need for their individual purposes, they will find that they want to keep discovering more about the world.

Figure 9.1: Mohammed, Abdulrahman and Ali discuss book choices

Chapter 10

Final Days

Each dropping book, depending on its size, makes a unique sound when it lands in the boxes. The children, who helped to classify and place the books in the beginning of the year, are helping to pack them away, closing down the year and my stay at this school. All the books that meant so much to our history, so much of what we did and thought—Chris Van Allsberg's *The Stranger*, one of Jayson's favorites; *Walk the Dog*, that supported Abubakar, Derek and Rosemary's first steps to reading; the wacky *Dragon's Fat Cat*, by Dav Pilkey, that inspired Brenda and Rosalinda, *Hansel and Gretel* that uncovered the worrisome circumstances of Etienne's life—all packed into these boxes with our memories. Jayson and Etienne, working together find *Abiyoyo* and stop to relive the scary times it inspired. *I Remember Somalia. . . .* I look around at my students and wonder how they will remember these books and our talks, and what the memories will create stirred together in their minds over time. This is the last day of school, and we're spending a relaxed day together. We've had our culminating activities for the year, the play, a potluck with the parents, and a field trip to the zoo where many parents made the trip easier and livelier. Today is dedicated to good-byes and an informal celebration of all that the children have learned. This morning after everyone sat down, and instead of calendar activities, I suggested that we could make an exceptional schedule of what to do today since it would be our last time together. This is what the children decided:

SCHEDULE

- Calendar
- Reading
- Writing
- Read aloud
- Help to put books into boxes (my request)
- Relay races and playing with toys in the room

The calendar was easy for them now, and never could, it seems, be eliminated. "Do you remember how hard this used to be?" I asked. "You couldn't say the days, you didn't know the ones and tens and hundreds...." "We didn't know nothing," says Jayson, and they laughed at their former ignorance. Etienne says, "Now we know everything." They laughed again with pleasure and approval. Part of every morning has been singing and today they wanted to sing as usual, all of their favorite songs instead of our usual focus on one: "Shake Your Brains," "See Me Beautiful," "I Think You're Wonderful" and "The Wheels on the Bus" for the whole-body movements. They outgrew "Five Little Ducks" long ago, and a few more of the earliest songs they learned. Next, following their schedule for today, which somehow corresponded closely to the regular one, we had stories. As a group they urged me to read *Mrs. Wishy Washy*, among others. I should have suggested that they write to Joy Cowley, the author long ago. She would have enjoyed their letters of appreciation I'm sure. They also asked for *Abiyoyo* one more time. While we read and talked together, Ali sat with Mrs. Vega, having chosen to read a story to her. Some children, Etienne, Jayson, Tamathor, had stories they'd written and wanted the class to hear, and the children agreed to hear them. They were especially attentive when Etienne read. They wanted to hear what he had written this time, as they always did. They had questions about the stories for the authors, appropriate laughter, murmurs of fright when Etienne read, and comments that showed how well they'd followed the readings. This didn't last long. They were eager to get on to the reading workshop, especially to sit with a friend or friends and read anything they wanted—a book, charts, old group stories, rhymes—anything at any level. It was a special day. I never failed on such days to ask myself, "How could I make everyday like this?" but I think we got as close to it as I could manage. They did need to read at appropriate levels to gain increasing competence, and the discipline was helpful. With their increasing competence came more pleasure, pride and confidence. What these children accomplished in a year was impressive. They learned to communicate in oral and written English, became literate, had a good sense of quantity, and began to understand the marvelous complexity of life and that it could be studied—that it's amazing and wonderful. As I looked around this morning, I saw happiness, the simple pleasure of being together and at knowing things. I could see it on their faces and in the competent way they addressed the materials and one another in the room. They knew what to do, and they knew what to say. I've heard a lot of teachers say, "This is the best class I've ever had" at the end of a school year, and I'm no different. That's how I feel today; it's "akin to love," and my heart is full of it as I look around the room at the animated faces I will never see again. I will worry about Mufdi and Etienne; Mufdi that he will be secure and belong, and Etienne that he will survive. I will wonder about Abubakar and Abdulrahman for political reasons: how will life treat them? Abdulrahman is academically quick and has a supportive family, but he's an African immigrant with a proud and independent nature. Will people understand? And Abubakar—much the same, without the academic bent: he's confident and funny, but not passive. Will his teachers understand? Will strangers be good to these two boys? Ali, what will happen to him next year? Will he have the support he needs to continue his recent awakening? Ivan, so quiet; how will he fare? Derek and Jayson—I don't feel concerned. I'm pretty sure that they will be fine. The four girls in the room, Sara, Glenda, Tamathor, Brenda and a fifth, the departed Rosemary—I think they'll be fine as well. They are sturdy and smart, and I can say with pleasure, literate; Tamathor's parents will protect her and watch her closely.

Chapter 11

Conclusions

When I began to write this book my focus was what the children learned and how they learned it, especially how they learned to read, write and speak English, but when I began to describe the process tangential elements kept meddling and demanding inclusion. It looked as if I wouldn't be able to finish without giving them some attention. As I pulled together these as-yet unconnected ideas and memories into forms I could discuss, some of them became entire chapters and brought surprising insights—many more than allegedly tangential elements requiring some attention would have brought. Others I recognized as themes, like individualized instruction.

Most of the insights were related to the emotional parts of the learning process. I realized as I wrote that the children's education had never been simply a matter of using the right teaching strategies; the process and the children were much more complex than that. The role of emotion in the children's achievement was as important as teaching strategies and was integral to every aspect of the day, so important that it demanded explicit attention.

Once I realized this, I remembered how much thought and attention I'd actually given to the children's emotional well-being and the conditions that led me to give it that much attention. My students were wary, even frightened when they first came to school, and with their fear a subtle kind of bullying appeared. A classroom environment with this emotional mood wasn't conducive to exploration or cooperation and creativity, so before I could begin to help them learn what they were capable of learning, school had to be a place where they wanted to be, and each child had to want to learn. Figuring out how to promote freedom, emotional safety, and mutual respect among the children took explicit attention, and the story of their growth in the class environment needed to be explained if a complete picture of their first-grade education was to be drawn. Happiness at school, where heavy old tradition lugubriously slogs through the halls and probably in our educator brains, didn't appear automatically. Creating it took thought, time and attention. It required looking at the curriculum and making it speak the children's language every day, finding a way to establish a classroom where unkindness is unthinkable, and establishing the principle that each person's voice is valuable.

Although schools aren't involved in all aspects of students' lives, teachers and other staff members are with children for an important part of their day. Educators can influence how children feel about themselves in school and how they are viewed by their peers, factors that significantly affect children's futures and academic achievement. Serious attention to the affective school environment is possible in a crowded school agenda if it can be systemic, with values stated, children trained to show how it looks in action and follow through all year by every staff member. If a child is crying or looks miserable it is helpful to find out why and to try to help with the problem rather than to do something quickly so the child will stop crying. If children are quarreling or fighting, time-out or a trip to the principal's office won't stop a similar problem from happening again. These quick remedies don't solve problems or create insight that will last beyond the one moment.

On the other hand, being alert to how children treat one another and teaching them the value of kindness and inclusion with a schoolwide effort can produce more enduring results, especially important where language is a focus. When children enjoy one another and feel safe, their instinct is to communicate with one another, exactly what is needed for their language and cognitive development. The positive effects on student learning are worth the investment of time and thought. Apart from pragmatic reasons, there is a dream of a peaceful society where people know how to talk to one another, and it too is worth the investment of time and thought.

My original focus, what the children learned and how they learned it, was for me the most interesting and creative part of my job. I combined curricular goals with my assignment to "just get them speaking English." I approached language study through a focus on academic subjects and interpreted task-based language education to be tasks that would begin the children's academic education right away. I was excited about a new challenge when I accepted the job, eager to prove that children learning in a new language are not disabled, and eager to try to give them the strong start I thought they needed. Their language acquisition would be a consequence of their academic study, a strategy that my experience had shown to be the most productive and attractive way for people to learn languages. Subjects that genuinely interested them would allow my students to learn what other first graders were expected to know and would have the added benefit of producing language that went beyond basic, functional communication. These subjects would create a genuine reason to communicate, and the target language would be required to do it.

This kind of language instruction wasn't as casual as it sounds, nor as spontaneous. I had an explicit plan for language instruction and that was to locate and create a need for language growth in everything we studied. I made sure that the demand for low-frequency words and certain language constructions was a part of every lesson, and used the language with them when I explained what they would be doing. Then, when they were busy with discovery, they used this language for their work and I'm convinced that they retained it more than they would have from traditional language and vocabulary lessons that focused on language isolated from an authentic context. The activities naturally required repetition with understanding.

It also helped that they knew they were learning a language and were aware of their processes. If I corrected a grammatical construction or suggested, "This is all right; I know what you mean, but it isn't really how people say it in English," they understood. Asking them how they said the same thing in their languages helped them to see the similarities and differences in languages and promoted metalinguistic awareness. They paid attention to language, to English and their own languages, and noticed their structures—except when they were talking; then they were too focused on communication to let anything interrupt them.

As for literacy, it was something they wanted and worked eagerly to master. I adapted many reading strategies of mainstream teachers for my ELL students. Some, like phonics and phonemic-awareness strategies, for example, were relatively easy to use without much adaptation, except to make them fun. This instruction was priceless for beginning English-language instruction as well. Others, literature-based reading and book talks, for instance, required more thought and problem-solving on my part. I needed to incorporate strategies that promoted as much language growth and comprehension as possible for my students so they could participate. As it turned out, once very basic language was acquired and English sounds became familiar through the phonemic awareness and phonics studies, paired with early recitation of simple songs and poems, reading books and having conversations about books contributed to the children's language—its structure and vocabulary. This mix, a hybrid of whatever teaching strategies would do the work, is what led to the children's reading, writing and oral language development.

It's the hybrid nature of my instruction that I think made it effective for my students and me. I wasn't following someone else's program. I read, took classes, observed, and thought, and then did what was comfortable and seemed appropriate for the children in my class and for the kind of person that I am. I realize that I was lucky that no one imposed much on me. This was in part because no one expected much of ELL children at first, a blessing welldisguised, because proving that they could indeed learn, and a lot, was a good portion of my pleasure in the work. It's tiresome to hear all the time, "Oh, they're ELL students. They won't be reading," to have to beg for book sets for an ELL classroom, or, to hear all the time "The ELL kids won't be able. . . ." These are comments to disprove and bury, and doing it is deeepy satisfying.

With their diverse backgrounds and preparation for school, the children responded, I believe optimally, to individualized instruction. They felt confident and motivated, and I could be sure that they were learning as much as possible. Individualized instruction allowed me to guide them as they needed without wasting anyone's time—mine or theirs. Record-keeping and individual assessments were easy to keep up-to-date under this system, and were important tools that supported my work with the children. Individualized instruction worked, and its management worked in our classroom because it was tailored to us,—the children and me.

The other subjects—science, social studies, art, math and music—were fun when children could study the things in life that fascinate them, or when I found a way to link children's interests to required curriculum. These subjects lend themselves to active learning and the information is interesting: the unexpected composition of soil, the varied ways people live around the world, voting, how things grow, how larva turn into butterflies. . . . They are subjects for which vocabulary growth naturally develops, and so does the propositional grammar that makes ideas with the words. Language learners don't need to be proficient in order to begin learning right away at school. With guidance they learn the language on the way to learning other subjects.

Alas, education isn't about teaching alone. There were, and still are, political faces to my job that everyone knows and still argues. The primary one is whether immersion is good for children, and that question has at least two completely different frames of thought. One is that English immersion, especially initial reading, is too hard on immigrant children; their identities are at risk, and it is easier for them to learn to read in their heritage languages because there is less to learn. Therefore, they should be in bilingual classes. In addition, English is a colonizers' language and colonizes the children's minds as it is learned. The second and nearly opposite point of view is that the children would learn English more quickly in a mainstream classroom. It is unkind to separate them from the other children in schools.

The reality of how education operates in the United States is an important element in this conversation and isn't much considered. As far as I have seen, mainstream education has failed many ELL children. I've watched them sitting in classes copying from the boards while heritage English speakers were busy learning; I've seen them lonely, and I've seen them still struggling with reading well into middle school. The very sight of those struggling children was painful and frustrating to me. I was sure they could do more. Besides, in sheltered English immigrant children were only separated from English speakers. They were *with* children from many other cultures, and soon enough would be in classes with English speakers as well, only this time, in a position to work with them on equal terms.

As for bilingual classes, they were impossible in my district at the time; there weren't enough trained teachers to teach in the different languages, not even Spanish. And there are many bilingual classes with the same problems I've seen in many mainstream and immersion classes: teachers and administrators who underestimate the children's capacity to learn. I want to say that I believe bilingual classes are good for children, maybe better than sheltered immersion, but only if they're well done and have high expectations for students. When they are well done, they are in a prime position to preserve and employ immigrant children's languages and to make the most of their prior knowledge. I chose to participate in the Sheltered English program because I thought I could help children who are learning a language, and I knew that I would enjoy the students and the work. In this program the children had enough time with the language to get a solid start with it.

Mastering a language takes a lot of practice and exposure. If my students remember—and this is where family and community support are critical—to keep increasing their heritage language and English vocabularies after first grade and have adult support, and if they continue to enjoy reading, they should be prepared for future academic work in either language. Encouragement and tangible support at school would increase the chances of this outcome.

I'm nearly certain that most of my students will speak and read in at least two languages. The Spanish speakers may because I was able to help them apply English reading skills to Spanish texts, and the two languages have enough similarities to make the transition fairly transparent—some children applied what they learned about using sounds in English and started without any help at all. In addition, the community was large enough that they had ample opportunity to use the language. Most of the children and their families took frequent trips to their home countries in South America, driving by car or bus, a very positive language-support activity. There is also a constant flow of Spanish-speaking immigrants into the United States that refreshes the language, and there are numerous television and radio stations across the nation that broadcast in Spanish.

The Arabic speakers as well seemed on their way to competence in English and Arabic. Community activists had established a Muslim school for afternoons and Saturdays that all my Arabic-speaking children, except Mufdi, attended. Salam will read Arabic because he had already started before coming to an American school, and because his parents will continue to help him. I'm sure that Mufdi will, thanks to his mother, his scholarly inclinations and family values, and Abubakar, Abdulrahman and Tamathor will as well, all attending the Muslim school, and all from families that want to maintain heritage culture and language. Ali might if his parents enroll him as they planned, and if they are encouraged in their relationship with the schools; help from school for his reading will be important. The Internet offers great opportunities for Arabic language use when it is available.

Hung's mother was one of the parents who at first worried that she should start speaking only English to him, but was also one of the parents who were pleased to hear the value of speaking the heritage language at home. She continued to speak Vietnamese to Hung and had found someone to tutor him in reading Vietnamese. All of the children, in order to read capably in their heritage languages, will need to speak them and continue to grow vocabularies in them. I'm optimistic about them in this regard. A supportive community and wise parents have already made a big difference.

Further maintaining a high level of heritage language and English vocabulary and conceptual growth seems like a challenge that communities, including schools, could solve if they shared the value that a fully educated multilingual population is desirable. If children are going to be educated in an English-speaking system, they need strong English-language skills—practice and exposure. Maintaining their heritage languages has the same requirements. The question to resolve is where and how the exposure will occur. Schools, families and communities will have to cooperate so that there will be enough time for each language. A half-way effort at school won't help the children and may keep them from learning as much as they could. For optimal development, it is important to add languages and skills, not to replace the students' heritage language and culture with another; too much is lost.

Finally, knowing more than one language enriches lives in many ways and may be a passport to wisdom and peace. Learning languages often includes learning about cultures as well, and this broader view is what brings hope for a more peaceful world. I can't imagine losing my language completely and replacing it with another. Who would I be if I spoke one language and my grandparents and parents another? Would this affect my chances for a confident, creative life?

If it is true that language is important to identity, and if the public decides that teaching languages and preserving heritage languages is valuable, who would these multilingual people be, our children grown into adults? The old view of language education for "others," those outside the inner-circle of English speakers, can't be what communities hope for today as they educate their children: citizens of a local area who are useful to their new employers—if they are lucky. I for one hope that instead my students will be open-minded, liberated and active *world* citizens who will care about what happens to every person on the planet, including the people around them wherever that might be, whether they be artists, plumbers, entrepreneurs or scholars. In that sense they can choose to be "useful, handy, and helpful," and to acquire knowledge with that end in mind.

References

Aldis, D. (1989 Version). *Raffi songs to read: Five little ducks.* New York: Crown.

Allen, P., Cummins, J., Harley, B., & Swain, M. (Eds.). (1990). *The development of second language proficiency.* New York: Cambridge University Press.

Allington, R. (Ed.). (2002). *Big brother and the national reading curriculum.* Portsmouth, NH: Heinemann.

Appiah, K. (2006). *Cosmopolitanism: Ethics in a world of strangers.* New York: Norton.

Au, K. (1993). *Literacy instruction in multicultural settings.* Belmont, CA: Wadsworth.

August, D., & Hakuta, K. (Eds.). (1997). *Improving schooling for language-minority children: A research agenda.* Washington, D.C.: National Academy Press.

Barner, B. (2000). *Walk the dog.* San Fancisco: Chronicle Books.

Barrett, M. (1999). *The development of language.* East Sussex, UK: Psychology Press.

Beck, L., McKeown, M., & Kucan, L. (2002). *Bringing words to life.* New York: Guilford Press.

Biancarosa, G., Dechausay, N., & Noam, G. (2003). *Afterschool education: Approaches to an emerging field.* Cambridge, MA: Harvard Education Press.

Birch, B. (2002). *English l2 reading: Getting to the bottom.* Mahwah, NJ: Lawrence Erlbaum Associates.

Boiarsky, C. (Ed.). (2003). *Academic literacy: Helping under prepared and working class students succeed in college.* Portsmouth, NH: Boynton/Cook Publishers.

Boyarin, J. (Ed.). (1993). *The ethnography of reading.* Berkeley, CA: University of California Press.

Brenner, A. (2002). *Idols behind altars: Modern Mexican art and its cultural roots*. Mineola, NY: Dover Publications.

Brown, H. (2001). *Teaching by principles: An interactive approach to language pedagogy* (2nd ed.). White Plains, NY: Longman.

Brown, H. (2004). *Language assessment: Principles and classroom practices*. White Plains, NY: Longman.

Brown, P., & Levinson, S. C. (1978/1987). *Politeness: Some universals in language usage* (Rev. ed.). Cambridge, UK: Cambridge University Press.

Bruner, J. (1996). *The culture of education*. Cambridge, MA: Harvard University Press.

Bruner, J. (2002). *Making stories: Law, literature, life*. Cambridge, MA: Harvard University Press.

Burns, S., Griffin, P., & Snow, C. (Eds.). (n.d.). *Preventing reading difficulties in young children*. Washington, DC: National Academy Press.

Burns, S., Griffin, P., & Snow, C. (Eds.). (2005). *Knowledge to support the teaching of reading: Preparing teachers for a changing world*. San Francisco: Jossey-Bass.

Buruma, I., & Margalit, A. (2004). *Occidentalism: The West in the eyes of its enemies*. New York: Penguin Books.

Calderwood, P. (2000). *Learning community: Finding common ground in difference*. New York: Teachers College Press.

Calkins, L. (1994). *The art of teaching writing* (Revised ed.). Portsmouth, NH: Heinemann.

Calkins, L. (2001). *The art of teaching reading*. New York: Longman.

Carini, P. (2001). *Starting strong: A different look at children, schools, and standards*. New York: Teachers College Press.

Chamot, A., & O'Malley, J. (1994). *The CALLA handbook: Implementing the cognitive academic language learning approach*. Boston: Addison-Wesley.

Collins, K. (2003). *Ability profiling and school failure: One child's struggle to be seen as competent*. Mahwah, NJ: Lawrence Erlbaum Associates.

Compton-Lilly, C. (2003). *Reading families: The literate lives of urban children*. New York: Teachers College Press.

Costa, A., & Kallick, B. (2000). *Habits of mind*. Alexandria, VA: Association for Supervision and Curriculum Development.

Cowley, J., & Fuller, E. (1999). *Mrs. Wishy Washy*. United States: Penguin Young Readers Group.

Cran, W., MacNeil, R., & McCrum, R. (1986). *The story of English.* New York: Viking.

Crawford, J. (1995). *Bilingual education: History politics theory and practice* (3rd ed.). Los Angeles: Bilingual Educational Services.

Csikszentmihalyi, M. (1996). *Creativity: Flow and the psychology of discovery and invention.* New York: Harper Collins.

Cuban, L., & Tyack, D. (1995). *Tinkering toward utopia: A century of public school reform.* Cambridge, MA: Harvard University Press.

Cummins, J. (2000). *Language, power and pedagogy: Bilingual children in the crossfire.* Clevedon, England: Multilingual Matters.

Cummins, S., J.and Schecter (Ed.). (2003). *Multilingual education in practice: Using diversity as a resource.* Portsmouth, NH: Heinemann.

Delpit, L. (1995). *Other people's children: Cultural conflict in the classroom.* New York: The New Press.

Dickinson, D., & Neuman, S. (Eds.). (2002). *Handbook of early literacy research.* New York: The Guilford Press.

Du Bois, W. (1903). *The souls of black folk.* New York: Barnes and Noble Classics.

Duckworth, E. (1996). *The having of wonderful ideas.* New York: Teachers College Press.

Duckworth, E. (Ed.). (2001). *"tell me more": Listening to learners explain.* New York: Teachers College Press.

Edwards, C., Forman, B., & Gandini, L. (Eds.). (1998). *The hundred languages of children: The Reggio Emilia approach — advanced reflections* (2nd ed.). Westport, CT: Ablex Publishing.

Eisner, E. (1994). *Cognition and curriculum reconsidered* (2nd ed.). New York: Teachers College Press.

Eldredge, J. (1995/2005). *Teach decoding: Why and how* (2nd ed.). Upper Saddle River, NJ: Pearson.

Elley, W. (1989). Vocabulary acquisition from listening to stories. *Reading Research Quarterly, 24,* 174–187.

Ellis, R. (1994). *The study of second language acquisition.* Oxford: Oxford University Press.

Espaillat, R. (1998). *Where horizons go.* Kirksville, MO: Truman University Press.

Evans, J. (Ed.). (2005). *Literacy moves on: Popular culture, new technologies, and critical literacy in the elementary classroom.* Portsmouth, NH: Heinemann.

Ferguson, R., Gever, M., Minh-ha, T., & West, C. (Eds.). (1990). *Out there: Marginalization and contemporary cultures*. Cambridge, MA: The MIT Press.

Fitzgerald, J. (1995). English as a second language reading instruction in the United States: a research review. *Journal of Reading Behavior*, 27(2).

Fountas, I., & Pinnell, G. (1996). *Guided reading: Good first teaching for all children*. Portsmouth, NH: Heinemann.

Freire, P. (1973). *Education for critical consciousness*. New York: The Seabury Press.

Gallistel, C., & Gelman, R. (1978/1986). *The child's understanding of number*. Cambridge, MA: Harvard University Press.

Ganske, K. (2000). *Word journeys: Assessment-guided phonics, spelling, and vocabulary instruction*. New York: The Guilford Press.

Gardner, H. (1991). *To open minds*. United States: Basic Books.

Gee, J. (2004). *Situated language and learning: A critique of traditional schooling*. New York: Routledge.

Giroux, H. (1997). *Pedagogy and the politics of hope: Theory, culture, and schooling*. Bolder, CO: Westview Press.

Gleason, J. (2001). *The development of language* (Fifth ed.). Boston: Allyn and Bacon.

Graham, C. (1979). *Jazz chants for children*. Oxford: Oxford University Press.

Graves, D. (1999). *Bring life into learning: Create a lasting literacy*. Portsmouth, NH: Heinemann.

Graves, D. (2002). *Testing is not teaching: What should count in education*. Portsmouth, NH: Heinemann.

Hadaway, N., Vardell, S., & Young, T. (2002). *Literature-based instruction with English language learners*. Boston: Allyn and Bacon.

Hadley, A. (1993). *Teaching language in context* (2nd ed.). Boston: Heinle and Heinle.

Harris, M. (2003). *Colored pictures: Race and visual representation*. Chapel Hill, NC: University of North Carolina University Press.

Hill, C., & Larsen, E. (2000). *Children and reading tests*. Stamford, CT: Ablex.

Hindley, J. (1996). *In the company of children*. York, ME: Stenhouse.

Hughes, H. (1958/2002). *Consciousness and society*. New Brunswick, NJ: Transaction Publishers.

Inkpen, D. (1998). *Harriet*. Hauppauge, NY: Barrons Juveniles.

Jacobs, J., & Tunnell, M. (2000). *Children's literature, briefly* (2nd ed.). Upper

Saddle River, NJ: Prentice Hall.

Juarez, B. (2006). *Apuntes para mis hijos*. Mexico: Fondo de Cultura Económica.

Kaplan, C. (1989). *Tikki Tikki Tembo a musical play*. St. Louis, MO: Milliken.

Keats, E. (1964). *Whistle for Willie*. New York: Penguin Books.

Kennedy, B., & Minami, M. (Eds.). (1991). *Language issues in literacy and bilingual/multicultural education*. Cambridge, MA: Harvard Educational Review.

Koch, K. (1970). *Wishes, lies, and dreams: Teaching children to write poetry*. New York: Harper and Row.

Krashen, S. (1993). *The power of reading: Insights from the research*. Englewood, CO: Libraries Unlimited.

Krashen, S. (2003). *Explorations in language acquisition and use*. Portsmouth, NH: Heinemann.

Krashen, S., & Terrell, T. (1983). *The natural approach: Language acquisition in the classroom*. Essex, England: Pearson Education.

Levy, F., & Murnane, R. (1996). *Teaching the new basic skills: Principles for educating children to thrive in a changing economy*. New York: The Free Press.

Lilla, M. (2001). *The reckless mind: Intellectuals in politics*. New York: New York Review Books.

Mathews, J. (1994). *I remember Somalia: Why we left*. Portsmouth, NH: Heinemann.

McCarty, T. (Ed.). (2005). *Language, literacy, and power in schooling*. Mahwah, NJ: Lawrence Erlbaum Associates.

McCormick, S. (2003). *Instructing children who have literacy problems* (4th ed.). Upper Saddle River, NJ: Pearson Education.

McKay, S. (2002). *Teaching english as an international language*. Oxford: Oxford University Press.

McWilliam, N. (1998). *What's in a word: Vocabulary development in multilingual classrooms*. Staffordshire, UK: Trentham Books.

Meier, D. (1995). *The power of their ideas.: Lessons for America from a small school in Harlem*. Boston: Beacon Press.

Moats, L. (2000). *Speech to print: Language essentials for teachers*. Baltimore: Paul H. Brookes Publishing.

Moorehead, C. (2002, June 13). Lost in Cairo. *The New York Review of Books*.

Ninio, A., & Snow, C. (1996). *Pragmatic development: Essays in developmental science*. Boulder, CO: Westview Press.

Noddings, N. (2002). *Educating moral people: A caring alternative to character education*. New York: Teachers College Press.

Noddings, N. (2003). *Happiness and education*. Cambridge, UK: Cambridge University Press.

Páez, M., & Suárez-Orozco, M. (Eds.). (2002). *Latinos: Remaking America*. Berkeley, CA: University of California Press.

Pérez, B., et al. (Eds.). (2004). *Sociocultural contexts of language and literacy* (2nd ed.). Mahwah, NJ: Lawrence Erlbaum.

Pilkey, D. (1992). *Dragon's fat cat*. New York: Orchard Paperbacks.

Pollock, M. (2004). *Colormute: Race talk dilemmas in an American school*. Princeton, NJ: Princeton University Press.

Pressley, M. (2002). *Reading instruction that works: The case for balanced teaching* (2nd ed.). New York: The Guilford Press.

Ready, T., Edley, C., & Snow, C. (Eds.). (2002). *Achieving high educational standards for all: Conference summary*. Washington, D. C.: National Academy Press.

Roediger, D. (2005). *Working toward whiteness: How America's immigrants became white*. Cambridge: MA: Basic Books.

Rogoff, B. (1990). *Apprenticeship in thinking: Cognitive development in social context*. New York: Oxford University Press.

Rosenblatt, L. (1938). *Literature as exploration* (5th ed.). New York: The Modern Language Association.

Said, E. (1993). *Culture and imperialism*. New York: Vintage.

Seeger, P. (2001 version). *Abiyoyo*. New York: Simon and Schuster Children's Publishing.

Sen, A. (2006). *Identity and violence: The illusion of destiny*. New York: Norton.

Shaywitz, S. (2003). *Overcoming dyslexia: A new and complete science-based program for reading problems at any level*. New York: Alfred A. Knopf.

Siegler, R. (1991). *Children's thinking* (2nd ed.). Englewood Cliffs, NJ: Prentice Hall.

Smith, F. (1988). *Joining the literacy club. further essays into education*. Portsmouth, NH: Heinemann.

Smith, F. (1998). *The book of learning and forgetting*. New York: Teachers College Press.

Snow, C., & Verhoeven, L. (Eds.). (2001). *Literacy and motivation: Reading engagement in individuals and groups*. Mahwah, NJ: Lawrence Erlbaum Associates.

Stanovich, K. (2000). *Progress in understanding reading: Scientific foundations and new frontiers.* New York: The Guilford Press.

Suárez-Orozco, C., & Suárez-Orozco, M. (2001). *Children of immigration.* Cambridge, MA: Harvard University Press.

Tucker, S. (1997). *Word weavings. writing poetry with young children.* Glenview, IL: Good Year Books.

Valencia, R. (Ed.). (2002). *Chicano school failure and success: Past, present, and future* (2nd ed.). New York: RoutledgeFalmer.

Vygotsky, L. S. (1978). *Mind in society: The development of higher psychological processes.* Cambridge, MA: Harvard University Press.

Warner, G. (1990 version). *The boxcar children.* Morton Grove, IL: Albert Whitman and Company.

Wilson, E. (1940). *To the Finland station.* New York: New York Review Books.

RETHINKING CHILDHOOD

JOE L. KINCHELOE & GAILE CANNELLA, *General Editors*

A revolution is occurring regarding the study of childhood. Traditional notions of child development are under attack, as are the methods by which children are studied. At the same time, the nature of childhood itself is changing as children gain access to information once reserved for adults only. Technological innovations, media, and electronic information have narrowed the distinction between adults and children, forcing educators to rethink the world of schooling in this new context.

This series of textbooks and monographs encourages scholarship in all of these areas, eliciting critical investigations in developmental psychology, early childhood education, multicultural education, and cultural studies of childhood.

Proposals and manuscripts may be sent to the general editors:

> Joe L. Kincheloe
> c/o Peter Lang Publishing, Inc.
> 29 Broadway, 18th floor
> New York, New York 10006

To order other books in this series, please contact our Customer Service Department at:

> (800) 770-LANG (within the U.S.)
> (212) 647-7706 (outside the U.S.)
> (212) 647-7707 FAX

Or browse online by series at:
> www.peterlang.com